T0330463

Evolution, Organization and Economic Behavior

Evolution, Organization and Economic Behavior

Edited by

Guido Buenstorf

University of Kassel, Germany

Edward Elgar

Cheltenham, UK • Northampton, MA, USA

Published by
Edward Elgar Publishing Limited
The Lypiatts
15 Lansdown Road
Cheltenham
Glos GL50 2JA
UK

Edward Elgar Publishing, Inc.
William Pratt House
9 Dewey Court
Northampton
Massachusetts 01060
USA

A catalogue record for this book
is available from the British Library

Library of Congress Control Number: 2012930578

ISBN 978 1 84980 628 2

Typeset by Servis Filmsetting Ltd, Stockport, Cheshire
Printed and bound by MPG Books Group, UK

Contents

v

Figures

Tables

Contributors

Zakaria Babutsidze is Assistant Professor at the Department of Economics, SKEMA Business School, and Economist at the Department of Innovation and Competition, Observatoire Français des Conjonctures Économiques, Sciences-Po Paris, France.

Markus C. Becker is Professor at the Strategic Organization Design Unit, Department of Marketing and Management, University of Southern Denmark.

Ron A. Boschma is Professor of Regional Economics and Director of the Urban and Regional Research Centre Utrecht, Utrecht University, the Netherlands. He is also affiliated with the Spatial Economics Research Centre of the London School of Economics, United Kingdom.

Guido Buenstorf is Professor of Economics at the University of Kassel, Germany.

Thierry Burger-Helmchen is Professor of Management Science at EM Strasbourg, University of Strasbourg, and member of the Bureau d'Économie Théorique et Appliquée research centre, University of Strasbourg, France.

Uwe Cantner is Professor of Economics at the Friedrich Schiller University of Jena, Germany, and the University of Southern Denmark, Odense, Denmark.

Christian Cordes is Professor of Economics at the University of Bremen, Germany.

Michael S. Dahl is Professor of the Economics of Entrepreneurship and Organizations at the Department of Business and Management, Aalborg University, Denmark.

Herbert Dawid is Professor at the Department of Business Administration and Economics and the Institute of Mathematical Economics, University of Bielefeld, Germany.

Koen Frenken is Professor in Economics of Innovation and Technological Change, Eindhoven Centre for Innovation Studies, Eindhoven University of Technology, and a Fellow in Economic Geography at the Urban and Regional Research Centre Utrecht, Utrecht University, the Netherlands.

Pernille Gjerløv-Juel is a PhD Fellow at the Department of Business and Management, Aalborg University, Denmark.

Werner Güth is Director of the Strategic Interaction Group, Max Planck Institute of Economics, Jena, Germany.

Philipp Harting is a PhD student at the Department of Business Administration and Economics, University of Bielefeld, Germany.

Hartmut Kliemt is Professor of Philosophy and Economics at the Frankfurt School of Finance and Management, Germany.

Stefan Krabel is a Research Associate at the Institute of Economics, University of Kassel, Germany.

Patrick Llerena is Professor at the Bureau d'Économie Théorique and Appliquée, University of Strasbourg, and Directeur Général at Fondation Université de Strasbourg, France.

1. Introduction

Guido Buenstorf

1 EVOLUTIONARY ECONOMICS AS BEHAVIORAL ECONOMICS OF INDIVIDUALS AND ORGANIZATIONS

Evolutionary economics is behavioral economics – it studies the behavior of individuals and organizations in economic contexts. Evolutionary economists share parts of their research agenda with (other) behavioral economists and with management scholars, and the more the three communities interact, the more they can each learn from the others. These three premises underlie the present collection.

That evolutionary economics is behavioral economics is by no means a new idea, but has been proposed – and practiced – for more than 100 years before these lines were written. The starting point of evolutionary economics can be dated to 1898, the year when Thorstein Veblen posed his famous question: 'Why is economics not an evolutionary science?'. Veblen's programmatic essay chastised economics for not engaging in a causal analysis of economic processes, which to him was the essence of evolutionary thinking (Veblen, 1898; see also Hodgson, 1998). To do so presupposed studying the behavior of human agents, who after all are 'the motor forces of the processes of economic development' (Veblen, 1898, p. 388).

For Veblen, the rational choice approach of neoclassical economics emerging at the time – portraying human agents as 'lightning calculators of pleasures and pains', as he sardonically put it (p. 389) – would not do the job. His alternative vision of economic agency was derived from contemporary instinct psychology (see Cordes, 2007, and the references therein). In this view, the individual agent's desires, thoughts and behavioral dispositions are not exogenously given and permanently fixed, but are the dynamic 'products of his hereditary traits and his past experience' (Veblen, 1989, p. 390). Thus, to understand the behavior of human agents we have to ask how they became what they are. And to answer this question both individual learning experiences and the phylogenic processes that shaped human nature in the species' evolutionary history need to be taken into account. This perspective, even though developed in the late nineteenth century, comes very close to contemporary views in evolutionary economics.

Understanding human agents as products of their past, moreover, leaves room for interaction with and learning from other agents. For Veblen, economic agents are not isolated decision makers. Their goal-oriented activities unfold in the context of their cultural environment, which is in turn modified through the activities of individual agents. Firms are a relevant part of the cultural context shaping (and being shaped by) individual behavior. It is therefore not surprising that Veblen's perspective on economic agency provided the theoretical foundation on which other American institutionalists built their critique of labor relations and corporate cultures prevailing in US corporations at the time (Cordes, 2007).

Joseph Schumpeter (1934; first published in German in 1911), the other founding father of evolutionary economics, likewise saw the need to understand human behavior to make sense of economic development. His innovative entrepreneur – the driver of Schumpeterian economic development – is a multifaceted individual. The entrepreneur's complex motivational structure could hardly be more different from the utilitarian agent of the rational choice approach who optimizes an income–leisure trade-off. It is not the expectation to make a profit from successful innovation that motivates Schumpeter's entrepreneur, and he (sic!) does not calculate a return on investment. Rather, he is restless and driven by the will to achieve, to win against his competitors, and to 'found a private kingdom' (Schumpeter, 1934, p. 93).

Nonetheless, as Witt (2002) has succinctly pointed out, in Schumpeter's (1934) elitist theory of economic development all interesting behavioral facets are limited to the entrepreneur. Both competing 'mere managers' and consumers are portrayed as passive, and much of the challenge faced by the entrepreneur is to overcome the obstacles posed by a social environment hostile to innovations. Thus, the behavioral perspective is clearly present in the younger Schumpeter, yet it remains sketchy and far from being fully explored. Furthermore, the process of invention is not part of Schumpeter's (1934) theory. Schumpeterian entrepreneurs are innovators, not inventors. Their creative activity is limited to discovering the economic opportunities provided by ideas that already pre-exist outside the market sphere. The Schumpeterian entrepreneur is likewise not necessarily a capitalist, firm owner or manager. As a consequence, how entrepreneurial ideas are realized in business firms is not part of Schumpeter's theory, either.

As is well known, firms came to play a dominant role in Schumpeter's later theorizing. Following the historical ascent of the industrial research and development (R&D) laboratory, in *Capitalism, Socialism and Democracy*, Schumpeter (1942) argued that the locus of innovation had mostly shifted from individual entrepreneurs to large corporations. A less noticed change in Schumpeter's thought relates to the motivation underlying innovative activities. He now portrayed business firms as profit oriented, and while they were not argued to be profit *maximizing*, they require the prospect of monopoly profits to be induced to engage in innovative activities. Otherwise, in spite of its important role in *Capitalism, Socialism and Democracy*, the firm essentially remained a black box in Schumpeter's later work.

This is very different in Richard Nelson and Sidney Winter's seminal *Evolutionary Theory of Economic Change* (1982), which started the modern tradition of evolutionary economics. Nelson and Winter's conception of evolutionary economics focuses on competition in innovative markets. As a consequence, firms are at the center of interest. Taking up ideas developed in the Carnegie tradition (for example, March and Simon, 1958; Cyert and March, 1963), the rule-based character of firms' decision making is stressed. As Winter (1971, p. 239) had put it in an earlier article, 'firms establish decision rules and apply them routinely over extended periods'. These organizational routines, which also encompass the 'relatively constant dispositions and strategic heuristics that shape the approach of a firm to the nonroutine problems it faces' (Nelson and Winter, 1982, p. 15), are at the heart of Nelson and Winter's theory of the firm.

Nelson and Winter thus shift the focus of evolutionary economics from individual to organizational behavior, which is of primary relevance to explain competition in markets. To be sure, the book does contain an entire chapter dedicated to a discussion of individual skills, drawing extensively on insights from cognitive psychology. However, individual skills are seen as an analogue to organizational routines, and they are mainly discussed to motivate the subsequent discussion of how partially tacit organizational routines underlie the coordinated performance of firm organizations.

The routine concept also provides the link to the selection concept borrowed from biology. Winter (1971) had already argued that selection is a meaningful concept in industrial economics only if some dimension of firm activity can be found that is long-lived enough for selection to operate upon, and suggested firms' decision rules as a suitable candidate for such a concept. In Nelson and Winter (1982), the routine-based theory of organizational behavior is combined with agent-based simulation models to develop an alternative growth theory based on competing heterogeneous firms operating in innovative markets. Characteristic of their evolutionary model is that the development of firms (and, as a consequence, industries) is informed by their past: '[t]he condition of the industry in each time period bears the seeds of its condition in the following period' (ibid., p. 19). Continuity in firm behavior is further enhanced by assuming satisficing behavior of firms. Firms' primary objective is to preserve their routines, and they only search for improved processes when profits fall below their aspiration level.

The analogy between market competition and natural selection is prominent in the Nelson–Winter book, and there is liberal use of biological rhetoric (such as characterizing 'routines as genes'; p. 134). At the same time, the authors explicitly disavow the idea that market competition is driven by precisely the same processes as natural selection, or even the objective to develop a more general theory of evolution. Likewise, they make no attempt to link presently observable human behavior to past evolutionary processes shaping human nature during the phylogeny of the human species. This is a striking difference to Veblen's vision of evolutionary economics, but also – as will be seen immediately – to another strand of modern evolutionary economics.

It was only a few years after Nelson and Winter (1982) that an independent line of evolutionary economic thought was started in Germany by Ulrich Witt. In a book that was never translated into English, Witt (1987) endeavored to provide individualistic foundations of evolutionary economics. Conceptualizing evolutionary economics as a general approach to the study of emergent novelty and dynamic change in the economy, Witt set out an ambitious agenda that went far beyond industrial economics. Underlying his approach are two premises. First, that the scattered evolutionary ideas in economics (in addition to Schumpeter, the Nelson–Winter approach, as well as some contributions by German-speaking authors, Witt discusses at length the (neo-)Austrian school of Friedrich von Hayek, Israel Kirzner and others) lack a unifying theoretical foundation. And second, that this foundation needs to be provided by a sufficiently general theory of individual behavior and human interaction. Evolutionary biology is highly relevant in this perspective of evolutionary economics – not to provide a template for evolutionary processes in the economic sphere, but because the behavioral dispositions and cognitive capacities of contemporary agents were shaped during human phylogeny. Witt's general conception of evolutionary economics thus comes closer to that developed by Veblen than either to Schumpeter's or Nelson and Winter's views.

Where Nelson and Winter (1982) drew their primary inspiration from organizational theory, Witt (1987) is heavily influenced by behaviorist and cognitive psychology. He develops a rich account of individual economic agency based on inherited traits as well as a variety of learning processes.

For example, in the field of consumer behavior, Witt proposes that humans share a universal set of innate wants and needs. (These ideas were later elaborated in Witt, 2001.) This genetic endowment, however, is only a starting point for the acquisition of new desires as well as increasingly sophisticated ways of satisfying them. Learning results from individual experience but also from vicarious learning based on observing the behavior of role models (Bandura, 1986). Learning from role models allows for some individuals to have a disproportionately strong impact on how views in their community develop.

In Witt's behavioral model, idiosyncratic individual framing of the environment and the human capacity to learn from observing others are linked to provide an account of self-reinforcing dynamics of convergent worldviews in communicating communities, and likewise increasingly different worldviews between groups that do not communicate. In several contributions, Witt (1998, 1999, 2000) applies his general behavioral model to the theory of the firm. He suggests that successful founders act as role models. In face-to-face interaction, they are able to shape the worldviews of employees and effectively diffuse their own view of the firm's mission and strategy in the firm. This process of 'cognitive leadership' helps ensure coordinated activities in the firm. To the extent that the entrepreneur's views are internalized by employees, it also helps to keep opportunistic behavior at bay. As the firm grows, face-to-face interaction becomes increasingly difficult to sustain for the entrepreneur. This provides an endogenous cause of firm development, which may take one of several directions: increased monitoring and formalization of procedures (routines), delegation of leadership functions to second- and third-tier managers, or even spin-off activities by disenchanted employees.

These ideas may be interpreted as providing an – admittedly indirect – link from Schumpeter's entrepreneur to Nelson and Winter's view of organizations. If Schumpeterian entrepreneurs establish firms to pursue their innovative ideas, they may imprint their own ideas on employees. As entrepreneurial visions differ, so will the worldviews of employees and, as a consequence, the organizational routines emerging in the firm. Witt's cognitive leadership may thus help account for the heterogeneity of firm routines and capabilities that is observable in many industries.

Since the 1980s, accounting for individual behavior in various contexts has been a core subject in evolutionary economics. In particular, numerous authors have focused on the learning of human agents and incorporated learning into the analysis of various economic processes (see, for example, Dosi et al., 2005, for a survey). In this way, our understanding of an important aspect of economic behavior has been enhanced substantially. Learning is a natural candidate as a focal point of evolutionary economics, as it is inherently a dynamic process unfolding over time. To the extent that learning is done deliberately in order to attain some objective, learning moreover links the process perspective of evolutionary economics to the intentional character of most economic activities. Learning agents may be forward looking, and an evolutionary economics focusing on learning is not restricted to modeling individual or organizational agents as passive objects of (however specified) selection processes.

The evolutionary analysis of learning has often been linked back to conceptual research originating outside economics. One important link is provided by the work on genetic algorithms and evolutionary strategies modeled after principles of evolutionary processes in nature. These algorithms were originally developed as applied (normative) problem-solving devices, but they have also informed a (positive) theoretical literature on learning in economics (see Brenner, 1998, for a critical discussion). Another link is with complexity theory, notably the notion of adaptive search in fitness landscapes (Kauffman, 1993). For example, building on Herbert Simon's (1962) notion of nearly decomposable systems, Frenken et al. (1999) show that satisficing may be superior to optimization in complex search spaces when search time is a relevant performance parameter (which is certainly plausible in innovative markets). Finally, learning is a key driver of the dynamics in the agent-based computational modeling approach, which has been found to be well-suited for evolutionary economics. Learning can relate to the actions taken by agents according to some specified decision rules, or it can relate to the parameters or even structure of these rules (Dawid and Harting, ch. 6, this volume).

2   NEW OPPORTUNITIES FOR INTERACTION AND MUTUAL LEARNING

Since the foundations of the modern approach to evolutionary economics were developed in the 1980s, there have been various developments in economics more generally that open new opportunities for fruitful interaction between evolutionary and 'other' economists. Most importantly, with the ascent of laboratory experiments as a socially acceptable empirical practice in economics, behavioral economics has gained increasing traction in the broader discipline. Numerous results have been established in the lab that are hard to reconcile with the rationality axioms of standard economists or at least with the generally accepted notions of what rational decision making implies (see Wilkinson, 2007). The perspective on economic agency that informs at least some of the contributions to this line of research is quite congenial to evolutionary economics.

Not only have economists outside the evolutionary camp rediscovered an interest in actual human behavior, going beyond axiomatic rational choice and taking seriously findings from other social sciences such as psychology. Economists have also begun to link human behavior to the inherited nature of the human cognitive apparatus. The most visible development in this context is neuroeconomics (see Camerer et al., 2005). Based on their interdisciplinary interaction with neuroscience, economists have come to accept that human behavior is multidimensional, and that, for instance, decisions may vastly differ according to whether they are made by automatic or controlled processes, or with different involvement of the brain's affective system. These insights lead at least some economists to conclude that '[t]he way the brain evolved is critical to understanding human behavior' (ibid., p. 25). And even in Chicago, economists have realized that when real-world agents fail to conform to the predictions of the rational choice model, the policy implications of that model may not be appropriate in a variety of real-world contexts (Thaler and Sunstein, 2003).

In this way, more than 100 years after Veblen's (1898) programmatic essay, economics may eventually be on its way to becoming an evolutionary science. En route there is still much that evolutionary economics has to offer to the rest of the discipline. Organizational behavior tends to be underexplored by behavioral economists, and likewise the issue of how complex macro-level patterns emerge from the micro-level interaction of individual agents. Evolutionary economics has a long and rich tradition of empirical studies of how firms, markets and industries develop. The body of empirical insights thus developed will be an important ingredient toward a better understanding of organizational behavior, which is more difficult to replicate in the lab than individual decision making. Closely related – and equally important to understand industrial dynamics – is the evolutionary research on innovation based on the insight that real-world knowledge is generally *not* a public good that can be costlessly replicated. On the demand side of markets, the recent upswing of behavioral economics has yet offered little in terms of an improved theory of consumer behavior. Similar to innovation, here is a real opportunity for evolutionary economics to have an impact on how economics develops in the future.

At the same time, behavioral economists are working on ideas that are highly relevant to evolutionary economics – such as the attempt to develop a general (and mathematical) theory of satisficing, a potentially powerful challenge to the engrained rational choice model of standard economics. In the same vein, the empirical work on subjective well-being not only challenges conventional welfare economics. It may also integrate insights into the substance and dynamics of evolved human needs and desires into notions of economic welfare.

Evolutionary economics has likewise much to learn from management scholars with their wealth of in-depth empirical knowledge about firms. In this context, a lively discussion and further refinement of the routine concept began at the intersection of evolutionary economics and the management literature (see, for example, Cohen and Bacdayan, 1994; Dosi et al., 2000; Becker, 2004; Becker et al., 2005). In particular, routines have been suggested as important repositories of organizational capabilities. The capability-based view of the firm emphasizes *strategic* capabilities, that is, capacities to use the firm's resources that are tied to a customer need, unique to the firm and hard to imitate by competitors (Teece and Pisano, 1994). As the knowledge base underlying organizational routines is partially tacit and not fully available to any single individual member of the firm, capabilities residing in organizational routines are often strategic in this sense.

In studying firm organizations, the routine concept is not the only contribution that evolutionary economists can bring to the debate. As noted in the previous section, there has been a long interest in evolutionary economics in the personality of the entrepreneur, and also in the cognitive and motivational dynamics within developing firms. In the field of industrial dynamics, evolutionary economics has made key theoretical and empirical contributions (Klepper, 1996, 2002; Klepper and Thompson, 2006). Again these interests resonate with recent developments outside evolutionary economics. For instance, entrepreneurship has emerged as a dynamic field of research that shares both its Schumpeterian roots and many specific research topics with evolutionary economics. Various contributions to entrepreneurship research are moreover informed by behavioral economics (for example, the work on entrepreneurial overoptimism by Lowe and Ziedonis, 2006), or even have a distinctly evolutionary flavor (such as the work on genetic foundations of entrepreneurship by Nicolaou et al., 2008). Both behavioral economists and management scholars are keenly interested in motivational aspects of labor relations and their repercussions on individual effort and firm performance (for example, Fehr and Schmidt, 2004, 2007; Sauermann and Cohen, 2010). Management scholars have also adopted concepts and methods from the evolutionary work on industrial dynamics. All these recent developments provide rich opportunities to enhance the state of knowledge in the economics of the firm. This seems all the more important not only because most economists outside the evolutionary community have so far shunned the evolutionary perspective on firms, but because economics has generally shown little interest in how firms actually behave and decide. That the field of management research has traditionally been open to many different theoretical inputs may make the dialogue even more fruitful.

This volume is intended as a contribution to the tripartite communication between evolutionary economists, behavioral economists, and management scholars. Each of the individual chapters of the volume takes up one or several aspects of the overlapping research agendas. Earlier versions of many of the chapters were presented at the 2009 European Meeting on Applied Evolutionary Economics (EMAEE) in the German city of Jena. To dedicate the 2009 EMAEE conference in Jena to this communication between the three communities was a straightforward choice for historical as well as present-day reasons. Historically, as is highlighted in both Markus C. Becker's and Uwe Cantner's chapters, Jena experienced a managerial natural experiment in the late nineteenth and early twentieth centuries that transformed the city into one of the world's earliest regional innovation systems. At the core of this experiment was Ernst Abbe, a scientist, Schumpeterian entrepreneur, philanthropist and architect of close interaction between public research and private-sector innovation at the regional level. Abbe's own management principles are surprisingly close to the evolutionary view of firm organizations (Buenstorf and Murmann, 2005). More recently, the Jena economics community formed by the Friedrich Schiller University and the Max Planck Institute of Economics has engaged in the close interaction between evolutionary economics, behavioral economics, and the economics of entrepreneurship and innovation.

3   PART I: ECONOMIC BEHAVIOR: INDIVIDUALS AND INTERACTIONS

The present volume is organized into three parts. The first part consists of four chapters focusing on individual agents and their interactions. Werner Güth and Hartmut Kliemt (Chapter 2) set the stage with a discussion of boundedly rational decision making under uncertainty. Their conceptual chapter is one element of a broader research agenda that aims to provide a mathematical formulation of satisficing behavior in the Simonian tradition (see, for example, Güth, 2007, 2010). Güth and Kliemt suggest that when deciding under uncertainty, real-world agents do not normally maximize their expected utility based on assigning probabilities to the possible states of the world they may encounter. Instead, agents selectively focus their attention on specific scenarios about what may happen (including other agents' decisions) and form aspiration levels of what outcomes would be satisfactory in the selected scenarios. In this framework, a choice option is 'optimal' if there is no alternative option that yields higher utility under one of the scenarios considered by the agent while yielding at least the same utility under all other scenarios. Optimal aspirations profiles are such that they can just be satisfied by the respective choice option in all selected scenarios.

In the Güth–Kliemt framework, boundedly rational agents do not make decisions that are dominated by alternatives in the set of considered scenarios. However, bounded rationality will not normally lead agents to choose *the* optimal decision (among all possible ones), but only *a* satisficing one based on the scenarios taken into consideration. The authors also argue that preferences cannot be deduced from observable actions. In their view, economics as a discipline needs to experience a 'cognitive turn' like the one made decades ago by psychology, and develop theories about how preferences are actually formed by human agents. Finally, they employ the abstract framework developed in the chapter to delineate conditions under which external advice may help boundedly rational decision makers to arrive at improved decisions.

Seeking 'a middle ground between the methodological individualism of many social sciences and methodological collectivism' (pp. 39–40), Christian Cordes (Chapter 3) shifts the focus from the individual agent to the interaction of many agents. Cordes argues that cultural phenomena are emergent macro-level phenomena resulting from micro-level interaction, while they in turn shape the behavior of these interacting agents. Insights from anthropology provide the theoretical foundation of the chapter. Cordes emphasizes humans' unique capacity to understand others as intentional agents, which underlies our social learning abilities, as the key micro-level foundation of culture. Drawing on dual inheritance theory, he suggests that a bias toward cooperative behavior was established in the human psychological setup during a period of gene–culture coevolution. In addition to this 'direct' bias in favor of cooperation, human nature is characterized by other biases that helped boundedly rational agents make functional decisions during human phylogeny. Specifically, anthropologists have identified biases toward conformist behavior and the imitation of successful role models.

Based on the theoretical considerations about evolutionary influences of human behavior, Cordes then develops a model of how new cultural traits can diffuse in a population of interacting agents. The model provides a coherent behavioral foundation for the logistic diffusion pattern that is well known from empirical diffusion studies, yet difficult to reconcile with sequences of purely individual rational choices from a set of given alternatives. In a broader context, models of the same basic structure – starting at the level of individual behavior but also incorporating the reverse causality from population-level processes back to the individual level – are suggested as fruitful tools for understanding social phenomena.

The consumption models developed by Zakaria Babutsidze in Chapter 4 are of the type advocated by Cordes. The main objective of the chapter is to alert readers to the importance of interaction among agents in studying consumer behavior: as personal communication and peer effects are important drivers of consumer decision making, neglecting interaction patterns in consumption may lead to false inferences about aggregate demand patterns and also to erroneous policy (or business strategy) recommendations.

Babutsidze uses two stylized model contexts to illustrate this point. In a model of global interaction resulting in frequency-dependent adoption patterns (analogous to the conformity bias in Cordes's model in Chapter 3), accounting for interaction leads to dramatic changes in the long-run market shares of the competing products. In contrast, in Babutsidze's second model local interaction is shown to affect the model's transitional dynamics. Consumers in this model are assumed to acquire skills enhancing their valuation of the consumed good (as is predicted by Witt's (2001) approach to consumer behavior). Consumer skills derive both from the agents' own experiential learning and from their interaction with neighboring agents (who may consume a different variety of good). Babutsidze shows that the effectiveness of advertising for one variety depends on the relative ease with which consumers can acquire skills relevant to the product (its 'user friendliness'). More importantly, how user friendliness relates to the effectiveness of advertising is determined by the strength of interaction. Without social learning, advertising is most effective if products are similar. With local interaction, effectiveness is enhanced by product heterogeneity in user friendliness. Interestingly, this effect is stronger for intermediate than for extreme levels of interaction. Babutsidze suggests that since learning is always a dynamic process unfolding over time, effects such as those shown in his exemplary models should be of particular interest to evolutionary economists.

The first part of the book is concluded by an empirical chapter by Stefan Krabel (Chapter 5) that turns to norms and attitudes in public research. This is a particularly well-suited context to study the evolution of agents' behavior, as norms in public research have changed considerably over the past decades. Traditional standards of 'open science' (Merton, 1968; Dasgupta and David, 1984) have increasingly been challenged by new demands on researchers and universities to prove their relevance by producing results that can be commercialized. Under these conditions, the chapter asks whether individual age, peer effects and organizational tradition have empirically measurable relationships to individual norms and incentives perceived by scientists. In other words: has the focus on technology transfer and 'entrepreneurial universities' affected the way researchers think about science and their own role as scientists?

To answer this question, Krabel presents results from a survey of researchers working at the Max Planck Society, Germany's foremost public research organization dedicated to basic research. The chapter thus differs from the thrust of the empirical work on university technology transfer, which has primarily been based on patent and publication data – and has therefore been unable to detect changes in attitudes and perceived incentives. By focusing on a single basic research-oriented organization, it is moreover able to control institutional differences (for example, stemming from differences in technology transfer strategies), doing so in a context where researchers are under comparatively little organizational pressure to partake in commercialization activities. The empirical findings indicate that a substantial shift in norms and perceived incentives may indeed be underway. Older researchers are more likely to subscribe to the norms of 'open science', and perceive systematically lower reputational effects of commercialization, than their younger peers. A candidate for a (partial) explanation is also provided, as individual attitudes closely reflect those of peers working in the same institute.

4   PART II: THE EVOLUTION OF FIRMS

The three chapters of Part II deal with the behavior and development of firm organizations. It is here that evolutionary economists can most fruitfully interact with management scholars. Indeed all three chapters – each in its own original way – apply ideas and concepts from management to the evolutionary analysis of firms.

As noted in Section 1 above, agent-based computational modeling has been a prominent modeling approach in evolutionary studies of industries and entire economies ever since Nelson and Winter (1982). The strength of this approach – being able to model rich behavioral dynamics of a variety of heterogeneous, interacting agents – has also resulted in a key challenge: how to select decision rules for the agents that are grounded in well-established behavioral findings, and yet come up with a model whose dynamics are reasonably transparent? Herbert Dawid and Philipp Harting (Chapter 6) suggest that a consensus on this question would improve the 'external' usefulness of agent-based models for practical applications. It would also enhance the 'internal' validity of results by facilitating robustness tests and the comparison of results from alternative models. The authors propose a 'management science approach' to the modeling of firm behavior. The essence of this approach is to implement 'relatively simple decision rules that match standard procedures of real-world firms as described in the corresponding management literature' (p. 109). The approach is illustrated by the assumptions about production and pricing decisions employed in a large agent-based macro model that the authors co-developed in a collaborative research project.

The similarity of Dawid and Harting's management science approach and the original approach taken by Nelson and Winter (1982) is striking. After all, the notion of organizational routines originated from the prior findings established in the Carnegie tradition that firms tend to rely on stable and often quite straightforward heuristics to deal with recurrent tasks and problems. Against this backdrop, the contribution made by Dawid and Harting is to show how more complex agent-based models can be based along the same principles, and that well-established heuristics and decision rules are available from management science. In model building, these may be used for modeling firm behavior just as experimental findings can be used for modeling individual behavior.

'Clan control' (Ouchi, 1979) is a management approach to solve the ubiquitous problem of organizational control, that is, to ensure that the actual decisions made in a firm conform to the objectives of the firm's top management. Clan control attempts to align the objectives of managers and employees based on commitment, traditions, socialization and stable membership. It is well-suited to manage R&D operations because individual output is difficult to measure and, given the inherently uncertain character of R&D, specific behaviors to attain the organization's objectives cannot be prescribed.

But how does clan control actually become established in a firm? This question, which is obviously highly relevant to understand firm development, is center-stage in the contribution by Markus C. Becker (Chapter 7). Becker traces the emergence of clan control in the empirical context of Carl Zeiss, which pioneered microscope making in the nineteenth century and has remained one of Germany's most prominent firms in the optical industry to this day. He shows that the firm's management – most importantly Ernst Abbe – employed a variety of means to install a control system consistent with the notion of clan control. Commitment was fostered by mutual agreement on the relevance of precision; science-based product innovation was turned into a tradition (and subsequently codified in binding statutes prescribing detailed management principles for the Zeiss firm); firm members were socialized in master–apprentice relationships based on intense face-to-face communication; and stable membership was fostered by labor relations aiming at long-term (frequently, lifelong) employment.

In the broader theoretical context, clan control can be understood as a specific type of higher-level organizational routine (a strategic heuristic). The Zeiss example indicates that organizational control systems develop over time in a firm organization and have a lasting character. Becker's chapter can thus be read as an empirical case study of how routines emerge in the firm. At the same time, the chapter contributes to the crucial yet underresearched topic of how entrepreneurial ventures transform into organizations less strongly dependent on any single individual.

Chapter 8 by Thierry Burger-Helmchen and Patrick Llerena is conceptual in character. With organizational learning, the chapter discusses a crucial prerequisite of sustained competiveness and an important driver of firm development. The authors' point of departure is what may be considered the economic essence of the firm: creating and capturing value. Burger-Helmchen and Llerena suggest that creating value has an individual as well as an organizational dimension. At the individual level, creating value is linked to the creation of new knowledge, which in turn is linked to interaction with other individuals (often other employees of the same firm). At the organizational level, creating value involves finding appropriate divisions of knowledge and labor both within and across the boundaries of the organization.

Based on how knowledge and labor are divided, firms may differ in their capacity to create value through exploration (acquiring new knowledge) and through exploitation (using their existing knowledge). In turn, both forms of organizational learning are favored by different conditions in terms of network structures, trust, and specialization in knowledge about the design of goods and services. To manage the alternative learning processes, Burger-Helmchen and Llerena suggest a focus on creative individuals. These may be either internal or external to the firm organization, and contractual relationships with them may be either of a more transactional or of a more relational character. The suitable form of contractual arrangement along these two dimensions depends on the value and uniqueness of the respective individual's human capital. Within the firm, somewhat different implications for the suitable work structures, forms of remuneration and learning opportunities follow from considerations related to the divisions of labor and knowledge.

5   PART III: EVOLVING FIRMS AS DRIVERS OF ECONOMIC DEVELOPMENT

Part III contains three chapters that are also concerned with evolving firms, but emphasize the broader implications they have for the development of regions and entire economies. Chapter 9 by Koen Frenken and Ron A. Boschma presents a verbal model that is inspired by Herbert Simon's work on firm growth, and simultaneously looks at the growth of firms and regions. The point of departure is Schumpeterian innovators coming up with product innovations. These innovators decide, first, whether to stay with their current employer (leading the employer to establish a new product division), to join another existing firm, or to start a new spin-off firm. Second, they decide whether to remain in the region where they presently work, move to another region, or settle in a 'new' (in the context of the respective industry) region.

Assuming that the likelihood of staying in the same firm (region) increases with the technological relatedness of existing and new products, and that innovators are likewise attracted by firms (regions) already active in related product markets, the branching model proposed by Frenken and Boschma is able to capture some well-established stylized facts from industrial dynamics. The branching process results in related diversification trajectories at the firm and regional levels. Moreover, if there is a core–periphery structure in the space of products (as is suggested by recent empirical evidence), growth opportunities will depend on the current position in product space. Firms and regions located in densely populated parts of product space will then have better growth prospects than those located in the product periphery. The chapter, which provides a rich source of opportunities for further theoretical and empirical research, concludes with a discussion of how technological relatedness can be identified in empirical data.

In the ensuing Chapter 10, Pernille Gjerløv-Juel and Michael S. Dahl scrutinize the economic importance of the spin-off process, which is one of the processes driving the branching model developed by Frenken and Boschma. Their chapter is a vivid example of the fruitful interaction between evolutionary economics and the research on strategic management in the realm of industrial dynamics. The chapter starts by observing that numerous studies by evolutionary economists and management scholars have found spin-offs to be more long-lived than other startups. Arguing that its job-creating potential is a crucial reason why policy makers are interested in entrepreneurship, Gjerløv-Juel and Dahl ask whether spin-offs are also superior as providers of employment, and compare job creation and job destruction over the first nine years for the two types of new firms.

Gjerløv-Juel and Dahl employ arguments from organization ecology and evolutionary economics to predict that compared to other startups, spin-offs command a larger pool of capabilities due to their pre-entry experience. Accordingly, they enter the market at larger size, which helps isolate them from the liability of newness. As a group they are more homogeneous in their growth performance, and have a stronger positive effect on employment than other startups.

An empirical investigation at the level of the entire Danish economy covering close to 30,000 startups created between 1995 and 2206 (22.5 percent of which are spin-offs) finds support for these predictions. When entering the market, spin-offs are larger than other startups. They experience a smaller hazard of exit, and also show less variation in growth rates. Interestingly, while their rate of net job creation is larger (as predicted), this is not because spin-offs grow faster, but because fewer of them exit, which leads to a lower rate of job destruction. Gjerløv-Juel and Dahl illustrate the economic relevance of these differences for the oldest cohorts in their sample, which can be traced for at least eight years. With increasing age, spin-offs account for a consistently increasing share of the total employment created by the new firms. For every 100 spin-offs started, total employment amounts to 211 workers after eight years, while for every 100 other startups, only 134 workers are employed. In the view of Gjerløv-Juel and Dahl, these differences are large enough to think about entrepreneurship policies targeted to spin-offs.

The final chapter by Uwe Cantner on the post-transition economic development of the Jena region has elements of the Frenken–Boschma branching model as well as the spin-off process highlighted by Gjerløv-Juel and Dahl – with a twist, since Cantner's account involves an extraordinary degree of Schumpeterian creative *destruction*. Moreover, one of the most important protagonists in the development studied by Cantner is the firm of Carl Zeiss, which has already provided the empirical context for Markus C. Becker in Chapter 7.

The Jena region has received substantial attention for its ascent after 1989 in popular as well as scholarly literature. Against this background, Cantner first specifies in what sense Jena is really special, referring to a series of empirical studies he conducted with various associates. As Cantner relates, Jena's post-transition record is spectacular not in terms of economic prosperity, but in terms of innovativeness, most notably innovation based on cooperation among local agents. The roots of cooperative innovation are found in the restructuring of the Zeiss firm, which during socialist times had been nationalized and turned into a huge conglomerate (a 'Kombinat') with close to 30,000 employees. The majority of these employees lost their job in the transition process, but they still provided the backbone of the region's post-transition innovative performance – as inventors working in successor firms, scientists in public research, or founders of 'enforced' spin-offs.

Cantner presents evidence from social network analysis showing that during the post-transition years the regional innovation system in Jena became larger, less fragmented, more centralized, and more strongly oriented to intraregional linkages. The comparatively dense network structure is associated with an increasingly coherent base of technological knowledge. Bilateral cooperation is not very persistent, while being positively associated with labor mobility. These patterns are explained by mutual trust based on sharing a common background at the Zeiss Kombinat.

The regional case study presented by Cantner touches upon several interesting points that may provide new research opportunities where evolutionary economists may successfully leverage earlier evolutionary ideas and concepts. For example, it indicates that not only the transition from entrepreneurial activity to a routine-based firm is a relevant research topic, but also the reverse transition from the firm to entrepreneurial activity. This transition is of course at the center of the research on spin-offs and their regional repercussions. However, spin-offs are mostly studied in the context of young and innovative industries where success breeds success. We know much less about how entrepreneurial activities may contribute to a systematic rejuvenation of obsolete industries, and to structural change in regions and countries where such industries are located. In a more historical perspective, we have observed that Schumpeter's prediction that the corporate R&D laboratory would replace individual entrepreneurship was outlived by the re-emergence of the high-tech startup. However, there is little in terms of a general theory why this would have been the case, and under what conditions yet another transition from a 'Schumpeter Mark I' to a 'Schumpeter Mark II' could be expected. Yet another issue that Cantner touches upon is that during the spin-off juggernaut that Jena experienced after 1989, the corporate culture that Ernst Abbe instilled at the Zeiss firm in the early twentieth century seems to have transcended the corporate boundaries of Zeiss, informing the regional business culture more broadly. This is an indication that individual entrepreneurial leadership may be extremely long-lasting and powerful, which calls for further study by behavioral evolutionary economics.

6   CONCLUDING REMARKS

The chapters collected in this volume can obviously make only limited, selective contributions to the ongoing research agenda of evolutionary economics. They do so each in their own style and with their own focus. Nonetheless, a common message emerges from the set. The intersection of evolutionary economics, behavioral economics, and management is a rich source of research opportunities. Tapping into this source will enable researchers to find better answers to the questions that (not only evolutionary) economists have long been tackling. Significant progress has already been made; still more can be done in the future.

REFERENCES

Bandura, A. (1986), *Social Foundations of Thought and Action*, Englewood Cliffs, NJ: Prentice-Hall.
Becker, M.C. (2004), 'Organizational routines: a review of the literature', *Industrial and Corporate Change*, **13**: 643–77.
Becker, M.C., N. Lazaric, R.R. Nelson and S.G. Winter (2005), 'Applying organizational routines in understanding organizational change', *Industrial and Corporate Change*, **14**: 775–91.
Brenner, T. (1998), 'Can evolutionary algorithms describe learning processes?', *Journal of Evolutionary Economics*, **8**: 271–83.
Buenstorf, G. and J.P. Murmann (2005), 'Ernst Abbe's scientific management: theoretical insights from a nineteenth-century dynamic capabilities approach', *Industrial and Corporate Change*, **14**: 543–78.
Camerer, C., G. Loewenstein and D. Prelec (2005), 'Neuroeconomics: how neuroscience can inform economics', *Journal of Economic Literature*, **43**: 9–64.
Cohen, M.D. and P. Bacdayan (1994), 'Organizational routines are stored as procedural memory', *Organization Science*, **5**: 554–68.
Cordes, C. (2007), 'The role of "instincts" in the development of corporate cultures', *Journal of Economic Issues*, **41**: 747–64.
Cyert, R.M. and J.G. March (1963), *A Behavioral Theory of the Firm*, Oxford: Blackwell.
Dasgupta, P. and P.A. David (1994), 'Toward a new economics of science', *Research Policy*, **23**: 487–521.
Dosi, G., L. Marengo and G. Fagiolo (2005), 'Learning in evolutionary environments', in K. Dopfer (ed.), *The Evolutionary Foundations of Economics*, Cambridge: Cambridge University Press, pp. 255–338.
Dosi, G., R.R. Nelson and S.G. Winter (2000), 'Introduction: the nature and dynamics of organizational capabilities', in G. Dosi, R.R. Nelson and S.G. Winter (eds), *The Nature and Dynamics of Organizational Capabilities*, Oxford: Oxford University Press, pp. 1–22.
Fehr, E. and K.M. Schmidt (2004), 'Fairness and incentives in a multi-task principal–agent model', *Scandinavian Journal of Economics*, **106**: 453–74.
Fehr, E. and K.M. Schmidt (2007), 'Adding a stick to a carrot? The interaction of bonuses and fines', *American Economic Review Papers and Proceedings*, **97**: 177–81.
Frenken, K., L. Marengo and M. Valente (1999), 'Interdependencies, nearly-decomposability and adaptation', in T. Brenner (ed.), *Computational Techniques for Modelling Learning in Economics*, Boston, MA/Dordrecht, Netherlands/London: Kluwer, pp. 145–65.
Güth, W. (2007), 'Satisficing in portfolio selection: theoretical aspects and experimental tests', *Journal of Socio-Economics*, **36**: 505–22.

Güth, W. (2010), 'Satisficing and (un)bounded rationality: a formal definition and its experimental validity', *Journal of Economic Behavior and Organization*, **73**: 308–16.

Hodgson, G.M. (1998), 'On the evolution of Thorstein Veblen's evolutionary economics', *Cambridge Journal of Economics*, **22**: 415–31.

Kauffman, S. (1993), *The Origins of Order: Self-organization and Selection in Evolution*, Oxford and New York: Oxford University Press.

Klepper, S. (1996), 'Entry, exit and growth, and innovation over the product life cycle', *American Economic Review*, **86**: 562–83.

Klepper, S. (2002), 'Firm survival and the evolution of oligopoly', *RAND Journal of Economics*, **33**: 37–61.

Klepper, S. and P. Thompson (2006), 'Submarkets and the evolution of market structure', *RAND Journal of Economics*, **37**: 861–86.

Lowe, R.A. and A.A. Ziedonis (2006), 'Overoptimism and the performance of entrepreneurial firms', *Management Science*, **52**: 173–86.

March, J.G. and H.A. Simon (1958), *Organizations*, Oxford: Blackwell.

Merton, R.K. (1968), 'The Matthew effect in science', *Science*, **159**: 56–63.

Nelson, R.R. and S.G. Winter (1982), *An Evolutionary Theory of Economic Change*, Cambridge, MA and London: Belknap Press of Harvard University Press.

Nicolaou, N., S. Shane, L. Cherkas, J. Hunkin and T.D. Spector (2008), 'Is the tendency to engage in entrepreneurship genetic?', *Management Science*, **54**: 167–79.

Ouchi, W.G. (1979), 'A conceptual framework for the design of organizational control mechanisms', *Management Science*, **25**: 833–48.

Sauermann, H. and W.M. Cohen (2010), 'What makes them tick? Employee motives and firm innovation', *Management Science*, **56**: 2134–53.

Schumpeter, J.A. (1934), *The Theory of Economic Development*, Cambridge, MA: Harvard University Press.

Schumpeter, J.A. (1942), *Capitalism, Socialism and Democracy*, New York: Harper & Brothers.

Simon, H.A. (1962), 'The architecture of complexity', *Proceedings of the American Philosophical Society*, **106**: 467–82.

Teece, D. and G. Pisano (1994), 'The dynamic capabilities of firms: an introduction', *Industrial and Corporate Change*, **3**: 537–56.

Thaler, R.H. and C.R. Sunstein (2003), 'Libertarian paternalism', *American Economic Review Papers and Proceedings*, **93**: 175–9.

Veblen, T. (1898), 'Why is economics not an evolutionary science?', *Quarterly Journal of Economics*, **12**: 373–97.

Wilkinson, N. (2007), *An Introduction to Behavioral Economics*, Basingstoke: Palgrave Macmillan.

Winter, S.G. (1971), 'Satisficing, selection, and the innovating remnant', *Quarterly Journal of Economics*, **85**: 237–61.

Witt, U. (1987), *Individualistische Grundlagen der Evolutorischen Ökonomik*, Tübingen, Germany: Mohr-Siebeck.

Witt, U. (1998), 'Imagination and leadership – the neglected dimension of an evolutionary theory of the firm', *Journal of Economic Behavior and Organization*, **35**: 161–77.

Witt, U. (1999), 'Do entrepreneurs need firms? A contribution to a missing chapter in Austrian economics', *Review of Austrian Economics*, **11**: 99–109.

Witt, U. (2000), 'Changing cognitive frames – changing organizational forms: an entrepreneurial theory of organizational development', *Industrial and Corporate Change*, **9**: 733–55.

Witt, U. (2001), 'Learning to consume – a theory of wants and the growth of demand', *Journal of Evolutionary Economics*, **11**: 23–36.

Witt, U. (2002), 'How evolutionary is Schumpeter's theory of economic development?', *Industry and Innovation*, **9** (1–2): 7–22.

PART I

Economic behavior: individuals and interactions

2. To weigh or not to weigh, that is the question: advice on weighing goods in a boundedly rational way

Werner Güth and Hartmut Kliemt

1 CONCEPTUALIZING PURPOSEFUL ACTION UNDER UNCERTAINTY

Proverbially, except for death and taxes, nothing is certain in this world. More technically speaking, since control over consequences is always imperfect, a choice must be represented formally as the problem of selecting a function that maps states of the world into a list of possible consequences. What actors expect to emerge under their choices is, of course, dependent on their knowledge and information. Their preferences over the set of functions depend on their desires as well. The desires along with beliefs determine how they will rank lists (functions) over states of the world regarded as possible.

Classical decision theory assumes that the beliefs of the individual decision maker will determine probabilities $p_j \geq 0$ for all states j such that $p_1 + \ldots + p_n = 1$ results. Using $p = (p_1, p_2, \ldots, p_n)$ to denote the vector of probabilities for lists $E = (E_1, E_2, \ldots, E_n)$, we can combine probabilities and lists: $E/p = (E_1/p_1, \ldots, E_n/p_n)$; where, of course, '$E_j/p_j$' is to be read as 'result E_j with probability p_j'. Finally, provided that certain axioms are fulfilled, a utility index u and probabilities p exist such that individual preferences over any two lists $E = (E_1, E_2, \ldots, E_n)$, $K = (K_1, K_2, \ldots, K_n)$ will yield: $u(E/p) \geq u(K/p)$ iff K/p is not preferred to E/p; where $u(E/p) = p_1 u(E_1) + \ldots + p_n u(E_n)$ and $u(K/p) = p_1 u(K_1) + \ldots + p_n u(K_n)$.

According to one traditional view of the matter, one should start from functions that adopt the same value E_j for each of the states of the world $j = 1$ to $j = n$. Once we can rank such 'constant functions' leading to homogeneous lists, we can try to form the ranking of heterogeneous lists of entries on this basis. 'Reducing' the problem of ordering heterogeneous lists to the primary ordering of constant functions is misleading, however.

On the one hand, it takes certainty as a primitive notion even though it is merely a limiting state of decreasing uncertainty. On the other, it nurtures the illusion that the reason for preferring one list to the other would be rooted in original utility assignments. However, as everybody knows, yet tends to forget, utility in the sense introduced here is merely representative of preferences. It is not among the reasons for preferring one alternative to another. What appears to be the outcome of an aggregation of utilities is in fact not.

The ranking of heterogeneous lists may be described in utility terms as if it were the result of an aggregation, but the choice-making actors themselves need neither aggregate nor maximize. In their conscious decision making they can pursue completely different aims. Only the result of their reasoning will be such that it can be represented as maximizing an aggregation function provided that their choice making over functions (mapping the states of the world into results) would comply with certain axioms of rationality or consistency.

Normatively, the axioms might be defended on behalf of some a priori intuitions. However such an a priori, in a broad sense 'intuitionist' approach to explicating 'rationality' is philosophically and economically unsatisfactory. Rather than from ideal intuitions, the explication should start reasonably close to real human decision behavior and actual human practices (as, for example, in Nelson Goodman's explication of inductive arguments; see Goodman, 1983). From there on an idealization such as 'full rationality' might be formed as a limiting case or perhaps rather a projection beyond the empirically feasible realm of 'bounded rationality' into what is in the last resort infeasible for humans.

Modern adherents of full rationality argue that only fully rational individuals will be able to avoid falling victim to problems as raised, for instance, by so-called 'money pumps'. (In the most simple case, with '>' or 'strictly preferred', we have $A > B$ and $B > C$ and $C > A$, such that a person holding A would trade it for a surcharge for B, then B for C, then C for A to start all over again, until the person is drained of money by paying the surcharges or changes the preference.) Yet in a world of boundedly rational individuals it is merely necessary to defend oneself against exploitation by boundedly rational rather than perfectly rational other individuals' abilities; for example, many possibilities to construe money pumps on others will remain 'uninvented'. Therefore the argument that 'competition' or 'evolution' must have weeded out all imperfections – of this or other kinds – seems far-fetched (even though the cross-connections between competitive adaptation, evolution and rationality are very interesting; see Aumann, 2000).

It seems rather obvious that maximization of expected utility is not representative of what goes on in the world. From the internal point of view of individuals who reason about how to choose in their decision-making process, (expected) utility does not play a role. Moreover, the behavior can be represented by a utility function only very rarely. Except for extremely simple or repetitive situations in which an evolutionary or adaptive selection process has singled out optimal behavior, the same holds true from the external point of view of an onlooker as well. Except for adaptations to simple repetitive situations, behavior cannot be represented as if it amounted to utility maximization (for an early exposition, see Schumpeter 1959, p. 80, on this restriction on the application of a maximization framework to individuals).

In the next step we shall use a very simple example of choice making in a lottery and then in a setting of portfolio selection. We use these simple examples since they illustrate in a transparent way what is at stake. Moreover, if our argument is plausible even in such simple cases, then it will certainly hold in all cases of more realistic complexity. Furthermore, the stylized deliberative processes that we propose as a model of the deliberation process antecedent to choice making are recognizably similar to real deliberations of real people (the continuity requirement of a good explication). This continuity will be an asset in particular when it comes to developing an understanding of and advice for real decision-making processes.

2 FROM LOTTERIES TO SCENARIOS

A Simple Lottery

Assume that a lottery ticket is offered to you. You can either win €1,000,000 or end up with nothing, €0. What you will get depends on two states, 1, 2. You cannot influence which state will apply. You can, however, influence results by choosing a function that maps the state that you cannot influence in a list of results you expect to emerge under that function. The function or option o maps the set of states $\{1,2\}$ into $\{€1,000,000, €0\}$. The list of values of that function has the form $E = (€1,000,000, €0) = [o(1), o(2)]$.

Even if probabilities $p = (p_1, p_2)$, existed with, say, $p_1 = 0.25$ and $p_2 = 0.75$, the typical boundedly rational actor would not use utility expectations to rank the lottery $E/p = (€1,000,000/0.25, €0/0.75)$ relative to other functions (actions/choices). The problem of the decision maker is not that monetary, E_j, and utility, $u(E_j)$ rankings, might diverge. For the decision maker, the problem is rather that he/she will end either with €1,000,000 or with nothing €0. Primarily the list (€1,000,000, €0) is what counts. The basic considerations of the decision maker are in terms of the 'scenarios': get (i) €1 million or (ii) €0, indicated by the list $o(1) = [€1,000,000], o(2)] = €0$.

Should a decision maker command the information $E/p = (€1,000,000/ 0.25; €0/1 - 0.25)$ and be asked whether he/she would be willing to pay €100,000 for such a lottery ticket, he/she could represent this as the choice between two options. Option o, buy $[€1,000,000/0.25; €0/(1 - 0.25)]$, or, o', not buy, with $o'(1) = €100,000, o'(2) = €100,000$. A decision maker who is in command of probability estimates that he/she deems reliable will not neglect them. Yet the decision maker will typically *not* use them to aggregate end results to some kind of *utility* expectation or other. The *monetary* expectation can and will in fact typically be merely one consideration among several. The representative utility emerges only after a ranking process comprising all of the other considerations has taken place. As opposed to the monetary expectation that is part of the reasoning, the index merely sums up considerations.

Some General Tools to Characterize Scenarios

Clearly the decision process of an individual may contain deliberations concerning relative frequencies of events and even assessments of probabilities. As a rule, real-world decision making will not start from such premises. Typically the decision maker as a planner will start by forming (i) a few scenarios and (ii) corresponding aspiration levels.

More precisely, let Z be a non-empty set of states of the world z. The states z are regarded by the actor as independent of all his/her choices. They are beyond his/her control. Let us assume that the actor treats the actions of other actors as beyond his/her control as well. Let S_{-i} denote the set of all possible combinations of such actions of other actors $j \neq i$. Then the set S_{-i} is the set of all lists $s_{-i} = (s_j)_{j \neq i}$ of action combinations of other actors.

The set of states of the world that are beyond the actor's control is given by $Z \times S_{-i}$. We assume that a boundedly rational actor will not consider all relevant states of the world $Z \times S_{-i}$. Actor i will selectively focus on merely a few scenarios. We assume that the scenarios are selected from $Z \times S_{-i}$. By putting a 'hat' on the symbols we indicate that a selection has been made and get the typical form of a scenario as $(\hat{z}, \hat{s}_{-i})$ with $\hat{z} \in Z$ and $\hat{s}_{-i} \in S_{-i}$.

A scenario from the set $Sc_i = \{(\hat{z}, \hat{s}_{-i})\}$ is a future state of the world that the actor singles out as relevant and worth his/her attention. We assume that Sc_i is selected as a proper subset from the set of state $Z \times S_{-i}$ whose emergence is perceived by the actor as beyond his/her control. Although the actor may not have any views on probabilities or relative frequencies, he/she regards as possible all $(\hat{z}, \hat{s}_{-i})$ with $\hat{z} \in Z$ and $\hat{s}_{-i} \in S_{-i}$. Only for those scenarios that show up in the selected set $Sc_i = \{(\hat{z}, \hat{s}_{-i})\}$ will the actor form aspiration levels $A(\hat{z}, \hat{s}_{-i})$, such as some minimum profit he/she aspires to realize.[1]

Let $U[o, (\hat{z}, \hat{s}_{-i})]$ denote the level of success of i, that emerges in scenario $(\hat{z}, \hat{s}_{-i})$ after choosing option o. The set of all choices of actors $i = 1, 2, \ldots, n$ can be written as $S_i \times S_{-i}$ with $o = s_i \in S_i$ and $\hat{s}_{-i} \in S_{-i}$. Fulfilling aspirations for the set of scenarios $Sc_i = \{(\hat{z}, \hat{s}_{-i})\}$ and the aspiration profile $A_i = [A(\hat{z}, \hat{s}_{-i})_{(\hat{z}, \hat{s}_{-i}) \in Sc_i}]$ for decision maker i then amounts to the choice of some option o:

(A) $\qquad U[o, (\hat{z}, \hat{s}_{-i})] \geq A(\hat{z}, \hat{s}_{-i})$ for all $(\hat{z}, \hat{s}_{-i}) \in Sc_i$

The aspiration profile A_i corresponds to a list E of desired results. If (A) holds good, all aspirations A_i are fulfilled by action o at the relevant level.

Should aspirations be too high, the decision maker on considering his/her options o will find out that condition (A) cannot be fulfilled. There are scenarios for which the decision maker's aspirations will not be met. This may happen in a natural way in a repeated action context. The boundedly rational actor may experience, on the one hand, that a scenario he/she has not taken into account emerges, and, on the other, that the results predicted for that scenario under the chosen option will not be brought about by that option. If the context is not one of the repeated action type, then feedback from real experience is impossible. In such cases a check on aspirations and empirical assumptions concerning the set of scenarios as well as the functions mapping those scenarios into results will require some kind of model-based simulation or other methods of critical deliberation (such as the well-known reflective equilibrium search; see Daniels, 1979, and originally Rawls, 1951). Note, however, that the methods brought into play are not of the decision-theoretic kind, at least not primarily so. What is necessary is critical thinking based on some methodology of theory formation which should ideally be evidence based (the relationships to so-called 'evidence-based management', EBM, are obvious). If anything, empirical theories on how the world lies, not decision theory *per se*, will do the trick.

The function U contains ordering information which sums up the evaluations of results of relying on option o under the scenarios taken into account. For simplicity's sake, we assumed that the values of U are scalars. Even then, evaluating decisions requires lists of results to be compared according to their relative ranking. If we are dealing with lists of scalars rather than single scalars, the very concept of optimality will have to take into account that the ordering of such lists is incomplete.

We refer to an option o^* as optimal in a way akin to the well-known criterion of efficiency as exhibited, for instance, by the Pareto principle. An option o^* is 'optimal' if there is no other option o fulfilling:

(O) $$U[o, (\hat{z}, \hat{s}_{-i})] > U[o^*, (\hat{z}, \hat{s}_{-i})]$$

for at least one scenario $(\hat{z}, \hat{s}_{-i}) \in Sc_i$ and

$$U[o, (\hat{z}, \hat{s}_{-i})] \geq U[o^*, (\hat{z}, \hat{s}_{-i})]$$

for all other scenarios $(\hat{z}, \hat{s}_{-i}) \in Sc_i$ envisaged by i.
If o^* is optimal, the corresponding 'optimal aspiration profile'[2] is:

$$A_i(o^*) = \{ U_i[o^*, (\hat{z}, \hat{s}_{-i})]_{(\hat{z}, \hat{s}_{-i}) \in Sc_i} \}.$$

The preceding formulation of optimality does not require probabilistic considerations as conventionally used to aggregate the ordering informa-tion of the list of ordering information into a scalar. If such information on probabilities is available and if the ordering information allows for aggregation, then, in the limit, a complete ordering of results may emerge. Taking into account probabilities in this or other ways is not ruled out. Yet, we insist that it is a delusion to assume that the reasoning of bound-edly rational individuals will always lead to complete orderings that then can be represented by a function adopting scalar values.

In particular, economists seem to be prone to falling into a trap here: although it is true that of a set of possible options in the end one must be taken in action, it is not true that the chosen action must weakly dominate all others in the preceding reasoning process. The chosen action must be perceived by a boundedly rational actor as undominated or efficient, but that will not tell that actor which of the several efficient actions he/she should take.

In short, to be rationally chosen, an option must be *a* (satisficing) rather than *the* rational one. The set from which the option is chosen may contain several alternatives that are undominated by any option (in or outside the set). The rational actor has good reasons not to choose a non-optimal action, yet has no compelling reason to choose a specific one from the set of optimal actions.

However, it is possible that among the scenarios $(\hat{z}, \hat{s}_{-i}) \in Sc_i$ taken into account by the actor some might be dominated in the larger set

$(\hat{z}, \hat{s}_{-i}) \in Sc_i$. If $(\hat{z}, \hat{s}_{-i}) \in Sc_i$ the actor finds this out and he/she will adapt his/her aspirations. Again there is no guarantee that all alternatives satisficing aspirations are optimal. Finally, should i be in command of probability assessments for some or all scenarios $(\hat{z}, \hat{s}_{-i})$ the actor can and will as a rule use that information. The actor i could, for example, choose one among those options $o*$ that are optimal (are not dominated according to (O)).[3]

Although a description of rational choice making in terms of scenarios, aspiration levels and searching for undominated, and in this sense optimal, ones among the satisfying alternatives is certainly closer to real human behavior than the conventional approach which presupposes a full or complete ordering of alternatives as revealed in action, it may still seem unrealistically complicated. As far as this is concerned one has to distinguish between the theoretical description of what is going on in functional terms and the action situation so described. The exemplary analysis of a simple portfolio decision may serve as an illustration of how the seemingly complicated mathematical description which is needed for the sake of precision in presentation is related to the simple underlying decision structure.

3 ILLUSTRATION BY A SIMPLE PORTFOLIO DECISION

Imagine an investor who intends to invest the fixed sum $e > 0$. The investor considers certain alternatives as viable and wonders which he/she should choose. Assume that the investor as a matter of fact abstracts the influence of other actors on him/her and perceives as relevant merely, 'B', 'boom', and, 'doom' or 'crash', 'C'. In short, i's model of the aspects of the world that i cannot influence $S_{-i} \times Z$ is reduced to Z. The typical element $(\hat{s}_{-i}, \hat{z}) \in S_{-i} \times Z$ is reduced to element $(\hat{z}) \in (Z)$. In the investor's model of the world, $\hat{s}_{-i}$ is taken to be constant or otherwise irrelevant.

The investor can invest e:

- in liquidity with return rate 1;
- in a risk-free investment with return rate $r (> 1)$; or
- in a risky prospect with return rate h resp. l, with $h > r > l$.

Rate $l (< r)$ will apply if C occurs and rate $h (> r)$ if the state of the world is B. The aspirations will fulfill $A(C) \leq A(B)$ since $h > l$.

Let x, y and z, respectively, refer to investments in liquidity, risk-free and risky assets with $x, y, z \geq 0$ and $x + y + z = e$, then the portfolio (x, y, z) fulfills aspirations if:

(A) $x + yr + zl - e \geq A(C)$ and $x + yr + zh - e \geq A(B)$.

Due to $r > 1$, bounded as well as full rationality both require $x = 0$. In this case we have $y = e - z$ and condition (A) becomes:

$$e(r - l) + z(l - r) \geq A(C) \text{ and } e(r - l) + z(h - r) \geq A(B)$$

or

$$\frac{e(r - l) - A(C)}{r - l} \geq z \geq \frac{A(B) - e(r - l)}{h - r}.$$

Optimality (O) in this case implies:

$$\frac{e(r - l) - A(C)}{r - l} = z = \frac{A(B) - e(r - l)}{h - r},$$

since otherwise there could always be an improvement along one dimension without a loss along the other one. Under optimality we have a linear relationship between $A(C)$ and $A(B)$. In Figure 2.1 we have the aspiration level $A(C)$ as abscissa and the aspiration level $A(B)$ as ordinate. The line of all portfolios with $x = 0$ links $z = e$ with $z = 0$. It graphically shows the set of all optimal portfolios. The simplex with vertices $x = e, z = 0$ and $z = e$ contains the aspiration profiles $(A(C), A(B))$, corresponding to the gains from the portfolios in the simplex $\{(x, y, z): x, y, z \geq 0 \text{ and } x + y + z = e\}$. Consequently all aspiration profiles $(A(C), A(B))$ on or below the line that emerges for $x = 0$ can be fulfilled, yet only those on the line linking $z = e$ with $z = 0$ do so optimally. The more the actor invests in the risky activity the more his/her success will obviously depend on which of the two scenarios B, C will in fact apply. If $z = e$, vulnerability or at least dependence is maximal, while for $z = 0$ the result will emerge regardless.

The example shows how a rather clear concept of bounded rationality can be formulated on the basis of a process of scenario formation, aspiration formation and subsequent search for aspiration fulfillment. This does not rule out perfect rationality. Along with probabilistic reasoning, it admits it as a limiting or somewhat extreme case.

Clearly the example is just that, an example. It provides a particularly simple illustration of basic aspects of a simple rationality model

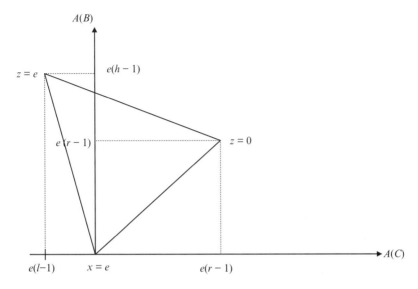

Figure 2.1   Aspiration profiles in a simple portfolio decision

that contains both basic descriptive as well as basic normative elements. Descriptively, a process of successive aspiration adaptation could be characterized in terms of the model. Should actors be confronted with the situation repeatedly, they should adapt their aspirations to higher levels if they find that such aspirations can be fulfilled with ease and the actors should adapt them downwards should they confront severe difficulties – or high costs – in fulfilling them or not be able to fulfill them at all. Normatively, it might be pointed out that a minimally rational actor would not choose dominated, non-optimal options. Yet there is no way to say with good reasons which of the several optimal ones are best. This would require comparisons across scenarios and between several manifestations of an individual in the scenarios. Even though most of us tend to assume otherwise, such intrapersonal comparisons are almost as problematical as interpersonal ones.

4   INTER- AND INTRAPERSONAL COMPARISONS

The scenario-specific aspiration adaptation sketched above may also be interpreted in terms of relations between decision-making entities. Rather than assuming that there is a single person who imagines the different scenarios as experienced by the same person, we can assume as well that that person imagines different manifestations of him/herself. Contingent on the particular scenario, that person conceives of him/herself as a different self.

More specifically, when choosing option *o*, the choice maker knows that his/her decision will affect a class of manifestations of his/her own future self. The well-being of each of the selves is important to the decision maker, yet the self weighing the effect of the future prospects is not identical to any of the several future selves (on weighing goods, see Broome, 1991; see also Parfit, 1984). In the specific example of Section 3, the investor in his/her role as a planner considers how his/her decisions will affect future manifestations of him/herself denoted by *c* and *b*. Decisions for which there exists another decision improving the lot of both, of *c* and of *b*, should and will be rejected out of hand by a planner who is rational in the sense explicated here. The act is dominated by an alternative no matter what the state of the world turns out to be according to the random variable representing the course of natural events. With the remaining alternatives, the decision maker can improve the lot of one future self only at the cost of worsening that of another self as emerging in at least one other state of the world.

Even though most of us have a conception of personal identity that seems to require that we treat all future selves equally, we do not follow up on that self-conception by aggregating. A typical rational planner considering his/her own future selves may shy away from a fully fledged intrapersonal comparison of the well-being of future selves. In his/her role as a planner, he/she might not have criteria to compare the well-being of *c* with that of *b*. Real human beings are not very good at imagining their own future satisfactions or happiness and in fact know this. A rational planner, even in view of his/her own future selves, may therefore adopt a cautionary strategy when it comes to singling out options as optimal choices.[4]

Obviously a strategy of maximizing the minimum expected of future satisfaction can make sense for planners who are confronting genuine uncertainty about how their own future selves will be affected by decisions of the present self. The Rawlsian view on the privileged role of the so-called 'maximin principle' may have derived some of its intuitive plausibility from such self-experiences. In any event, to assume that there is some kind of complete ordering of Pareto-efficient alternatives – Pareto efficient for the collectivity of the many future selves – amounts to assuming away the true problem of a rational planner.

Rather than running some simple calculation on expected utility, the rational planner has to construct some kind of ordering in the first place.

The utility index will represent preferences correctly only if utility is representative of preferences 'all things considered'. Yet the 'things' have to be considered in the first place. In particular, risk attitudes must have been included in what is represented by the index. As far as this is concerned, intra- and interpersonal assessments may be seen as being more or less in the same boat. Furthermore, philosophers have argued that those who accept intrapersonal aggregation should accept interpersonal aggregation as well. However, contrary to what most philosophers seem to assume, both forms of aggregation may be equally impossible rather than equally possible.

5   AGGREGATION IN ACTION?

Economists, who insist on using the concept of revealed preference as external description, aim to keep complicated, and in any event subjective, cognitive processes out of their science. With little exaggeration one might actually claim that they still have to make the 'cognitive turn' as occurs in psychology when overcoming behaviorism. Now, we should, of course, stick to the emphasis on empirical testing of theories that was one of the driving forces of the anti-speculative movement of behaviorism. Yet we should reject the simple-minded behaviorist attitude toward the role and interpretation of theoretical terms such as 'preference'. Sound empirical theories do not require that their theoretical terms can be directly mapped on observations. In the case of preferences it is not necessary to translate the concept into directly observable behavior as in revealed preference concepts (on this, see Sen, 1973 [1982]). Even if this may be useful for some purposes – which we do not deny – it is inadequate for the purpose of reasoning about options as in the case at hand.

The adherent of the traditional rationality model might still object that in the end one option must be chosen. Like in the case of Achilles who knows from seemingly flawless logic that he will never be able to overtake the tortoise, choice makers may take consolation in the fact that in the end they will act. Instead of *solvitur ambulando* (it will be solved in walking) we have *solvitur agendo* (it will be solved in action). The inability to aggregate according to reasons across several dimensions of a problem is resolved by taking action. And, even though we may not be able to defend taking a specific action in terms of reasons for taking that action, we can have the resolve to take some action.

It can be argued that even though the actors may not be able to state the relative weight of the dimensions of value – they have no stated preferences to that effect – we may still take them 'not at their word but at their actions'. We can *ascribe* to them preferences *as if* revealed by choices. Such preferences as revealed in choice can be used as stenographic representations of the results of individual choice making. However, actors can reveal preferences by their actions only if we ascribe to them a kind of consistency and rationality that may in fact be completely beyond them. In particular, the consistency would have to apply to multiple selves all being of the same mind.

Comparable considerations apply to collective decision making and to evaluating collective results. In such contexts the problems will be solved in action as well. Some collective result with a distribution of advantages and disadvantages emerges. Some individuals are made better off and some worse off. But this does not mean that the weighing is based on a deliberate weighing process in the minds of the actors. To assume that some kind of plan is executed by the collectivity as a whole when a collective result emerges from the actions of several individuals amounts to a mere postulate or an ascription of an 'as if'.

Planners who have to prepare choices – on behalf of some collectivity of selves, own or other – from an internal point of view are not describing the choices from the outside or from an external point of view. Adopting an internal point of view to their preferences is not revealed in choice. Planners have to make up their mind and as 'doers', have to make the choice. The problem is exactly that planners will be of several minds so to speak when they consider how alternatives will affect their future selves (related to this, see Ainslee, 1992). The whole conception of aggregating across scenarios becomes questionable if it is meant to represent what is going on in the mind of a rational planner. If preferences are not taken to represent choices as made by the acting individual but rather as reasons entering into the choice-making process, their role is completely different from that of a behavioral representation.

6   COUNTING NUMBERS?

The specific example of 'drug' as presented by philosophers (originating in Taurek, 1977) may illustrate what is at stake here. A person can either help some person who needs five units of a life-saving drug or five other persons who each need one unit of that drug. If the first option, *o*, is chosen, one person will survive and five others will die. If the second option, *o′*, is chosen, one person will die and five will survive. What will happen does not depend on a chance event. It all depends on actions that the decision maker in his/her role as a planner can plan and put into action. Even if the planner refuses to use the greater number as a criterion in the deliberations that lead to a plan, he/she will nevertheless in the end have to choose. After the fact, the decision maker would either have chosen the smaller or the larger number. Therefore, he/she would have acted either as if the numbers do count or as if the numbers do not count.

It may seem that at least in action aggregation cannot be avoided. We encounter 'revealed aggregation' in our acts. However, for those opposing deliberate aggregation in reasoning the necessity to act does not imply that we may ascribe to the actor as a planner that he/she is reasoning in terms of weighing. The planner may adopt either or neither stance as far as aggregation is concerned. The actor does what the actor has to do: that is, take some action. That necessity rather than the deliberation which of the actions to take is the overwhelming factor.

After the fact, the actor can still reasonably insist that there is no moral reason that could justify either one of his/her actions. It is not clear at all that from such actions a certain conception of what is morally good can be inferred. There may be no revealed morality. We perhaps cannot infer anything of the kind. Both acts may seem morally defendable to an actor. Sometimes he/she would take the one and sometimes the other action. Given the tragedy of the situation, the deliberations may amount to the same as involving a pseudo-random generator (on the difficulty to do this strategically as a boundedly rational actor, see Güth et al., 2005). This may be just right since many people seem to prefer throwing a coin in a case such as the one discussed above. This means that besides or on top of the two options considered so far, the third one of throwing a coin is added to the choice set. This seems to change the problem significantly. It becomes possible to provide an equal chance for each of the individuals affected by the decision of the choice maker. To provide that chance rather than some aggregation of utilities weighted by probabilities is driving the argument.

The equal chance option is a relevant additional alternative for the planner. Yet, after the coin has been tossed, the planner still has to act. Since the tossing of the coin does not in itself cause his/her subsequent choice, the actor is responsible for either following the signal of the coin or not. To derive the actor's intentions from his/her acts would be questionable. The actor might have tossed a coin and all that can be observed are his/her actions afterwards. Perhaps after several such choices we may infer that the actor acts randomly. If so, we would, however, hardly assume that we could know from his/her actions that the actor subscribes to some norm of equal chances. We simply do not know from his/her actions which are the norms that he/she as a planner would observe from an internal point of view.

We need to develop a theory of boundedly rational deliberation including its own theoretical terms and hypotheses. From this theory we can then derive certain implications for observable behavior. These implications lead to predictions in observational language that can be checked against the evidence. This is completely different from keeping mental processes in the dark, and to ascribe to what remains a black box some 'preference order', as if it were revealed as a reasoning (which it is not).

7 CONCLUDING REMARKS

The preceding has been a largely conceptual exercise. Conceptual exercises are sometimes just that. In other cases they provide tools that can be used to formulate tailor-made models of actual practice. Such models represent what is going on in the world in a transparent and useful way if the conceptual scheme is a good one.

We believe that boundedly rational actors do indeed proceed in ways close to thinking in terms of scenarios. If this is in fact true then it becomes possible to suggest conceivable improvements of practices described. After all, the description of the practices in the theoretical language renders them more transparent. In this case, as in other cases, the proof of the pudding is in the eating, that is, in applying the concepts in practice.

We would in general be optimistic that a focus on scenarios will help to improve decisions. We should hasten to acknowledge, however, that the focus on scenarios is not helpful because of the general nomological knowledge it would provide. There is no such directly applicable general knowledge involved. The conceptual scheme is not primarily a store of general knowledge, but rather a store for local knowledge. Once that knowledge is represented in the general terms developed before, some advice derived from similar situations might carry over. It is here that the usefulness of the conceptual scheme lies. The models based on it are not general but are 'local' or tailor-made. They allow for reflections on actual practices and possibly their improvement. They do so by representing them in a stylized way in a precise language, not by providing general rules or hypotheses.

More specific tools are represented in Table 2.1.

Table 2.1   Room for advice in different decision contexts

Classification	Type of behavior	Formal characteristics: (S, A) for situation $\{Z, S_{-i}, O, U[o, (z, s_{-i})]\}$
Advice necessary	Aspiration cannot be fulfilled	There is no option o with (A) $U[o, (\hat{z}, \hat{s}_{-i})] \geq A(\hat{z}, \hat{s}_{-i})$ for all $(\hat{z}, \hat{s}_{-i}) \in S$
Advice urgent	Aspirations unfulfilled	(A) can be fulfilled, yet option o with $U[o, (\hat{z}, \hat{s}_{-i})] < A(\hat{z}, \hat{s}_{-i})$ for a scenario $(\hat{z}, \hat{s}_{-i}) \in S$
Advice viable	Aspiration fulfillment	Chosen option o fulfills (A)
Advice as incomplete or selective scenario analysis	Undominated aspiration	Chosen option $o*$ is optimal in fulfilling aspirations; i.e., there is no option o with (D): $U[o, (\hat{z}, \hat{s}_{-i})] > U[o*, (\hat{z}, \hat{s}_{-i})]$ for at least one scenario $(\hat{z}, \hat{s}_{-i}) \in S$ and $U[o, (\hat{z}, \hat{s}_{-i})] \geq U[o*, (\hat{z}, \hat{s}_{-i})]$ else
No definitive suggestion	Optimality as undominatedness	Option is optimal for (V) $S = ZxS_{-i}$ no constellation excluded
No room for counsel	Unique aspiration fulfillment	Option $o*$ resp. aspiration $A*$ is uniquely determined by (A): $U[o*, (\hat{z}, \hat{s} - i)] = A(\hat{z}, \hat{s}_{-i})$ for all $(\hat{z}, \hat{s}_{-i}) \in S$ with $S = ZxS_{-i}$, i.e. (V), $o*$ undominated, i.e. (D), and (B): i has probability estimates $p(z, s_{-i})$ for all $(z, s_{-i}) \in ZxS_{-i}$ and $o*$ maximizes $\sum_{(z,s_{-i}) \in ZxS_{-i}} p(z, s_{-i}) U[o, (z, s_{-i})]$
Nobody can unilaterally improve result	Strategic equilibrium	Decisions of all decision makers fulfill (A), (D), (V) and (B) All i have rational expectations $p(z, s_{-i})$; i.e. (R): all random events are expected by all i with identical probabilities i and all expect behavior correctly

NOTES

1. To keep things simple, we refrain from generalizing the argument to multidimensional aspiration levels, though this is viable in principle if often beyond the capabilities of a typical boundedly rational actor.
2. As will become clear from the discussion in Section 3, sets of profiles will be rather large if probabilities can be used to aggregate information.
3. The criterion of choice may be the maximum expected value as formed for some function U that allows for a kind of aggregation. Then the individual would act roughly like

the utility-maximizing actor of conventional theory. Something like this might typically hold if the actor were interested only in monetary results, risk neutral and in command of some external objective probability measure.
4.   Including some form of self-paternalism, see Schelling, 1984; Frank, 1988.

REFERENCES

Ainslee, G. (1992), *Picoeconomics*, Cambridge: Cambridge University Press.

Aumann, R.J. (2000), *Collected Papers I & II*, Cambridge, MA: MIT Press.

Broome, J. (1991), *Weighing Goods: Equality, Uncertainty and Time*, Oxford: Basil Blackwell.

Daniels, N. (1979), 'Wide reflective equilibrium and theory acceptance in ethics', *Journal of Philosophy*, **76**(5): 265–82.

Frank, R. (1988), *The Passions within Reason: Prisoner's Dilemmas and the Strategic Role of the Emotions*, New York: W.W. Norton.

Goodman, N. (1983), *Fact, Fiction and Forecast*, Cambridge, MA: Harvard University Press.

Güth, W., Y. Kareev and H. Kliemt (2005), 'How to play randomly without random generator: the case of maximin players', *Homo oeconomicus*, **22**(2), 231–55.

Parfit, D. (1984), *Reasons and Persons*, Oxford: Oxford University Press.

Rawls, J. (1951), 'Outline of a decision procedure for ethics', *Philosophical Review*, **60**: 177–90.

Schelling, T.C. (1984), *Choice and Consequence*, Cambridge, MA: Harvard University Press.

Schumpeter, J.A. (1959), *The Theory of Economic Development*, Cambridge, MA: Harvard University Press.

Sen, A.K. (1973 [1982]), 'Behaviour and the concept of preference', in *Choice, Welfare and Measurement*, Oxford: Basil Blackwell, pp. 54–73.

Taurek, J. (1977), 'Should the numbers count?', *Philosophy and Public Affairs*, **6**(4): 293–316.

3. Emergent cultural phenomena and their cognitive foundations

Christian Cordes

1 INTRODUCTION

The social sciences have long been occupied with the 'micro–macro problem' (for example, Jackson, 2002; Dopfer and Potts, 2004).[1] If, when formulating a theoretical concept, we start from individual behavior, as most economists do, how can we ever get to a proper account of society-scale – emergent – phenomena? On the other hand, if we start with collective institutions, as many sociologists do, how do we account for individual behavior? We show in this chapter that a theory of cultural evolution addresses and integrates a micro and a macro level (see Henrich and Boyd, 1998): (i) at a cultural level it is shown how cultural variants spread and persist within a population via processes of cultural learning; and (ii) at the genetic evolutionary level the conditions are analyzed under which natural selection favors the psychological mechanisms underlying the cultural evolution of groups. To understand the evolution of the psychological mechanisms that shape culture, it is necessary to analyze how individual psychology shapes the cultural environment and how that environment conditions the behavior that people acquire. Moreover, we show how the theory of gene–culture coevolution clarifies the recursive connection between humans' innate psychological predispositions and the macro-level institutions in which humans are always embedded.

To provide some additional insights into the dynamic aspects of multilevel cultural evolution, the chapter presents a model of the transmission of cultural contents via processes of social learning, and expounds how these influence the diffusion of novelty in a population. As will be shown, cultural transmission is biased; people tend to acquire some cultural variants rather than others.[2] The process of cultural transmission is influenced and constrained by humans' evolved psychology which shapes what we learn, how we think, and whom we imitate. The proposed model seeks a middle ground between the methodological individualism of many social sciences and methodological collectivism. This is done by relying on a population-based model of cultural evolution and insights on human cognition stemming from evolutionary biology, anthropology, cognitive science, and other disciplines that serve as this approach's micro foundation.

Given such a 'naturalistic' approach, which implies a behavioral model of human agents that is based on our knowledge about human nature, it can be argued that the Darwinian theory of biological evolution is relevant for the social sciences in a very basic sense: the human species is, after all, a result of natural (Darwinian) evolution. However, this relevance does not directly affect the analytic concepts of theorizing in the social sciences. Natural evolution has shaped the ground and still defines the constraints for human-made, or cultural, evolution. The historical process of cultural evolution can therefore be conceived as emerging from, and being embedded in, the constraints shaped by evolution in nature. Darwinian theory explains the origins of cultural evolution in human phylogeny and fosters the understanding of the lasting influence of innate elements, dispositions, and programs on behavior, which are results of the forces of natural selection and which impose limitations on cultural evolution (Witt, 2003, chap. 1; 2004). Evolutionary selection has established a set of cognitive devices that influence human behavior (for example, Singer, 2000). From this perspective, the biologically evolved foundations of social cognition, learning, and reasoning directly enable and affect cultural evolution with its own modes of transmission and its much faster pace. Therefore, Darwinian concepts explain the origins of the human adaptation for culture and the lasting influence of certain evolved cognitive traits (see Cordes, 2004). They cannot, however, do justice to cultural evolution in general and socioeconomic evolution in particular, which follow their own rules (Cordes, 2006).

The remainder of this chapter is organized as follows: the next section will introduce some of the evolved cognitive dispositions that take effect in cultural transmission. Section 3 demonstrates how gene–culture coevolution gives rise to uniquely human cognitive features. The dissemination of cultural novelty in a population given certain biases in cultural learning that originate from evolved cognitive dispositions are the subject matter of a formal model in Section 4. Section 5 concludes this chapter.

2 THE MICRO FOUNDATIONS OF CULTURAL TRANSMISSION PROCESSES

During their evolution, humans adapted for culture in ways other primates did not.[3] Biologically evolved novel forms of social cognition and cultural learning formed the micro foundation for cultural evolution and exclusively human ways of behavior. The key adaptation has been the one that enabled humans to understand other individuals as intentional agents like the self – a capability necessary for reproducing someone else's behavioral strategies (Tomasello, 1999). The sophisticated human skills of social cognition, such as imitative learning, do not just mimic the surface structure of an observed behavior. They also mean a reproduction of an instrumental act understood intentionally. Humans do not just reproduce the behavioral means but also the intended end to which the behavioral means was applied. This unique cognitive skill of human beings underlies behavioral patterns such as joint attentional activities, discourse skills, learning to use tools, the creation and use of conventional symbols, and the participation in, and creation of, complex social organizations and institutions. These species-unique aspects of human cognition are socially constituted. This means that human social organization is an integral part of the process that resulted in the special characteristics of human cognition (see also Section 3). The partly innate, partly learned behavioral repertoire is the basis on which cultural evolution rests. Social–cognitive learning is a crucial element here (Bandura, 1986, chap. 2). It allows for a fidelity of transmission and diffusion of behaviors and information among the members of a population not feasible in genetic transmission (see Kruger et al., 1993). It also enables humankind to accumulate a multitude of modifications in the course of socioeconomic evolution and to pool collective cognitive resources both contemporaneously and over historical time.

Although culture evolves according to its own mechanisms, humans have not transcended biology. Therefore, a deeper understanding of emergent cultural phenomena necessitates an analysis of the underlying human cognitive learning capacities. Cultural transmission is based on complex psychological mechanisms that are likely to have been shaped by natural selection (Henrich and Boyd, 1998).[4] To grasp cultural macro phenomena it is important to understand the nature of these evolved psychological mechanisms – the micro foundation of culture – because they determine which cultural variants spread and persist in human groups.

Most variation between human groups is cultural: genetically similar people live in similar environments showing different patterns of behavior due to different, culturally acquired cultural variants. What is more, individuals living in the same group tend to behave in similar ways and hold similar moral values, which is partly due to conformist cultural transmission (see below). These cultural variants are transmitted within social groups by various forms of social learning. On a micro level, Boyd and Richerson (1985) and Richerson and Boyd (2005, p. 99) have conceptualized cultural transmission as the product of a series of analytically separable cognitive learning mechanisms or transmission biases that allow humans to effectively and efficiently acquire cultural variants in a complex cultural environment. Evolutionary considerations suggest that humans' cognitive dispositions consist of learning rules that preferentially select and evaluate sensory data from prescribed subsets of externally produced information (see also Henrich and Boyd, 1998). These learning heuristics provide 'rules of thumb' that bias humans toward certain cultural variants without exhaustively examining the immense amount of available social and environmental information. The addition of cultural transmission creates many more links between individuals and the populations they live in. Therefore, human culture is an example of an emergent macro phenomenon for it is based on social learning processes taking place on a micro level.

One of the psychological mechanisms in cultural transmission is the well-studied conformist bias (for an overview, see Aronson et al., 2002, chap. 8; Kameda and Diasuke, 2002; Henrich, 2004; Richerson and Boyd, 2005, p. 120). This bias uses the commonness or rarity of a cultural variant as a basis for choice. Due to the conformist bias, agents pick the cultural variant that is used by most of the models in a population (see also Henrich and Boyd, 1998). Boyd and Richerson (1989) show that a tendency to acquire the most common behavior exhibited in a society was adaptive in a simple model of evolution in a spatially varying environment, because such a tendency increases the probability of acquiring adaptive cultural variances. Moreover, a fairly modest conformist bias will maintain intergroup variation in the face of fairly high intergroup migration rates, an important feature in models of cultural group selection (see Section 3). Conformist transmission belongs to the class of frequency-dependent biases and has been a simple heuristic that improves the chance of acquiring the locally favored cultural variant (Boyd and Richerson, 1985, p. 216; 1989). In general, frequency-dependent bias will occur if the probability that social learners acquire a variant depends nonlinearly on the frequency of the variant among the set of models. Especially if the environment changes slowly and the information available to an individual is poor, a strong reliance on social learning evolves that favors a strong conformist tendency. There is a synergistic relationship between the evolution of imitation and the evolution of conformism. The fact that humans can imitate implies that conformism is likely to be an important component of human social learning.

The boundedness of human rationality in the face of a complex world often induces individuals to adopt culturally transmitted behaviors without independent evaluation of their outcomes (Richerson and Boyd,

2001). The constrained psychological resources of human actors are a fundamental part of cultural evolution. This implies that these approaches abandon the assumption that agents rationally choose utility-maximizing items from a given set of alternatives. Instead, it is assumed that an important force in learning is social observation. Agents are aware of only a fraction of the available information. Therefore, imitating or learning from others is one of the most important means by which humans finesse these bounds of rationality (Boyd and Richerson, 1993). This can lead to adaptive but also myopic choice among the cultural variants observed.[5]

Conformist transmission implies that on the (micro) level of an individual there is a propensity to preferentially adopt the cultural traits that are most frequent in the population, that is, at the population level, conformist transmission causes more common traits to increase in frequency. On the other hand, the frequency of a trait among the individuals within the population – a macro-level property – provides information about the trait's adaptiveness. Therefore, in the case of conformist transmission, the frequency of a cultural variant, a population property, affects its probability of being imitated by individuals (see Richerson and Boyd, 2005, p. 247).

Moreover, anthropologists have likewise found that the choice of cultural traits is based on the observable attributes of the individuals who exhibit the trait (ibid., p. 69). In human phylogeny, selection favored social learners who have been able to evaluate potential models and copy the most successful among them, thereby saving the costs of individual learning (see also Rogers, 1983; Henrich and Gil-White, 2001; Labov, 2001). Hence, model-based learning includes a predisposition to imitate successful or prestigious individuals. In general, a model-based bias results if social learners use the value of a second character that characterizes a model (for example, prestige) to determine the attractiveness of that individual as a model for the primary character (for example, a certain behavior). This method of evaluating different cultural variants is likely to be much less costly than directly evaluating these variants (Boyd and Richerson, 1985, p. 135). In Section 4, this bias will be used, among others, to model the diffusion of novelty in a population.

Finally, individuals are more likely to adopt some cultural variants based on their content (ibid., p. 135; Richerson and Boyd, 2005, p. 69). Such a content-based or direct bias can result from the calculation of costs and benefits associated with alternative variants or from cognitive structures that cause people to preferentially adopt some cultural variants rather than others, that is, it results from cues that arise from the interaction of specific qualities of a cultural variant with our social learning psychology. This procedure is likely to entail some kind of experimentation on the part of the agent.[6] In general, a cultural transmission rule is characterized by direct bias if one cultural variant is more attractive than others. A directly biased transmission creates a force that increases the frequency of the culturally transmitted variant that is favored by the bias. A relatively weak direct bias can have important effects on the frequency of different cultural variants in a population. An example of a direct bias – favoring cooperative cultural traits – will be the subject matter of the next section.

To provide another example, Cordes (2005) has, with reference to hypotheses from evolutionary psychology, argued that there are specialized psychological mechanisms that have evolved during human phylogeny to solve cognitive problems linked to the making and using of tools. These mechanisms show considerable content sensitivity with respect to observational learning of how to apply tools and play a role in directing attentional processes. Thus, innate cognitive dispositions contribute to what information will be subject to profound contemplation, what information will easily diffuse within a population of agents, and whether it may be an input to creative activity. Such a bias influences culturally engendered and institutionalized attitudes toward, for example, productive and useful work, the compliance with certain cultural norms, or the aesthetic sense for an appreciation of skill and dexterity.

As a consequence of these thoughts, biological, Darwinian concepts account for some of the aspects of the relation between individual and collective phenomena (see Richerson and Boyd, 2005, p. 247). This is a feature of many biological concepts since the basic biological theory already includes the genetic level, individuals, and populations, that is, what happens to individuals affects the population's properties and vice versa. The cultural transmission biases mentioned above are a case in point.

3   INTERACTIONS BETWEEN THE CULTURAL AND GENETIC LEVELS: THE DUAL INHERITANCE THEORY

The dual inheritance theory provides another explanation for important facets of the recursive relationships between a (genetic) micro and a (cultural) macro level. It explains the evolution of uniquely human cognitive dispositions that are not amenable to a purely reductionist approach.

The central tenet of evolutionary theory is that behavior of organisms should maximize genetic fitness. Furthermore, as a corollary of this principle, natural selection leads to cooperation among large numbers of individuals only if they are genetically closely related. With the exception of humans, this result seems consistent with the available data (Wilson, 1975). In human organizations, cooperation – including among non-relatives – readily emerges spontaneously in small- and medium-sized groups. Cooperation seems to be a kind of first choice for human actors.[7] This disposition is rare in nature, if not uniquely human. The question is then, what are the origins of this inclination toward cooperation? If genes spread because they enhance the survival and reproduction of their carriers, how can altruistic/cooperative behavior evolve at all? Existing genetic evolutionary approaches – that focus on the genetic micro level – cannot explain the degree of prosociality (cooperation, altruism, moralistic punishment) observed in humans.

In order to understand this phenomenon, we require a theory that explains why humans, but not other organisms, are capable of large-scale cooperation among non-relatives. Boyd and Richerson (1982, 2002) and Richerson and Boyd (2005) propose that the disposition for cooperation has evolved by a process of cultural group selection. Humans are also unique in the degree to which they depend upon socially transmitted information, that is, culture – a macro-level phenomenon, to create complex adaptations (see also Tomasello, 1996). While genetic variation between human groups is very hard to maintain due to intergroup migration, cultural variation between groups can resist the destruction of intergroup variation.[8] The fact that cultural variation can more easily respond to group selection is due to mechanisms peculiar to culture that maintain variation even when migration rates are appreciable. One of these mechanisms in cultural transmission that culturally homogenize groups is the conformist bias mentioned above; another is the role model bias. Other cultural processes, such as symbolic markers of group identity, also tend to limit the flow of ideas from group to group (McElreath et al., 2003). Moreover, the patterns of group formation and group competition in small-scale societies satisfy the requirements of cultural group selection models (Soltis et al., 1995). As a result, the capacity for culture enables behavioral equilibria consisting of combinations of cooperation and punishment that are not available to genetic evolutionary processes.

The ancestors of modern humans became highly cultural in the Middle Pleistocene, perhaps 250,000 years ago (McBrearty and Brooks, 2000). If cultural group selection became an appreciable evolutionary force about that time, it would have set in motion a process of gene–culture coevolution.[9] The prevalent level of cooperation based upon the prevailing social transmitted institutions in a group would exert selection on innate human social dispositions, that is, here we have a direct interaction between a micro (genes) and a macro (culture) level resulting in a certain cognitive setup of human agents. Over many generations this coevolutionary dynamic generated a social psychology that facilitated cooperation. This coevolutionary dynamic makes genes as susceptible to cultural influences as vice versa (Richerson and Boyd, 2005, p. 191).

We imagine a long period of repeated gene–culture coevolutionary cycles in which primitive social institutions, such as the rule to treat cousins like brothers, became established in populations, and in turn exerted a coevolutionary response, for example, down-regulating testosterone production when confronted with relatively distantly related males who might be mating competitors. Once males became a little more docile, then a more tolerant culturally transmitted norm that encouraged cooperation between still more distantly related males might invade. Over many generations this coevolutionary dynamic generated a cognitive setup that facilitated cooperation, sometimes even with strangers. By systematically altering the social (macro) environment in favor of prosocial phenotypes, cultural processes create the conditions for natural selection to favor prosocial genes on a micro level, for example, genetically coded dispositions for in-group altruism, cooperation, and punishment (see Boyd and Richerson, 1982). By focusing on competition among cultural groups, these models demonstrate how the cultural transmission of behaviors related to cooperation may explain otherwise puzzling patterns of human prosociality.

The selective mechanisms involved in this process can favor quite different behaviors from those favored by selection on genes alone. As a result, any gene that contributed to prosocial behavior or anti-social conduct would have undergone selection by coevolution. Culturally evolved social environments favored an innate psychology that is suited to such environments, for example, a psychology aiming at gaining social rewards and avoiding social sanctions.[10] In this way, cultural institutions set up a moral community.[11] The complex societies of the sort we live in began to evolve only about 5,000 years ago, too little time for much, if any, evolution of the innate aspects of our social psychology. Hence, complex societies are based upon the cultural evolution of institutions that use our tribal social predispositions as their raw material (Richerson and Boyd, 1999).

In this context, cultural group selection meets a fundamental evolutionary principle: costly group-beneficial behavior cannot evolve unless the benefits of this behavior flow non-randomly to individuals who carry the genes that give rise to the behavior. Moreover, the evolution of moralistic strategies has been guided by cultural group selection – a macro-level property – for cooperative traits and represents another crucial mechanism in creating cultural differences between groups: the coevolutionary process between genes and culture is maintained by a system of moral rules that sanction bad behavior and reward good behavior. 'Good' genes get rewarded and 'bad' genes penalized by culturally transmitted norms; in this case not by group selection acting directly on the genes. Nevertheless, in the end, the innate elements of human social psychology act much as if they had been subject to group selection. The theory of punishment (for example, Fehr and Gächter, 2002) describes how the evolved willingness to punish non-conformists – even at a cost to oneself – renders a potentially powerful tool in homogenizing social groups and group competition.[12]

Groups with prosocial moralistic norms for cooperation had a considerable advantage over other, competing groups (Henrich, 2004; Richerson and Boyd, 2005, p. 214). By producing multiple behavioral equilibria, including group-beneficial equilibria, cultural evolution generates a macro-level mechanism of equilibrium selection that can favor prosociality on the micro level of an individual. Cultural group selection favors not only the evolution of prosocial predispositions, but also the harder element of altruistic punishment of individuals who violate cultural norms. Successful social institutions are based on humans' propensity toward cooperation reinforced by altruistic punishment, rewards, moral suasion, and social role models, often codified in culturally transmitted norms and rules. Furthermore, institutions have to cope with the problem that there is always a not-insignificant selfish minority that has to be coerced into cooperating. Some sort of policing system must exist to counteract this threat (Oström, 1990; Fehr and Gächter, 2000; Richerson and Boyd, 2001). Monitoring, rewarding, and punishment systems are necessary to prevent an increase of selfish behavioral strategies and a collapse of cooperation. These systems function best when they crowd in good behavior in those tempted to defect without crowding out cooperation on the part of those inclined to cooperate. To understand these facets of human behavior, an analysis of the recursive relationship between cultural and genetic transmission is inevitable.

As a result, the coevolutionary selection of genes has given rise to a direct bias taking effect in cultural transmission: the evolved inclination toward group-beneficial or cooperative cultural contents. The gene–culture, or micro–macro, coevolutionary approach provides an explanation for the human capacity of large-scale cooperation in various domains. Human social learning abilities produce cultural evolution and behavioral equilibria not available to genetic transmission alone. Then, cultural group selection acted on these alternative behavioral equilibria. In the next section, we develop a model of cultural transmission that relies on biases in social learning to explain the diffusion of novelty in a population.

4   THE DIFFUSION OF NOVELTY AS A CULTURAL MACRO PHENOMENON

Evolutionary models of cultural change allow one to deduce the population-level evolutionary consequences of individual-level psychologies, decision rules, and behaviors (McElreath and Henrich, 2007). At the same time, the population affects individuals. The micro-level learning biases of individuals taking effect in cultural transmission, which have been discussed in Section 2, have consequences for the population-level dynamics of cultural change. A simple formal model of cultural evolution that draws on a model developed by Henrich (2001) can depict this interrelationship and explain an important stylized empirical fact – the diffusion of novelty in a population via processes of social learning. The human ability to acquire novel behaviors by observation is the reason why cultural change, that is, the diffusion of new cultural variants, is cumulative. This contrasts with rational choice models in the social sciences: a core element of these is that individuals rationally choose among given alternative behaviors by performing cost–benefit analyses using payoff-relevant data.

To understand how a population's culture evolves, we need to account for the processes that increase the frequency of some cultural variants, for example, a novel practice, idea, or technology, and reduce that of others, for example, established ways of behavior. A complex interplay of such processes will constantly affect any population's culture. In this context, the agents' behavioral repertoire is crucially influenced by processes of social learning. In the following, we illustrate how these considerations can be translated into a stylized mathematical model (as points of origin for this method, see Cavalli-Sforza and Feldman, 1981; Boyd and Richerson, 1985). The starting point of the analysis is the empirical observation that robust 'S-shaped' cumulative adoption curves are typically observed in the spread of novel practices, ideas, and technologies. Diffusion rates first rise, then fall over time; a period of rapid adoption is sandwiched between a slow takeup and satiation. These diffusion curves emerge as an empirical phenomenon from the diffusion of innovations literature and their general shape captures the temporal dynamics encountered in a wide range of diffusion studies (see, for example, Rogers, 1983; Henrich, 2001). Why do things diffuse slowly if an innovation is advantageous from the beginning? Rational choice models cannot account for these temporal dynamics of the diffusion of an advantageous novelty, especially for the long time lag until the adoption dynamic 'takes off', that is, the 'long tails' of the S-shaped diffusion curves. However, as will be shown in the following, models based on biased cultural transmission can reproduce these empirical patterns.

Within the scope of this model, we shall focus on three cultural evolutionary forces that bias transmission, can be traced back to evolved cognitive dispositions, operate at the individual level, and have been described above (see Section 2): the model-based or prestige bias, the conformity bias, and a direct bias. In general, cultural transmission biases are forces that arise because people's psychology makes them more likely to adopt some cultural contents rather than others, thereby changing the frequency of the different types of cultural variants in the population.[13] In this context, biases can consist of an innate component and/or a cultural component acquired in an earlier episode of social learning (Richerson and Boyd, 2005, p. 66).[14] To model the transmission of a dichotomous cultural trait we begin by labeling the variants, say 'Trait 1' and 'Trait 2', where Trait 1 represents the new technology, behavior, or idea and Trait 2 the existing cultural variant. Tracking only two traits is sufficient to capture the essentials of a typical diffusion process. The state of the population is determined by the frequency of agents with the new variant Trait 1, labeled p, which denotes the frequency of the novel Trait 1 in this population (0 in the beginning); $1 - p$ is the frequency of Trait 2 (1 in the beginning). Now, the task is to find a recursion equation in discrete time that allows us to predict the frequency of p in the next stage of the transmission process given its frequency in the present stage. Cultural transmission takes place between the members of a population. The model is of the form:

$$p_{t+1} = p_t + \text{cultural evolutionary forces (biases)}.$$

We take a population perspective, that is, we look at a population of potential adopters. In a large population, each individual encounters one potential 'cultural model' during each time cycle. During each time step, individuals acquire information on the relative payoffs of the two alternatives, whereby it is assumed that Trait 1 – the innovation – is superior to Trait 2 with respect to payoffs. To characterize the evolution of the population, the model must allow us to predict the changes in the frequency of cultural variants in the course of time. We derive a recursion that determines p in the next time step, given the value of p in this period. This is done by specifying the probability that a particular set of role models makes an individual to acquire the cultural variant Trait 1.

A direct bias or a model-based bias is represented by the variables r_1 and r_2 in Table 3.1, that is, agents compare the r-value of their cultural variant with the model's or the trait's r-value. In the case of the prestige or model-based bias, an individual compares his/her prestige to the prestige of the potential cultural model and switches and adopts the trait of the

Evolution, organization and economic behavior

Table 3.1   *Probability of an agent acquiring Trait 1 or Trait 2 given a particular model and the cultural variant held by the agent*

Culture variant of		Frequency of pairings	Probability that an agent acquires Trait 1 or Trait 2	
Self	Model		Pr(*T*1)	Pr(*T*2)
1	1	p^2	1	0
1	2	$p(1-p)$	$\frac{1}{2}[1 + (r_1 - r_2)]$	$\frac{1}{2}[1 - (r_1 - r_2)]$
2	1	$(1-p)p$	$\frac{1}{2}[1 + (r_1 - r_2)]$	$\frac{1}{2}[1 - (r_1 - r_2)]$
2	2	$(1-p)^2$	0	1

more prestigious model. A direct bias causes an individual to compare his/her own trait to the qualities of the trait possessed by the cultural model. This gives the switching probabilities for each combination of cultural models (the term $r_1 - r_2$ ranges from -1 to 1). With these assumptions, the cultural transmission table shows the probability of agents acquiring Trait 1 or Trait 2, given a particular set of cultural role models (Self, Model).

For example, let $P(T1|T1T2)$ denote the conditional probability that an agent acquires Trait 1 given that he/she is exposed to a model with Trait 2 while holding Trait 1 him/herself. After inserting all possible conditional probabilities, the following equation shows the frequency of Trait 1 after transmission, p', given that it was p before transmission:

$$p' = p^2 P(T1|T1T1) + p(1 - p)P(T1|T1T2) + (1 - p)pP(T1|T2T1)$$

$$+ (1 - p)^2 P(T1|T2T2). \tag{3.1}$$

This term computes the frequency of each different set of social models, multiplies this by the probability that a particular set of social models results in an individual acquiring a particular cultural variant, and then sums over all possible sets of social models. The frequency of Trait 1 after cultural transmission is calculated by multiplying the probability of each pairing by the probability of ending up with Trait 1. This expression tells us how the frequency of the trait will change from one time step to another because of the social learning processes.

Inserting the conditional probabilities from Table 3.1, we can rewrite equation (3.1):

$$p' = p^2(1) + p(1 - p)\frac{1}{2}[1 + (r_1 - r_2)]$$

$$+ (1 - p)p\frac{1}{2}[1 + (r_1 - r_2)] + (1 - p)^2(0). \qquad (3.2)$$

Simplifying this, we get:

$$p' = p + (1 - p)p(r_1 - r_2) = p + p(1 - p)B \text{ (with } B = r_1 - r_2). \quad (3.3)$$

The model's r-values may also contain a conformist component that depends on the frequency of the trait in the current population, that is, agents use the frequency of a trait as an indirect indicator of its worth – a direct interaction between the micro and the macro level. On each encounter, individuals assess the relative frequency of the two traits. B now has two components, a constant part and a frequency-dependent part:

$$B = b(1 - \alpha) + \alpha(2p - 1). \qquad (3.4)$$

The conformist component of equation (3.4), $\alpha(2p - 1)$, varies between -1 and 1. When the frequency of the novel trait is low, this component is negative, which reduces the value of the total bias B. Whereas, when $p > 0.5$, this term increases the conformity bias, thereby favoring the dissemination of the more common trait. Here, α scales the weight given to the frequency of a behavior relative to other biases in social learning, that is, b captures other biases, such as the direct or model-based biases introduced above and as shown in Appendix 3A (α varies between 0 and 1; b varies between -1 and 1).[15] We obtain:

$$p' = p + p(1 - p)[b(1 - \alpha) + \alpha(2p - 1)]. \qquad (3.5)$$

The recursion given by equation (3.5) models the change of p in the population in the course of time given three potential learning biases. By setting the parameters of the system, we can analyze its long-run behavior by conceptually iterating equation (3.5) recursively through successive time cycles. Its temporal dynamics are plotted in Figure 3.1.

These diffusion curves generated by the model for different values of the parameters nicely fit the empirically observed diffusion curves. Moreover, the conformity bias explains the slow growth of p during the initial stages of the diffusion process: it captures the empirical phenomenon of 'long tails' – the slow growth period in the beginning of diffusion – and the takeoff points, that is, when a 'critical mass' is achieved, the diffusion

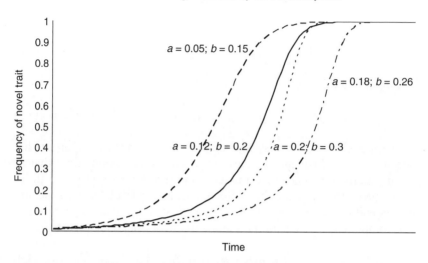

Figure 3.1   Spreading of a novel trait in a population via processes of biased cultural transmission for different values of α *(denoted by 'a' in the figure) and* b

process 'takes off' and the trait quickly reaches fixation (the takeoff frequencies lie between 0 and 0.5).[16] The existence of takeoff points supports the claim that social learning is a crucial force in the dissemination of novelty. Hence, the different S-shapes generated by this social learning model resemble a wide range of the empirical adoption curves (see Henrich, 2001). This similarity suggests that biased cultural transmission models capture an important component of human behavioral change. The models of cultural evolution consistently produce the particular S-dynamics found throughout the literature.

Therefore, adoption dynamics, that is, the diffusion of innovations of all kind, indicate that biased cultural transmission (social learning) is the predominant force in behavioral change and sociocultural evolution in general, and not individual-level rational choice, trial-and-error learning, or cost–benefit analysis as is assumed in many theoretical approaches in the social sciences. Unless payoff information related to the different cultural traits is very clear, people rely on biased cultural transmission. What is more, cultural transmission can also explain the spread of maladaptive or costly behavior against the force of individual learning – such traits are prevalent in cultures throughout the world (Richerson and Boyd, 2005, p. 243).

5 CONCLUSIONS

Although many economists and other social scientists are working on how individuals make decisions and how behavior is acquired, many of them ignore how those decisions and mechanisms of learning aggregate at the population level. On the other hand, many analyses of collective institutions do not account for the micro determinants of individual behavior and the recursive relationship between these levels. As shown, evidence from evolutionary and cognitive science suggests that humans have an evolved psychology that shapes what we learn, perceive, and think (ibid., p. 4). These cognitive dispositions influence the kinds of cultural variants that spread and persist. Moreover, these approaches link the population dynamics of cumulative cultural evolution to the psychological mechanisms that shape social learning. Furthermore, this chapter has shown that humans have predispositions toward cooperation and group-beneficial behaviors that have resulted from a process of gene–culture coevolution, that is, the recursive interaction of a micro and a macro level (Boyd and Richerson, 1982).

In evolutionary models, the classical conflict between explanations at the level of individuals and explanations at the level of the society disappear (see, for example, Dopfer and Potts, 2004; McElreath and Boyd, 2007). Population models allow explanation and causation at both levels to exist in one theory (see also Jackson, 2002). They are about how individuals can create population-level effects which then influence individual behavior and vice versa. A model of cultural transmission has been proposed that can be considered as a step toward an applied science of cultural evolution – in this case in the context of diffusion dynamics of technologies, ideas, or behaviors. This learning model is rooted in human psychology, is evolutionarily plausible, and still produces the typical S-curves of most diffusion dynamics found in the literature under a wide range of general conditions.

Models of cultural evolution start with a theory based on individual behavior and also provide an account of society-scale phenomena. In the short run, individual decisions do not have much effect on institutions, but, in the long run, accumulated over many decisions, individual decisions have a profound effect on institutions – they are the driving force of cultural evolution. Delineating both the micro-level psychological mechanisms of cultural transmission, as well as the population-level processes to which they give rise and that again influence individual behavior, may further the understanding of a variety of important social phenomena (see, for example, Cordes et al., 2008). Evolutionary approaches to cultural evolution account for the basic structure of the relationship between individuals and the emerging collective properties of their societies.

NOTES

1. In their contribution to this debate, Dopfer and Potts add a mediating third – meso – domain to the analysis.
2. A cultural variant is defined as an idea, skill, belief, attitude, or value that is acquired by social learning and that influences an individual's behavior.
3. The following discussion draws on Cordes (2004).
4. In this context, biases can consist of an innate component and a cultural component acquired in an earlier episode of social learning (Richerson and Boyd, 2005, p. 66).
5. Therefore, rational choice is a weak process relative to cultural transmission in the construction of behavioral repertoires. For a similar argument in economics, see Eshel et al. (1998).
6. As long as this experimentation is not too expensive, it is plausible that directly biased transmission might evolve, as is indicated by abundant empirical evidence (for example, Lumsden and Wilson, 1981, p. 38; Rogers, 1983, p. 217; Labov, 1994). However, when it is difficult or costly to evaluate the consequences of the cultural variants available in the population directly, then frequency-dependent or model-based bias may be more advantageous.
7. See the abundant evidence from game theory and experimental economics (for example, Rubin, 1982; Güth and van Damme, 1998; Fehr and Schmidt, 1999; Bolton and Ockenfels, 2000; Fehr and Gächter, 2000).
8. The first aspect is the central problem of any genetic explanation of group selection.
9. To enable this process to start, a group-beneficial variant must become common in an initial subpopulation only once. Then, the conformist effect will favor its further increase by group selection.
10. Evidence from neuroscience, for example, shows that cooperation leads to the activation of brain regions involved in the release of dopamine and in pleasure behavior, thus reinforcing cooperation (Rilling et al., 2002). Cultural rules that are affectively evaluated in a positive way may be transmitted preferentially.
11. For an account of the evolution of relatively large, cooperative, egalitarian hunter-gatherer societies from smaller, less cooperative dominance structured ape societies, see Boehm (1999).
12. Moralistic punishment is a more plausible mechanism for the maintenance of large-scale cooperation than reciprocity. For an interesting transfer of this topic to the explanation of international political conflicts, see Witt (2001).
13. The forces of biased transmission acting on cultural variation are much stronger than those that shape genetic variation; they work on shorter timescales and are driven by psychological processes, not demographic events.
14. Each of these biases of cultural transmission arises from the attempts of social learners to evaluate the adaptiveness of the different cultural variants they are exposed to in a setting in which information is incomplete or costly to acquire (Boyd and Richerson, 1985). This does not imply that all biases are necessarily adaptive, especially in contemporary societies.
15. If α is large, few if any traits can spread in the population.
16. Conformist transmission also predicts socio-spatial clusters of similar traits any time the differences between the costs and benefits of alternatives are relatively small.

REFERENCES

Aronson, E., T.D. Wilson and R.M. Akert (2002), *Social Psychology*, Upper Saddle River, NJ: Prentice-Hall.

Bandura, A. (1986), *Social Foundations of Thought and Action*, Englewood Cliffs, NJ: Prentice-Hall.

Boehm, C. (1999), *Hierarchy in the Forest: The Evolution of Egalitarian Behavior*, Cambridge, MA: Harvard University Press.

Bolton, G.E. and A. Ockenfels (2000), 'ERC: a theory of equity, reciprocity, and competition', *American Economic Review*, **90**, 166–93.

Boyd, R. and P.J. Richerson (1982), 'Cultural transmission and the evolution of cooperative behavior', *Human Ecology*, **10**, 325–51.

Boyd, R. and P.J. Richerson (1985), *Culture and the Evolutionary Process*, Chicago, IL: University of Chicago Press.

Boyd, R. and P.J. Richerson (1989), 'Social learning as an adaptation', *Lectures on Mathematics in the Life Sciences*, **20**, 1–20.

Boyd, R. and P.J. Richerson (1993), 'Rationality, imitation, and tradition', in R.H. Day and P. Chen (eds), *Nonlinear Dynamics and Evolutionary Economics*, New York: Oxford University Press, pp. 131–49.

Boyd, R. and P.J. Richerson (2002), 'Group beneficial norms can spread rapidly in a structured population', *Journal of Theoretical Biology*, **215**, 287–96.

Cavalli-Sforza, L.L. and M.W. Feldman (1981), *Cultural Transmission and Evolution: A Quantitative Approach*, Princeton, NJ: Princeton University Press.

Cordes, C. (2004), 'The human adaptation for culture and its behavioral implications', *Journal of Bioeconomics*, **6**, 143–63.

Cordes, C. (2005), 'Veblen's "instinct of workmanship", its cognitive foundations, and some implications for economic theory', *Journal of Economic Issues*, **39**, 1–20.

Cordes, C. (2006), 'Darwinism in economics: from analogy to continuity', *Journal of Evolutionary Economics*, **16**, 529–41.

Cordes, C., P.J. Richerson, R. McElreath and P. Strimling (2008), 'A naturalistic approach to the theory of the firm: the role of cooperation and cultural evolution', *Journal of Economic Behavior and Organization*, **68**, 125–39.

Dopfer, K. and J. Potts (2004), 'Evolutionary realism: a new ontology for economics', *Journal of Economic Methodology*, **11**, 195–212.

Eshel, I., L. Samuelson and A. Shaked (1998), 'Altruists, egoists, and hooligans in a local interaction model', *American Economic Review*, **88**, 157–79.

Fehr, E. and S. Gächter (2000), 'Cooperation and punishment in public goods experiments', *American Economic Review*, **90**, 980–94.

Fehr, E. and S. Gächter (2002), 'Altruistic punishment in humans', *Nature*, **415**, 137–40.

Fehr, E. and K.M. Schmidt (1999), 'A theory of fairness, competition, and cooperation', *Quarterly Journal of Economics*, **114**, 817–68.

Güth, W. and E. van Damme (1998), 'Information, strategic behavior, and fairness in ultimatum bargaining: an experimental study', *Journal of Mathematical Psychology*, **42**, 227–47.

Harrington Jr, J.E. (1999), 'Rigidity of social systems', *Journal of Political Economy*, **107**, 40–64.

Henrich, J. (2001), 'Cultural transmission and the diffusion of innovations: adoption dynamics indicate that biased cultural transmission is the predominant force in behavioral change', *American Anthropologist*, **103**, 992–1013.

Henrich, J. (2004), 'Cultural group selection, coevolutionary processes and large-scale cooperation', *Journal of Economic Behavior and Organization*, **53**, 3–35.

Henrich, J. and R. Boyd (1998), 'The evolution of conformist transmission and the emergence of between-group differences', *Evolution and Human Behavior*, **19**, 215–41.

Henrich, J. and F.J. Gil-White (2001), 'The evolution of prestige: freely conferred deference as a mechanism for enhancing the benefits of cultural transmission', *Evolution and Human Behavior*, **22**, 165–96.

Jackson, W.A. (2002), 'Functional explanation in economics: a qualified defense', *Journal of Economic Methodology*, **9**, 169–89.

Kameda, T. and N. Diasuke (2002), 'Cost–benefit analysis of social/cultural learning in a nonstationary uncertain environment: an evolutionary simulation and an experiment with human subjects', *Evolution and Human Behavior*, **23**, 373–93.

Kruger, A.C., H.H. Ratner and M. Tomasello (1993), 'Cultural learning', *Behavioral and Brain Sciences*, **16**, 495–552.

Labov, W. (1994), *Principles of Linguistic Change: Internal Factors*, Oxford: Blackwell.

Labov, W. (2001), *Principles of Linguistic Change: Social Factors*, Oxford: Blackwell.

Lumsden, C.J. and E.O. Wilson (1981), *Genes, Mind, and Culture*, Cambridge, MA: Harvard University Press.

McBrearty, S. and A.S. Brooks (2000), 'The revolution that wasn't: a new interpretation of the origin of modern human behavior', *Journal of Human Evolution*, **39**, 453–563.

McElreath, R. and R. Boyd (2007), *Modeling the Evolution of Social Behavior: A Guide for the Perplexed*, Chicago, IL: University of Chicago Press.

McElreath, R., R. Boyd and P.J. Richerson (2003), 'Shared norms and the evolution of ethnic markers', *Current Anthropology*, **44**, 122–9.

McElreath, R. and J. Henrich (2007), 'Modeling cultural evolution', in R. Dunbar and L. Barrett (eds), *Oxford Handbook of Evolutionary Psychology*, New York: Oxford University Press.

Ostrom, E. (1990), *Governing the Commons: The Evolution of Institutions for Collective Action*, Cambridge: Cambridge University Press.

Richerson, P.J. and R. Boyd (1999), 'Complex societies: the evolutionary origins of a crude superorganism', *Human Nature*, **10**, 253–89.

Richerson, P.J. and R. Boyd (2001), 'The evolution of subjective commitment to groups: a tribal instincts theory', in R.M. Nesse (ed.), *Evolution and the Capacity for Commitment*, New York: Russell Sage Foundation, pp. 186–220.

Richerson, P.J. and R. Boyd (2005), *Not by Genes Alone: How Culture Transformed Human Evolution*, Chicago, IL: University of Chicago Press.

Rilling, J.K., D.A. Gutman, T.R. Zeh, G. Pagnoni, G.S. Berns and C.D. Kilts (2002), 'A neural basis for social cooperation', *Neuron*, **35**, 395–405.

Rogers, E.M. (1983), *Diffusion of Innovations*, New York: Free Press.

Rubin, P.H. (1982), 'Evolved ethics and efficient ethics', *Journal of Economic Behavior and Organization*, **3**, 161–74.

Singer, W. (2000), 'Response synchronization: a universal coding strategy for the definition of relations', in M.S. Gazzaniga (ed.), *The New Cognitive Neurosciences*, Cambridge, MA: MIT Press, pp. 325–38.

Soltis, J., R. Boyd and P.J. Richerson (1995), 'Can group-functional behaviors evolve by cultural group selection? An empirical test', *Current Anthropology*, **36**, 473–94.

Tomasello, M. (1996), 'Do apes ape?', in C.M. Heyes and B.G. Galef Jr (eds),

Social Learning in Animals: The Roots of Culture, San Diego, CA: Academic Press, pp. 319–46.

Tomasello, M. (1999), 'The human adaptation for culture', *Annual Review of Anthropology*, **28**, 509–29.

Wilson, E.O. (1975), *Sociobiology: The New Synthesis*, Cambridge, MA: Harvard University Press.

Witt, U. (2001), 'Between appeasement and belligerent moralism: the evolution of moral conduct in international politics', *Public Choice*, **106**, 365–88.

Witt, U. (2003), *The Evolving Economy: Essays on the Evolutionary Approach to Economics*, Cheltenham, UK and Northampton, MA, USA: Edward Elgar.

Witt, U. (2004), 'On the proper interpretation of "evolution" in economics and its implications for production theory', *Journal of Economic Methodology*, **11**, 125–46.

APPENDIX 3A

The r-values in the case of conformist transmission are:

$$r_1 = b_1(1 - \alpha) + \alpha\left(p - \frac{1}{2}\right) \tag{3A.1}$$

and

$$r_2 = b_2(1 - \alpha) + \alpha\left(1 - p - \frac{1}{2}\right). \tag{3A.2}$$

This gives us the total bias B:

$$B = r_1 - r_2 = (b_1 - b_2)(1 - \alpha) + \alpha(2p - 1) = b(1 - \alpha) + \alpha(2p - 1). \tag{3A.3}$$

4. Consumer learning through interaction: effects on aggregate outcomes

Zakaria Babutsidze*

1 INTRODUCTION

It is the nature of the capitalistic free market that the results of producer actions are ultimately anchored to consumer behavior. It is consumers who decide when to buy and what to buy, and how to respond to price or quality changes in products supplied to them. Thus, we believe that the analysis of any economic phenomenon should start with the analysis of consumer decisions.

Consumer behavior has been analyzed from many different perspectives. Various disciplines have used different types of approach at different levels of analysis. Hansen (1972) offers an interesting classification of these approaches. According to him the models can be divided into four groups. The first group consists of the psychological models which deal with the consumers at the individual level. The second group corresponds to social–psychological models which deal with individuals and their environment. The third group is sociological, and deals with the segments of society, while the fourth group is anthropological and deals with entire societies. Economics, being a social science, is somewhere close to the anthropological group. Therefore, what the discipline should aim at is to understand the behavior of consumer populations as a united system. This is crucial for deriving useful policy advice.

Thus, aggregate consumer behavior is of central importance. However, consumer society consists of heterogeneous, interacting consumers. And, as Hansen (ibid.) points out, the further you go in modeling from psychological toward anthropological models, the more important the aggregation issues become. In other words, it becomes harder to derive the aggregate behavior from the behavior of single agents. Therefore, economics resorted to overly simplified setups that omit important features of consumer populations. In this chapter we concentrate on one such feature and analyze what might be the result of omitting it from the modeling of consumer behavior.

Learning requires information. Information can come from various sources. Many consumer behavior models are rightly built on a multiplicity of sources of information about products available on the market. Information collected through these sources can be classified into two groups: internal and external information. Internal information is collected through immediate experience with products. Consumers themselves are responsible for interpreting the experience and giving it the form of the piece of information. External information reaches the consumer in the form of a piece of information. The literature in psychology (Fazio and Zanna, 1978) and marketing (Smith and Swinyard, 1983) suggests that, in general, weights attributed to internal information are higher than those put on external information. The latter nevertheless remains an influential driver of consumer choices (Bennett and Mandell, 1969; Duncan and Olshavsky, 1982). Myers and Robertson (1972) claim that consumers judge information sources according to the source's intention to inuence the information receiver. On this scale, personal communication among consumers scores highest among all the sources of external information (Hansen, 1972). Therefore, it is safe to claim that interaction with peers is the most valuable source of external information. This is confirmed by the overwhelming empirical evidence about intensity of interaction among consumers (Beatty and Smith, 1987; Gershoff and Johar, 2006).

Hence, interaction is an important driver of the consumer choice process, at least with regard to certain product classes (for example, consumer electronics). However, it has not attracted sufficient attention in economics. Although there are many models built on consumer interactions, to the best of our knowledge, there has been no investigation into the consequences of mis-specifying the consumer behavior model by omitting the interrelatedness of consumer choices. This chapter looks at the importance of modeling consumer interactions for deriving aggregate outcomes. We show that neglecting the modeling of interactions, in cases where consumers affect each other's choices, might lead to not only quantitative, but also serious qualitative mistakes in outcomes, and as a result in policy recommendations. This conclusion does not depend on the intensity of interaction. In fact, for certain aspects, a lower intensity of interaction might mean larger departures from replicating the actual behavior of the system.

In this chapter we discuss two examples and contrast results with and without consumer interactions. These two examples use different interaction mechanisms. They have a level of sophistication that is no more than the level of absolute necessity, in order to underline the main message of the chapter. Examples are designed to demonstrate that the omission of consumer interaction from modeling can modify both equilibrium and transitional properties of the system.

2   CONSUMER INTERACTION

Economists distinguish between two types of interaction: global and local. Interaction is global when forces generated by consumers affect every consumer in the economy. Interaction is local when different forces affect different consumers. This distinction is best demonstrated with the example of information. If information about the product, say an impression of a consumer, is somehow broadcast to all the consumers, interaction is global. If this information is communicated only to part of the society, interaction is local. Local interactions must have temporal stability of links. In other words, the same consumers should share information with the same subset of the population over time. These linkages are usually determined by the geographical location or social status (Cowan et al., 2004).

There are two major approaches to the analysis of local social interactions, the game-theoretic and the complex systems approaches. There are many game-theoretic setups in non-market (social) environments. Some of these games explicitly model social interactions between agents. The most prominent examples of this type of game are coordination games. These are the games with multiple pure strategy Nash equilibria that are Pareto rankable. Examples of such games include the 'prisoner's dilemma' and the 'battle of the sexes' (Cooper, 1998). In simple forms of coordination games, rationally playing agents choose Pareto inferior outcomes (Gibbons, 1992). The prospect of overcoming coordination failure with additional social interaction has been examined experimentally (Fehr and Gachter, 2000; Manski, 2000). Other examples of modeling social interactions from a game-theoretic perspective include minority games (Arthur, 1994) and household behavior games (McElroy, 1990). Although these setups are modeling agent interactions, the accent in these models is on individual behavior in the environment with interactions, rather than on aggregate outcomes. These models are not suitable for analysis of what happens when there is no interaction.

The most prominent applications of complex systems to the analysis of interactions are social networks. The modern-day graphical toolbox for the analysis of social networks was first developed in sociology (Coleman, 1964; Holland and Leinhardt, 1970). Recently the methodology has become popular in business and management (for example, Reingen et al., 1984; Brass et al., 1998). This methodology has great potential for empirical analysis (Burt, 2001). Although these models are concerned with aggregate implications, deriving them using social networks as the basis for agent interactions is somewhat complicated. The reason is that, like in any other complex system, small perturbations in the topology of networks lead to large differences in outcomes. A prominent contribution in this respect is due to Bala and Goyal (1998). However, with modern computational capabilities, the application of complex systems theories to economic problems becomes viable. Computational tools such as agent-based modeling can contribute a great deal to understanding important economic processes (Fagiolo et al., 2007).

These two approaches to local social interactions are usually used in combination in economics. For example, a great deal of effort has gone into analyzing network formation through game-theoretic setups. This line of research has been concerned with the formation of social (Bala and Goyal, 2000; Ehrhardt et al., 2007), as well as collaborative (Goyal and Moraga-Gonzalez, 2001) and buyer–seller networks (Wang and Watts, 2006). Besides, the games where agents are matched not randomly but through networks have also been developed. Here networks on which games are played can be exogenously given (Schelling, 1969; Epstein and Axtell, 1996) or endogenously formed (Fagiolo, 2005; Fagiolo and Valente, 2005).

The best-known and most widely analyzed incarnation of global social interactions are network effects (Katz and Shapiro, 1994). Network effects create additional incentives (or disincentives) for consumers to buy a product. These are usually modeled as consumers taking into account the popularity of the product. In the original interpretation, network effects increase the value of the product (technology, standard) with the number (share) of consumers due to technological incompatibility between alter-natives (Farrell and Saloner, 1985). However, the same mechanism can be used for modeling popularity weighting for any other reason. Furthermore, there can be cases when popularity does not increase, but rather decreases the incentive to purchase the product (think of status goods and upper classes wanting to distinguish themselves from the rest of society).

In today's information society it is not hard to imagine consumer inter-action becoming global. Today every piece of information can be easily shared through the internet, blogs and social networking sites. However, global interactions can have many more incarnations. Most types of con-sumption are relatively conspicuous (Veblen, 1899). And the information about the most popular items in consumption baskets spreads easily. This contributes to the growth of 'fad' behavior: popular products attract more buyers (for example, Young, 1993; Bernheim, 1994). Kim and Chung (1997) empirically find the positive effect of popularity. Raj (1985) finds that the popularity of products is further reinforced by a larger share of loyal buyers. The importance of network effects for social behavior is best demonstrated by the models of informational cascades (Bikhchandani et al., 1992). In these models of sequential decision making, bandwagon (or herd) behavior can emerge as an outcome (Banerjee, 1992).

There has been an interest in the literature about the difference between local and global information flows, or interaction more generally (Ellison, 1993; Brock and Durlauf, 2000; Glaeser and Scheinkman, 2000). Research has demonstrated that global interactions result in more ordered systems, properties of which are straightforward to analyze (Gonzalez-Avella et al., 2006). However, systems with local interactions result in richer, more complex dynamics and require more subtle analysis (Glaeser and Scheinkman, 2000; Babutsidze and Cowan, 2009).

The main concern of modern evolutionary economics is with the open-ended dynamics, with the evolution of systems. Learning through interaction can easily alter the course of development. Therefore, interactions become especially important here. Furthermore, in the case of local interactions, the interaction structure is shown to be an important determinant of system development (Watts and Strogatz, 1998). Taking into account different topologies of interaction structures complicates mathematical analysis of the systems. The openness of evolutionary economics to heterodox research techniques (for example, computations, numerical simulations) promises greater potential for the analysis of economic interactions under the general framework of evolutionary economics.

3   GLOBAL INTERACTION

Effects of global interactions, especially when modeled as network effects (Farrell and Saloner, 1986; Katz and Shapiro, 1994), are relatively well understood in economics. Moreover, as the interaction structure is simple compared to local interactions, these models can be fairly straightforward. Here we present a setup to demonstrate that small portions of consumer interaction can change the equilibrium outcomes of the model dramatically. Ignoring these effects in modeling is thus unacceptable.

This exercise builds on the model presented by Babutsidze (2009). Consider a simple setup with a finite number of consumers and products. Each consumer has a utility function defined over all the products: or rather, defined over the valuations that the consumer ascribes to the products available on the market. Valuation of a product for a consumer is the maximum price this consumer is willing to pay for this product. The overall size of the economy is constant. To simplify the analysis we abstract from differences in prices. We also exclude the possibility that prices change over time.

Following the discrete choice literature (Anderson et al., 1992), we assume that the utility function $U(V)$ is such that the probability of the consumer s to buy the product n is given by the multinomial logit function:[1]

$$p_n^s = \frac{e^{v_n^s}}{\sum_{i=1}^{N} e^{v_i^s}}, \tag{4.1}$$

where $v_n^s \, (\geq 0)$ is the valuation of the product n for consumer s and N is the number of products. These valuations can be different across population as well as across product space. However, they do not change over time.

We define the equilibrium as the state when the economy reaches a time-invariant market share distribution. As there is no dynamics in valuations, equation (4.1) will describe the equilibrium distribution of purchasing probabilities. As we are studying markets with constant size, we can, without a loss of generality, normalize its size to unity. This allows us to measure the market share of the product as the average purchase probability of this product across the consumer population by:

$$h_n = \frac{1}{S} \sum_{s=1}^{S} p_n^s, \tag{4.2}$$

where S is the number of consumers in the economy.

As purchase probabilities are time invariant (due to valuations being constant), equation (4.2) describes the equilibrium market share of the product. Then it follows that if there exists s for which $v_n^s \neq 0$ then product n will have a non-zero market share in equilibrium $(h_n > 0)$.

Now consider what happens when global consumer interaction is in place. In this case we assume that there are positive network effects, which means that consumers want to purchase more popular products. For demonstration purposes we also assume that at each time period the consumer takes the market share distribution from the previous period into account. Consider the case of a linear effect.[2] In this case we can write down the new purchase probability function:

$$\bar{p}_{n;t}^s = (1 - \bar{\mu})p_n^s + \bar{\mu}\bar{h}_{n;t-1}, \tag{4.3}$$

where $\bar{\mu}$ is the level/intensity of interaction, p_n^s calculated as in equation (4.1) n and $\bar{h}_{n;t}$ describes the market share distribution in the presence of learning through interaction. It is measured as:

$$\bar{h}_{n;t} = \frac{1}{S}\sum_{s=1}^{S}\bar{p}_{n;t}^s. \tag{4.4}$$

In this case, market shares will be dynamic, as consumers will be taking into account not only their valuations, but also aggregate popularity of the product when deciding which product to purchase.

If we use the same definition of equilibrium as in the case of no interaction, it is easy to verify that the equilibrium state of the economy changes dramatically. To see this, consider what happens to the market share of the product that is least popular initially. It is straightforward to see from equation (4.3) that no matter what the level of interaction is (as long as it is not absent, $\bar{\mu} > 0$), the purchase probability of this product decreases with time for every consumer in the economy. This implies that the market share of this product goes to zero in time-invariant state.

The above argument is valid for every product that has less than average market share. Their purchase probabilities go to zero with time. So, as time passes, the industry loses products. Therefore, its average market share increases. This induces more products to cross the fatal threshold and disappear from the market. This continues until only one product remains on the market. So, in equilibrium $\bar{h}_n = 0$, $\forall n$ for which $\exists n'$ such that $h_n < h_{n'}$.

It is worth noting again that the time-invariant state described above is the same for every economy irrespective of the intensity of interaction ($\bar{\mu}$). $\bar{\mu}$ controls only the time that is needed to converge to the equilibrium. And, in fact, lower values of this parameter imply a longer time necessary to reach the equilibrium.

4   LOCAL INTERACTION

In the previous section we presented a simple framework to discuss the effects of global interaction among consumers. This section is concerned with the effects of local interaction. This requires a slightly more elaborate model in order to discuss interaction effects.

Setup

This builds on the model presented in Babutsidze (2011). Consider an economy with many agents. Each consumer has an idiosyncratic valuation for every product at every time period. On the supply side, assume that there are two (substitute) products, with no quality difference, offered on the market. These are indexed by $n = 1, 2$.

Consumers are myopic: they make decisions by maximizing one-shot utility. The probability that the consumer s will choose product n at time t is a function of valuations that a given consumer holds for a given time period ($v^s_{1;t}$ and $v^s_{2;t}$).

Assume that the valuation for the product is proportional to consumer skill level ($k \in [0, 1]$), which we assume to be product specific. If a consumer's skill level is 1, he/she can utilize the given product to its maximum capacity, thus his/her valuation of the product will be equal to its maximum. We normalize this maximum to be equal to one, which effectively sets $v^s_{n;t} = k^s_{n;t}$. Thus, in contrast to the case with global interactions, consumer valuations change due to the learning process.

Consumers learn from two sources: through consumption and through socialization/interaction. Here, as you can see, we have an additional internal driver of valuations, in contrast to the case with global interactions. If we had not taken learning by consuming on board, consumer interaction would have modified the equilibrium of the system. However, with learning by consuming, equilibrium stays unchanged and gives us the opportunity to analyze changes in transitional dynamics, which is the purpose of this section.

We assume that learning by consuming happens at a decreasing rate and specify the learning function:

$$k^s_m = 1 - (1 - k^s_0)e^{-\delta m}, \tag{4.5}$$

which is the same for both of the products. In equation (4.5) δ is the speed of learning, k^s_0 is the initial skill level of agent s for the product under discussion and m is the number of consumption events prior to (and including) the current one.

From equation (4.5) we can derive the change in skill levels between two subsequent consumption events of the same product:

$$k^s_{m+1} - k^s_m = \gamma(1 - k^s_m), \tag{4.6}$$

where $\gamma = 1 - e^{-\delta}$.

Every time period t agent s chooses the product n for purchase with the probability given by equation (4.1). This, together with equation (4.6) allows us to write down the expected law of motion for consumption skills (still abstraction from interaction) as:

$$E_t(k^s_{n;t+1}) = k^s_{n;t} + \gamma_n(1 - k^s_{n;t})p^s_{n;t}. \tag{4.7}$$

An important thing to note with equation (4.7) is that the expected dynamics of skills, and therefore of valuations, depends on a product-specific speed of learning (γ_n). This parameter can be interpreted as user friendliness of the product. If γ_n is high, skill acquisition for the product is rapid, while in the case of low γ_n it takes a long time before the skill level of a consumer converges to its maximum.

Concerning consumer interaction, we assume that every consumer is interacting with a small and constant group of people. Through this inter-action the consumer can acquire product-specific consumer skills at some rate, if any of his/her friends has higher consumer skills for this product than he/she does. For the sake of tractability, assume that consumers are aligned on a circle and that each of them interacts with only two immediate neighbors (one on each side). The consumer can learn from only one neighbor in any period and we assume that he/she is choosing the most skillful neighbor in this certain product and if the consumer's skills are lower than those of that neighbor, he/she learns from the neighbor at rate μ. So, ignoring learning through consuming for a moment, the effect of consumer interaction on valuation can be written as:

$$k_{n;t+1}^s = k_{n;t}^s + \mu[\max(k_{n;t}^{s-1}; k_{n;t}^s; k_{n;t}^{s+1}) - k_{n;t}^s]. \tag{4.8}$$

To combine two forces of consumer learning assume that despite product choices, interaction affects the valuations of all the products in every time period. This means that consumers acquire some skills for every product in every time period (given that they have not reached the highest skill level and they are not the highest-skilled consumers in their neighborhood). Then, combining equations (4.7), (4.8) and equality $v_{n;t}^s = k_{n;t}^s$ gives the full specification of the model:

$$E_t(v_{n;t+1}^s) = v_{n;t}^s + \gamma_n(1 - v_{n;t}^s)p_{n;t}^s + \mu[\max(v_{n;t}^{s-1}; v_{n;t}^s; v_{n;t}^{s+1}) - v_{n;t}^s]. \tag{4.9}$$

It is important to note that the expected law of motion of the product valuations is product specific, as well as consumer specific. Thus we have $2 \times S$ of these equations.

Note also that ultimately, market share dynamics depend on the dynamics of valuations. It is easy to verify that, as $\forall s$ and $\forall n$, $k_n^s \rightarrow 1$ market share distribution becomes time invariant and market shares of both products converge to 50 percent. The equilibrium of the model does not depend on the parameters of the model. The parameters influence only transition toward the equilibrium.

As the concern of this section is transitional dynamics, we need to somehow quantify effects on it. For this reason we consider the responses of the system to the one-time shock. In other words, we compare how the system responds to a certain shock at the onset of an industry in the case of interaction and in the case of no interaction.

The shock that we choose to analyze can be interpreted as product promotion. Consider the situation when producers can positively affect consumers' purchase probabilities for their products. Intuitively one can see that in this model the effects of product promotion are anchored to skill acquisition. If the average consumer skill level in the population has not reached its maximum for product n, advertising will influence the probability of purchase of product n not only at a time when there is advertising, but also during the next periods as a higher purchase probability today ensures a higher rate of skill acquisition, which influences the purchase probability for the next period. Thus, as long as advertising is undertaken before the average skill level reaches unity, it has a long-lasting effect. On the other hand, if advertising takes place after everybody has learned how to utilize the product to its maximum capacity, it will not have any effect on the purchasing probability in subsequent periods.

We allow producers to advertise their products at the onset of the industry and analyze the system's response to producers' actions. We model the mechanics of advertising as follows. If in the case of no advertising consumer choice probabilities are given by equation (4.1), then in the case of advertising they are given by:

$$\hat{p}^s_{n;0} = \frac{A + e^{v^s_{n;0}}}{A + \sum_{i=1}^{N} e^{v^s_{i;0}}},\tag{4.10}$$

where A is the effect of advertising, which is constant across producers.

It takes simple algebra to notice that $\hat{p}^s_{n;0} > p^s_{n;0}$ as long as $A > 0$, which we assume is the case. From here we can deduce that $\hat{h}_{n;0} > h_{n;0}$. Following the temporal effect argument earlier, we can argue that as long as $(1/S)\sum_{s=1}^{S} k^s_{n;0} < 1$, $\hat{h}_{n;1} > h_{n;1}$. And in general, $(1/S)\sum_{s=1}^{S} k^s_{n;t-1} < 1 \Rightarrow \hat{h}_{n;t} > h_{n;t}$. So, advertising results in a market share gain over the extended period of time if a producer advertises during the first period when its product was put on the market.[3] Then we can measure the return to advertising as:

$$r_n = \sum_{t=0}^{\infty} (\hat{h}_{n;t} - h_{n;t}),\tag{4.11}$$

where r_n is the return on advertising for the product n. This is the measure that we use to study the difference in response of the consumer population to the shocks in the presence and absence of consumer interactions. In principle, we are studying the behavior of returns to product promotion for different constellations of γ parameters and different intensities of consumer interaction.

5 ANALYSIS

The interaction intensity parameter μ is unique to the economy. User friendliness, on the other hand, is product specific. And as we have two products on the market we have a pair of γs to work with. But because these products are competing with each other, intuitively the most important parameter would be the ratio of γs and not the values of single parameters themselves. Thus, for the analysis of the model we work with these ratios. This complicates the reporting of results. To solve this problem we design a peculiar set of scales for the presentation of simulation outcomes. The axis for the γ ratio, the ordinate in Figure 4.1, is constructed in such a way that it reaches 1 in the center, which means that two products are equally user friendly. This splits the axis in two. The upper half is a linear scale and reaches some maximum value (in this particular case, 5, which means that the value of the parameter is 5 times that of the value of the corresponding parameter of the competitor's product), while the lower

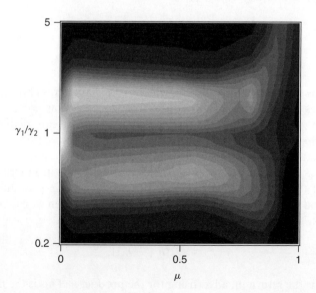

Figure 4.1   Dependence of returns to advertising on user friendliness and communication intensity

half symmetrically follows the upper one and takes values of 1 over the corresponding value from the upper section (thus, in this case the lower half of the axis goes to 1/5, which means that the value of the parameter is 5 times lower than the corresponding parameter of the competitor). To eliminate the differences in results due to the differences in absolute values of the parameter, parameter ratios are created by holding the average constant across the axis. This means that if the ratio of γs being equal to one is created by $\gamma_1 = 2$ and $\gamma_2 = 2$, then the ratio of 3 is created by $\gamma_1 = 3$ and $\gamma_2 = 1$ and the ratio of 1/3 is created by $\gamma_1 = 1$ and $\gamma_2 = 3$.

Figure 4.1 reports returns to advertising for the different values of μ and ratios of γ. Lighter shades of gray imply higher returns in this contour plot. In these calculations we fix the number of consumers to be 100 and $(\gamma_1 + \gamma_2)/2 = 2$.[4] These are the averages of 40 runs, standard deviations are very small. Every run covers the whole spectrum of γ ratios. At the beginning of every run we generate consumers and the initial skill distribution for each of the products, averages of which are equal to each other. After that, we run the economy as long as it takes advertising returns to become negligible for each γ ratio. The next run starts by generating the new skill-level distribution for the consumers (of course, the means of every run's skill distributions are equal).

The presentation scheme above (using the ratio of γs) allows us to solve another problem. The additional problem in discussing the effects of advertising in this setup is that both of the firms can advertise simultaneously. Thus, if we choose one of the firms and discuss returns to its advertising we shall have virtually two regimes to analyze: one when the competitor does not advertise and the other when the competitor advertises. These two regimes might produce not only quantitatively, but also qualitatively different responses to advertising. All in all, for each parameter constellation we shall have four values to analyze: returns to advertising for each firm when the competitor does not advertise, the same returns when the competitor does advertise. The plot in Figure 4.1 gives us the opportunity to read all four values simultaneously.

To see how we can read these values, note several facts. As our products are of similar quality and we do not want to give any aggregate initial advantage to any of them (therefore average initial skill levels are equal across products) in the absence of advertising, the market will be equally split by the firms at the initial state. Then, due to symmetry, if both of the firms advertise, initial market share should again be equally split. This means that returns to one of the firms for advertising when the competitor does not advertise, and returns of the competitor's advertising in response to the firm's advertising, will be equal. This reduces the number of observations needed to fully characterize the response of transitional dynamics

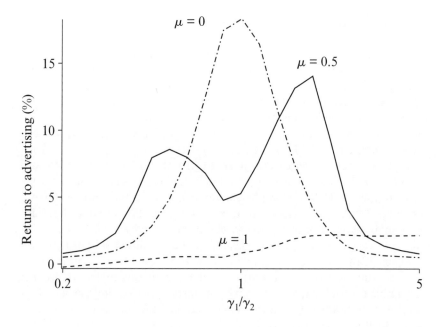

Figure 4.2   Cross-sectional cuts into Figure 4.1

to the advertising to two. But as the γ ratio axis is constructed in the way described above, every point on the graph has its corresponding point mirrored by the $\gamma_1/\gamma_2 = 1$ line. So, if we are considering the scenario when $\gamma_1/\gamma_2 = 0.5$, we can observe the second firm's perspective by swapping γs with places and looking at $\gamma_1/\gamma_2 = 2$.

The main conclusion that we can draw from Figure 4.1 is that the relation between the returns to product promotion and user friendliness of the product have a double-hump shape: starting from the relatively non-user-friendly product, as user friendliness increases initially so do returns to advertising, which fall after some time, reaching a local minimum when user-friendliness parameters of the two products are equal, then they rise and fall again. This profile is present as long as the communication level is away from zero. When $\mu = 0$ there is no double hump.

This result is better seen on Figure 4.2 where we plot three cross-sectional cuts into Figure 4.1: one when there is no communication ($\mu = 0$), one when the communication parameter μ is equal to 0.5, and one when the communication intensity is extremely high ($\mu = 1$). From Figure 4.2, one can clearly see that no communication results in a no double-hump shape in returns to advertising. Thus, we can conclude that the model results in qualitatively different behavior in the case where there is no interaction as opposed to when interaction among consumers is present.

To understand why this is the case, note that, technically, interaction in this particular example means skill spillovers across population. When there is no interaction, the dynamics is driven purely by the learning by consuming, and it is intuitive that returns to advertising increase with the similarity of the products. However, when there is communication in place, skills for the user-friendly product are pulled upwards even for the consumers that have not intensively consumed the product. Therefore, the absolute value (not only the ratio) of the higher γ drives the transitional dynamics. Of course if the difference between γs is too dramatic, advertising will not change much in the transition. This is due to the fact that with larger differences in product user friendliness, the effect of an initial shock becomes unimportant. However, when the difference is not too large, communication will increase returns to advertising for players. Interaction gives the edge to the user-friendly product. Then advertising effects propagate faster.

Intuitively, the explanation for this phenomenon can be found in the double nature of the advertising in our model: besides the fact that advertising ensures earlier consumers for the product, which are important for increasing the speed of the skill accumulation of this particular product, it also ensures fewer consumers, and slower skill accumulation, for the competitor. Thus, given the equal product qualities, if our product is more user friendly (relative to the competitor) the major contribution of the advertising returns is due to more consumers consuming our product, while the minor contribution is due to fewer consumers consuming the competitor's product. While if our product is (relatively) less user friendly, the major contribution becomes due to deterring part of the consumers consuming the competitor's user-friendly product, while the minor contribution is due to increased consumption of our product. This explains the double-peaked nature of the profile. Exactly at the middle these two forces are equal, but apparently their joint effect is smaller than when user-friendliness levels are different.

Thus, the conclusion one can draw from this section is that, similar to the global interactions, omitting local interactions from the modeling of consumer behavior can lead to misleading results and as a consequence in misleading policy advice.

6 SUMMARY AND CONCLUSION

This chapter has been concerned with effects that model mis-specification can have on deriving implications about the behavior of agent populations.

We have analyzed two simple models in order to discuss the difference in results between setups with and without consumer interaction. We have established that the omission of either global or local interactions among consumers might lead to incorrect results. Results of models with and without interactions can be not only quantitatively but also qualitatively different.

As a conclusion we can say that ignoring interaction among consumers is unacceptable for applications that base their insights on the behavior of consumer populations (that is, derivation of aggregate demand). As learning and information processing come to the forefront of economic research, more attention and resources should be devoted to interaction among consumers. Due to the implicit incorporation of time into learning processes, interaction is bound to have important effects on the dynamics of the system. Therefore, consumer interactions should become central in subfields of economics explicitly concerned with dynamics, such as evolutionary economics.

NOTES

* I wish to acknowledge the comments from the editor, Guido Buenstorf, as well as from Alex Coad, Robin Cowan and Marco Valente. They have helped me to improve the chapter.
1. Multinomial logit is a highly nonlinear function. Using linear mapping from valuations to purchase probabilities does not change the qualitative results of the chapter, but considerably increases the computational time.
2. The effects demonstrated here do not depend on the linearity assumption. The results actually become stronger with nonlinear effects, as long as they favor popular products.
3. The only case when this statement is not true is when $\forall s\, v_{n;0}^{s} = 1$, which we rule out as it does not involve any learning, and is thus not interesting.
4. Changing the number of consumers and/or the average levels of user friendliness does not change reported results.

REFERENCES

Anderson, S.P., A. de Palma and J.-F. Thisse (1992), *Discrete Choice Theory of Product Differentiation*, Cambridge, MA: MIT Press.

Arthur, W.B. (1994), 'Inductive reasoning and bounded rationality', *American Economic Review*, **84**(2), 406–11.

Babutsidze, Z. (2009), 'R&D behaviour and the emergence of fat-tailed firm size distributions', UNU-MERIT working paper 2009-056, Maastricht, Netherlands.

Babutsidze, Z. (2011), 'Returns to product promotion when consumers are learning how to consume', *Journal of Evolutionary Economics*, **21**(5), 783–801.

Babutsidze, Z. and R. Cowan (2009), 'Inertia, interaction and clustering in demand', UNU-MERIT working paper 2009-045, Maastricht, Netherlands.

Bala, V. and S. Goyal (1998), 'Learning from neighbours', *Review of Economic Studies*, **65**(3), 595–621.

Bala, V. and S. Goyal (2000), 'A noncooperative model of network formation', *Econometrica*, **68**(5), 1181–229.

Banerjee, A.V. (1992), 'A simple model of herd behavior', *Quarterly Journal of Economics*, **107**(3), 797–817.

Beatty, S.E. and S.M. Smith (1987), 'External search effort: an investigation across several product categories', *Journal of Consumer Research*, **14**(1), 83–95.

Bennett, P.D. and R.M. Mandell (1969), 'Prepurchase information seeking behavior of new car purchasers: the learning hypothesis', *Journal of Marketing Research*, **6**(4), 430–33.

Bernheim, B.D. (1994), 'A theory of conformity', *Journal of Political Economy*, **102**(5), 841–77.

Bikhchandani, S., D. Hirshleifer and I. Welch (1992), 'A theory of fads, fashion, custom, and cultural change as informational cascades', *Journal of Political Economy*, **100**(5), 992–1026.

Brass, D.J., K.D. Butterfield and B.C. Skaggs (1998), 'Relationships and unethical behavior: a social network perspective', *Academy of Management Review*, **23**(1), 14–31.

Brock, W.A. and S.N. Durlauf (2000), 'Interaction-based models', National Bureau of Economic Research working paper 258, Cambridge, MA.

Burt, R.S. (2001), 'Attachment, decay, and social network', *Journal of Organizational Behavior*, **22**(6), 619–43.

Coleman, J. (1964), *Introduction to Mathematical Sociology*, New York: Macmillan.

Cooper, R. (1998), *Coordination Games*, Cambridge: Cambridge University Press.

Cowan, R., W. Cowan and G.P. Swann (2004), 'Waves in consumption with interdependence among consumers', *Canadian Journal of Economics*, **37**, 149–77.

Duncan, C.P. and R.W. Olshavsky (1982), 'External search: the role of consumer beliefs', *Journal of Marketing Research*, **19**(1), 32–43.

Ehrhardt, G., M. Marsili and F. Vega-Redondo (2007), 'Emergence and resilience of social networks: a general theoretical framework', *Annales d'Économie et de Statistique*, (86), 1–13.

Ellison, G. (1993), 'Learning, local interaction, and coordination', *Econometrica*, **61**(5), 1047–71.

Epstein, J.M. and R. Axtell (1996), *Growing Artificial Societies: Social Science from the Bottom Up*, Cambridge, MA: MIT Press.

Fagiolo, G. (2005), 'Endogenous neighborhood formation in a local coordination model with negative network externalities', *Journal of Economic Dynamics and Control*, **29**, 297–319.

Fagiolo, G., A. Moneta and P. Windrum (2007), 'A critical guide to empirical validation of agent-based models in economics: methodologies, procedures, and open problems', *Computational Economics*, **30**, 195–226.

Fagiolo, G. and M. Valente (2005), 'Minority games, local interactions, and endogenous networks', *Computational Economics*, **25**, 41–57.

Farrell, J. and G. Saloner (1985), 'Standardization, compatibility, and innovation', *RAND Journal of Economics*, **16**(1), 70–83.

Farrell, J. and G. Saloner (1986), 'Installed base and compatibility: innovation, product preannouncements, and predation', *American Economic Review*, **76**(5), 940–55.

Fazio, R.H. and M.P. Zanna (1978), 'Attitudinal qualities relating to the strength of the attitude–behavior relationship', *Journal of Experimental Social Psychology*, **14**, 398–408.

Fehr, E. and S. Gachter (2000), 'Fairness and retaliation: the economics of reciprocity', *Journal of Economic Perspectives*, **14**(3), 159–81.

Gershoff, A.D. and G.V. Johar (2006), 'Do you know me? Consumer calibration of friends' knowledge', *Journal of Consumer Research*, **32**, 496–503.

Gibbons, R. (1992), *Game Theory for Applied Economists*, Princeton, NJ: Princeton University Press.

Glaeser, E.L. and J.A. Scheinkman (2000), 'Non-market interactions', NBER working paper 8053, Cambridge, MA.

Gonzalez-Avella, J.C., V.M. Eguiluz, M.G. Consenza, K. Klemm, J.L. Herrera and M. San-Miguel (2006), 'Local versus global interaction in nonequilibrium transitions: a model of social dynamics', *Physical Review E*, **73**, 1–7.

Goyal, S. and J.L. Moraga-Gonzalez (2001), 'R&D networks', *RAND Journal of Economics*, **32**(4), 686–707.

Hansen, F. (1972), *Consumer Choice Behavior: A Cognitive Theory*, New York: Free Press.

Holland, P. and S. Leinhardt (1970), 'A new method for detecting structure in sociometric data', *American Journal of Sociology*, **76**, 492–513.

Katz, M.L. and C. Shapiro (1994), 'Systems competition and network effects', *Journal of Economic Perspectives*, **8**(2), 93–115.

Kim, C.K. and J.Y. Chung (1997), 'Brand popularity, country image and market share: an empirical study', *Journal of International Business Studies*, **28**(2), 361–86.

Manski, C.F. (2000), 'Economic analysis of social interactions', *Journal of Economic Perspectives*, **14**(3), 115–36.

McElroy, M.B. (1990), 'The empirical content of nash-bargained household behavior', *Journal of Human Resources*, **25**(4), 559–83.

Myers, J.H. and T.S. Robertson (1972), 'Dimensions of opinion leadership', *Journal of Marketing Research*, **9**(1), 41–6.

Raj, S.P. (1985), 'Striking a balance between brand "popularity" and brand "loyalty"', *Journal of Marketing*, **49**(1), 53–9.

Reingen, P.H., B.L. Foster, J.J. Brown and S.B. Seidman (1984), 'Brand congruence in interpersonal relations: a social network analysis', *Journal of Consumer Research*, **11**(3), 771–83.

Schelling, T.C. (1969), 'Models of segregation', *American Economic Review*, **59**(2), 488–93.

Smith, R.E. and W.R. Swinyard (1983), 'Attitude-behavior consistency: the impact of product trial versus advertising', *Journal of Marketing Research*, **20**(3), 257–67.

Veblen, T. (1899), *The Theory of the Leisure Class: An Economic Study of Institutions*, New York: Macmillan.

Wang, P. and A. Watts (2006), 'Formation of buyer-seller trade networks in a quality-differentiated product market', *Canadian Journal of Economics/Revue Canadienne d'Économique*, **39**(3), 971–1004.

Watts, D.J. and S.H. Strogatz (1998), 'Collective dynamics of "small world" networks', *Nature*, **393**, 409–10.

Young, H.P. (1993), 'The evolution of conventions', *Econometrica*, **61**(1), 57–84.

5. Scientists' valuation of open science and commercialization: the influence of peers and organizational context

Stefan Krabel

1 INTRODUCTION

Over the past decades, universities and other public research organizations have faced the challenge of transforming themselves into 'entrepreneurial enterprises'. Observing the importance of academic research for science-based industries such as biotechnology or nanotechnology, policy makers called upon public research to make scientific achievements more relevant to industry (Slaughter and Leslie, 1997; Cohen et al., 1998). Facing these changed policy expectations for economic development and seeking new sources of income, universities and public research organizations escalated their involvement in technology transfer (see, for example, Powers and McDougall, 2005).

With the demand for commercialization efforts of scientists increasing, a scholarly debate has arisen whether and to what extent scientific norms are changing as a result. Existing studies highlight that in research a dual system of reward allocation has evolved (Dasgupta and David, 1994; Hong and Walsh, 2009). On the one hand, scientists still need to disseminate their results openly, for example, by publication, in order to prove their academic advances. Thus, in the spirit of the Mertonian norm of *communism*, many scientists freely share their research outcome and receive the recognition of peers when distinguished advances are achieved – adhering to the concept of open science (Merton, 1957; Hong and Walsh, 2009). On the other hand, a large percentage of scientists regard successful commercialization as a tool for gaining academic repute (Owen-Smith and Powell, 2004; Colyvas and Powell, 2007). The latter view is based on the rationale that scientists become increasingly visible and also attract external funding when research results are successfully commercialized. Thus, scientists are caught between two stools. They face two conflicting norms or values, namely the norm of open science and at the same time the increasing academic value of successful commercialization.

In this study, I analyze whether or not a shift from the traditional norm of open science toward more commercialization can be observed when regarding scientists' individual perceptions of academic values and norms. In order to do so I analyze whether there is a relationship between the age of individual academics and the maturity of their institution, and the perceived norm of open science and the perceived reputational gain of commercialization. Moreover, I analyze to what extent such norms are related to perceptions of peers within the same organization. Understanding the impact of social imprint in institutions on commercialization efforts is crucial for the assessment of the extent to which commercialization efforts are cultivated on the individual level. Thus, by investigating both the influence of age and social imprint a comprehensive picture is drawn of the extent to which a transformation process of academic norms can be observed.

In order to examine scientists' proclivity toward commercialization and its relationship to institution, age and peer influence, data obtained through survey interviews with scientists of the Max Planck Society (MPS) in Germany are analyzed. The data capture information about whether scientists have commercialization experience via patenting, licensing and research cooperation with private firms. Further, the data include scientists' assessment of reputational rewards resulting from commercialization and the role of open science. When the survey interviews were held, the MPS consisted of 78 autonomous institutes. Thus, it is possible to examine whether scientists' attitude toward commercialization is related to the opinions of institute peers, institute age and past commercialization experience. The rest of the chapter is structured as follows. Section 2 reviews literature on the reward system in science highlighting the development toward more commercial activity. Section 3 describes the empirical context of the MPS and the process of data generation. In Section 4, descriptive statistics and the empirical analysis on determinants of scientists' attitude toward commercialization are presented. Finally, Section 5 discusses the results and concludes.

2   COMMERCIALIZATION ACTIVITIES IN SCIENCE AND CHANGING ACADEMIC NORMS

The Shift Toward Increasing Commercialization Activities

Policy makers in the US and other industrial nations have recognized the possibility that technology transfer from public research to the private sector can enhance national and regional economic growth (see, for example, Jaffe, 1989; Mansfield, 1995; Link and Siegel, 2007, p. 108). Thus, in the face of stiffening economic competition and budget constraints, policy makers called on public research organizations to make scientific results more applicable to the private sector in order to make best societal use of the money spent in public research (Cohen et al., 1998). Policy initiatives such as the Bayh–Dole Act in the US and similar measures in other countries were introduced over the past decades to promote commercial use of academic knowledge. In order to foster commercialization efforts of scientists, policies aimed at strengthening scientists' intellectual property rights and their ability to make commercial use of their research results (see, for example, Mowery et al., 2001; Lissoni et al., 2007). Moreover, technology transfer offices and science parks were established in many universities in the US and in Europe in order to support technology transfer from science to industry via commercialization efforts of scientists.

In the course of evolving incentives for universities to commercialize knowledge, scientists needed to alter their work practices and become more engaged in commercialization activities. Tracking annual patent and license counts of universities over time, several studies show that commercial research output of scientists in many universities and other public research institutions has increased exponentially since the 1980s in both American (see, for example, Henderson et al., 1998; Jaffe and Lerner, 2001; Jensen and Thursby, 2001) and European (see, for example, Lissoni et al., 2007; Buenstorf, 2009) research institutions Mowery et al. (2001) argue that the transformation process of increasing commercialization in the US began even before the Bayh–Dole Act was introduced in 1980.

The majority of studies examining commercialization activities of scientists rely on data from official sources and examine the commercial research output of organizations and institutions (for examples, see Jensen and Thursby, 2001; Thursby and Thursby, 2002, 2003; Di Gregorio and Shane, 2003). As mentioned above, these studies report a substantial increase of commercialization activities on the organizational level, indicating that a transformation process has taken place on this level. Further, it is often shown that the distribution of commercialization activities is highly skewed, with few scientists being responsible for a relatively large proportion of commercialization activities (see, for example, Shane, 2004; Azoulay et al., 2007). Since studies on the organizational level might be strongly affected by a relatively small share of scientists, a comprehensive picture on the evolution academic norms and commercialization behavior demands a stronger focus on the individual scientists (Krabel and Mueller,

2009; Tartari et al., 2010). By studying to what extent individual scientists' perceived relevance of commercialization and open science is transforming, I aim to contribute to this gap in the literature.

Reputational Gains through Commercialization and the Norm of Open Science

Etzkowitz (1989) initiated research on the evolution of an entrepreneurial norm within the institutions of science. The study argues that while universities accept their economic role in society, it will be of educational value to researchers when they begin to interact frequently with the private sector. Researchers learn about the practical relevance and commercial potential of their research, which enables them to assess which lines of research are of high importance to the private sector. This knowledge can be passed on to research students, who are mainly educated for private sector firms. A similar view is expressed in several later studies, describing how technology transfer to the private sector is part of the public good mission of universities (see, for example, Glenna et al., 2007) and how commercialization efforts are a part of the tasks that researchers need to fulfill (Slaughter and Leslie, 1997). These studies imply that Merton's (1957) view that free distribution of scientific results is the only way to gain scientific reputation – through claiming priority in discovery – is no longer unchallenged. Instead, scientists' research output is evaluated according to two different criteria. On the one hand, scientists need to be able to do high-quality basic research and, on the other, they need to be able to adopt the entrepreneurial role of bridging this research to the private sector (Colyvas and Powell, 2007). Hackett (1990) and Dasgupta and David (1994) describe the dissemination of scientific results within the scientific community and commercial research output as two different value systems prevalent in science. These two opposing views are not mutually exclusive, though. Research productivity and commercial research output have been shown to be complementary rather than substitutes (Lowe and Gonzalez-Brambila, 2007; Buenstorf, 2009).

Despite the ongoing debate surrounding the fact that scientists are increasingly evaluated according to commercialization efforts, few studies have actually investigated how scientists individually perceive scientific reputation as being gained through commercialization. Among the rare exceptions are studies by Owen-Smith and Powell (2001, 2004). By analyzing personal interviews with more than 80 life scientists, these studies provide evidence indicating that scientists perceive a change of criteria by which scientific success is determined and rewards are allocated. The authors classify scientists into different categories according to their perception of whether the work of industry and academy overlap and to what extent academic reputation is related to commercial success. According to their typology, some scientists believe that the free distribution of scientific knowledge is the only way to gain scientific reputation. This view is related to the aforementioned norm of open science with the goal of widespread dissemination of findings, as expressed by Merton (1973) as well as Stephan (1996). Another group of scientists believes that the evaluation of scientific expertise is shifting toward higher recognition of commercial success. Scientists get noticed when they successfully commercialize new knowledge, and the revealed innovative potential serves as a signal that the underlying research is of high quality. This view is in line with Gittelman (1999) who argues that in applied areas such as biotechnology research, scientists are rewarded for commercialization.

Most of the aforementioned studies on changing values within the institution of science are either theoretical papers or based on case evidence regarding scientists from a specific institution or research field such as life or biotechnology scientists. Recently, studies by Roach and Sauermann (2010) and Tartari et al. (2010) have investigated the individual perceptions of scientists toward commercialization of research results. The study by Roach and Sauermann investigates survey data of over 2,000 academic scientists employed at 160 different US institutions and finds that the desire to contribute to society is a key motive for commercializing research. Further, scientists with a strong desire to contribute to society are more likely to carry out more applied research. Tartari et al. examine in a sample of 1,200 UK physics and engineering scientists how colleagues' attitudes toward commercialization and commercialization behavior influence scientists' individual attitudes and behaviors. Evidence from the latter study suggests that peer effects are strong while organizational-level effects are not found.

The present study follows a similar research outline; it investigates to what extent the academic norm of open science and the perceived reputational reward of commercialization by institute peers influence the respective attitudes of an individual scientist. Thus, this study contributes to our understanding of peer influence in scientists' assessment of academic norms. In view of the aforementioned study by Tartari et al. (2010), I hypothesize that peers do influence scientists' individual perceptions on the academic norm of open science and reputational gains through commercialization:

H1a: Scientists' individual perception of the relevance of open science for academic reputation is positively related to peers' perception of open science.

H1b: Scientists' individual perception of the relevance of commercialization efforts for academic reputation is positively related to peers' perception of reputational gains of commercialization efforts.

Further, the present study investigates to what extent scientific norms have indeed transformed from the 'old' Mertonian view that open science is the key to academic reputation toward the 'new' view that academic reputation depends to a substantial degree on commercialization efforts. In view of the literature reviewed above on the transformation process of scientific institutions it is likely that older organizations (or older organizational entities) have a stronger focus on the traditional norm of open science, while the perception that commercialization activities are seen as relevant is more pronounced in relatively new organizations. This hypothesis is based on the rationale that academic norms and values are difficult to change in existing institutions with a long tradition while new institutes can adapt new values more easily:

H2a: Scientists' individual perception of the relevance of open science for academic reputation is positively related to the maturity of the scientist's institute.

H2b: Scientists' individual perception of the relevance of commercialization efforts for academic reputation is negatively related to the maturity of the scientist's institute.

Apart from the maturity of institutions the individual scientist's age may also affect individually perceived values and norms. Younger scientists began their academic career when scientific institutions were already under pressure to produce commercial research outputs and transfer knowledge to the private sector. This reasoning is in line with a study by Stephan and Levin (1991) which provides evidence that scientists become less productive over their career life cycle and argues that later research activity appears to be investment driven. Thus, the younger a scientist is the more likely it is that she or he perceives high reputational gains from commercialization. On the contrary, in the transformation process of universities the Mertonian norm is increasingly diminishing. Consequently I hypothesize:

H3a: Scientists' individual perception of the relevance of open science for academic reputation is positively related to the scientist's age.

H3b: Scientists' individual perception of the relevance of commercialization efforts for academic reputation is negatively related to the scientist's age.

3 DATA

Sample: The Max Planck Society

With the purpose of examining the relevance of the norm of open science and the perception of reputational gains through commercialization success, the present study analyzes information gathered through structured interviews with 1,002 senior scientists of the Max Planck Society in Germany. The MPS consists of 79 research institutes and three additional research facilities in Germany that perform basic research in the natural sciences, life sciences, social sciences, and the humanities. Approximately 12,800 scientists are employed by Max Planck institutes, including professors, postdoctoral fellows, doctoral students, and guest scientists (as of January 1, 2010). Researchers are supported by roughly 3,000 non-scientific employees, responsible for administration and research assistance. Around 82 percent of the MPS's expenditure is met by public funding from the Federal government and the German states. The remaining 18 percent stems from donations, member contributions and from third-party funded projects. In 2009, the MPS had a total budget of €1.3 billion.

MPS institutes are focused on basic research. They are supposed to take up new and innovative research areas that German universities are not in a position to accommodate or deal with adequately. Thus, research at Max Planck institutes complements the work of universities and other research facilities in important fields. Scientists within the MPS are free to process their research topics as they feel the research should be done to accomplish scientific excellence. This enormous freedom is given to the researchers by the MPS as the Society seeks to do distinguished, basic research. Therefore, leading researchers from outside the MPS are appointed as directors of MPS institutes, the majority coming from abroad. MPS institutes are established in fields where world-class researchers can be attracted, and directors of MPS institutes are free to design their research topics and make decisions about resource allocation. The outcome of research conducted at MPS institutes is distinguished, as is documented by the 32 Nobel prizes awarded to MPS researchers since the Society was founded in 1948 (the information above was taken from Max Planck Society, 2009, 2010).

MPS scientists represent a suitable sample for the research topic of the present study as they are not influenced by institutional pressures to commercialize research findings. Moreover, it seems reasonable to assume that these scientists strive for academic reputation and research excellence. Scientific reputation, however, only matters for scientists who choose to stay in academia after obtaining their PhD degree. Therefore, the following empirical analysis will focus on senior researchers who decided to stay in academia after finishing their doctorate. Within the MPS, senior researchers can hold four different types of position: postdoctoral research fellows, group leaders, research professors, or directors. Group leaders are senior research scientists responsible for research groups while research professors are heads of independent junior research groups. Directors represent the leaders of the departments of the institutes.

Data Generation: The Max Planck Scientist Survey

The data used in this chapter are based on a survey conducted within the MPS between mid-October and mid-December 2007. Before performing the survey, I contacted the executive directors of each institute to ask for permission to interview the scientists. Most of the directors (67 out of 79 institutes existent in 2007) permitted me to conduct the interviews and provided me with the necessary contact information to scientists, whenever this was not publicly available.

The survey was conducted by TNS Emnid GmbH, a professional opinion research institute. Trained interviewers from TNS Emnid GmbH contacted every scientist in the population by phone. Participation in the survey was voluntary, so that the available scientists could refuse to participate at all, or skip any specific question. Scientists who could not be contacted with three calls as well as scientists who refused to participate were dropped from the study. The survey questions were specifically designed to analyze the extent of knowledge transfer by basic scientists, scientists' perception on the scientific reward system and the relation of both fields of interest.

The feasibility and reliability of the survey questions were tested and improved during a pilot study conducted in August and September 2007. Within this pilot study, randomly contacted scientists from various public research institutions in Germany were interviewed. In order to analyze scientists' assessments, the survey captures possible stimuli and barriers of scientific commercialization, as well as experience in commercialization activities such as patenting or cooperation. Additionally, the survey contains questions regarding scientists on research experience, industrial experience, education, demographics, and risk-taking behavior.

Variables

The main variables of interest reflect scientists' commercialization experience and their attitude toward commercialization. These variables are analyzed as dependent variables in the empirical analysis.

Dependent variables: open science identity and reputational gains from commercialization

Open science identity   This variable measures to what degree scientists perceive science as a public good to be made freely available to anyone. The measure is based on the degree to which scientists agreed on the following statement 'Your research results should be freely accessible to any other researchers and businesses'. Scientists were asked to what degree they agree or disagree with these statements given a five-point Likert-type scale, ranging from 1: 'Strongly disagree' to 5: 'Strongly agree'. Therefore, the variable is coded with integer values ranging from one to five with increasing affirmation to the statement. A further binary variable is created that takes a value of one if scientists either agree or strongly agree with the statement given, and a value of 0 if scientists report neutrality or disagreement with the statement.

Reputational reward from commercialization   In a similar fashion, the interviewed scientists were asked to what extent they agree or disagree with the statement: 'Commercialization activities increase the reputation of a scientist in your scientific community'. The same five-point Likert-type scale was applied and the associated variable is coded from 1 to 5 with increasing degree of agreement with the statement.

Again, a binary variable is created that distinguishes between the two groups of scientists who agree or strongly agree that commercialization increases reputation (coded as 1) and scientists who reported lower agreement levels (coded as 0).

As explanatory variables, information about scientists' research discipline, their research position and organizational environment, work experience as well as personal and idiosyncratic variables are included in the analysis.

Scientists' attitudes on the relevance of commercializing scientific results

Commercialization is common   In order to measure the importance of commercialization in scientific research fields, the survey included the following statement on commercialization activities within the scientist's research community: 'Commercialization activities are common in your field of research'. Another variable is created to distinguish between scientists who agree with that statement and those scientists who did not strongly agree with it. This variable is therefore binary, taking a value of 1 if scientists either agree or strongly agree with the given statement while taking a value of 0 when a lower agreement level with the statement is reported.

Commercialization experience

Research cooperation   Scientists' experience in research cooperation with private firms was measured with a rather broad definition of research cooperation. The surveyed scientists were asked whether they have cooperation experience comprising contract research for private firms, research collaboration with private firms or research joint ventures. Based upon this information, a dichotomous indicator is built which takes the value 1 if a scientist has such cooperation experience and 0 otherwise.

Patenting   Another binary variable indicates whether or not scientists have ever applied for a patent (1 = yes, 0 = no).

Research discipline

In order to measure scientists' research discipline, the surveyed scientists were asked in which discipline they obtained a doctorate. Out of the fine-grained information it is possible to characterize scientists' research fields in nine different categories. These categories are PhD *in: biology, chemistry, physics, economics/management law, social sciences, engineering, mathematics/computer science, medicine,* and *earth sciences.* For each category a binary variable is included that takes a value of 1 when a scientist has obtained a doctorate in the respective discipline and takes a value of 0 otherwise. Multiple answers were allowed as some scientists hold several doctorates.

Research position

Differences between the four different categories of senior researchers, namely directors of research units, research professors, group leaders and postdoctoral researchers are captured by inclusion of four binary variables indicating that a scientist belongs to the respective category. Thus, the variable *director* takes a value of 1 when a scientist is a director of a research unit and takes a value of 0 to indicate that a scientist does not hold such a position. By analogy, the four variables *director, professor, group leader* and *postdoctoral researcher* are created to indicate which category each researcher belongs to. Thus, the groups are mutually exclusive. In the following, postdoctoral researchers are used as the reference group.

Organizational environment

Within the MPS, each institute is autonomous while the aspiration of research excellence is demanded through the parent society and the generous research budget granted for all institutes. This specific setting allows an investigation of organizational peer influence, since the perceptions of institute peers serve as a reference.

Three variables capture the potential influence of peers on the respective assessments that commercialization is common within the scientist's field of research, that commercialization activities increase scientists' reputation in their field of research and that scientific results should be freely accessible to anyone. The variables capture the mean value reported to the respective statement by institutional peers. Scientists' own assessment is thereby excluded from this computation to ensure that the variable only measures the assessment in the working environment and not the respondent's own evaluation. For example, the variable *Institutional Peer Value: commercialization is common* measures the average value of the scientist's colleagues – from the same institute – (who participated in the survey) on the statement that commercialization is common within their field of research. By analogy, the two variables *Institutional Peer Value: commercialization increases scientific reputation* and *Institutional Peer Value: research results should be freely available* are computed.

Work experience

A further control variable captures prior work experience in the private sector. The variable *Work experience in the private sector* is binary indicating such experience by a value of 1 (= yes) while a value of 0 (= no) denotes that the respective scientists have never worked in private sector firms.

Personal and idiosyncratic variables

The empirical models also account for age, gender, nationality, and individual risk attitude. Scientists' *age* is taken into account by two variables denoting age in years and the squared value of age (*age2*) in years. Two further binary variables indicate scientists' *gender* (female = 1, male = 0) and scientists' nationalities (1 = German, 0 = foreign). The measure of *risk attitude* is adopted from the Socio-Economic Panel in Germany (Dohmen et al., 2005; Wagner et al., 2007). Respondents were told that they have hypothetically won €100,000 in a lottery and are faced with the chance of a risky but lucrative investment. They could invest nothing, 20 percent, 40 percent, 60 percent, 80 percent or their entire lottery winnings. According to the answers given, our risk variable takes six integer values from 0 to 5. A value of 0 denotes that the respondent would not invest anything and a value of 5 denotes that the scientist would invest the entire winnings.

4 RESULTS: DETERMINANTS OF SCIENTISTS' PERCEIVED ACADEMIC VALUES

Sample Characteristics and Distribution of Academic Values

The sample population for the survey consisted of 7,808 scientists working for the 67 MPS institutes that allowed us to survey their scientists. The dataset includes data from 2,604 interviews, a response rate of 33.35 percent. However, both doctoral students and senior researchers were interviewed as the survey aimed to answer several research questions. As this chapter focuses on academic values, doctoral students were excluded from the analysis; in Germany (as in most other European countries), many doctoral students leave academia after finishing their PhD, so an analysis of perceived academic reputation could be biased if PhD students were included. Further, senior scientists who chose to skip any question concerning a variable of interest have been dropped from the analysis. This procedure left a final sample of 1,059 senior scientists. Among these 1,059 scientists the correlations of the perceived value of open science, the perceived reputational reward from commercialization and commercialization experience via patenting or research cooperation are given in Table 5.1

The distribution of the norm of open science and perceived reputational reward from commercialization are given in Figures 5.1 and 5.2, respectively. Figure 5.1 indicates that a relatively large share of scientists agree or strongly agree that research results should be freely available to anyone. Thus, the distribution indicates that researchers give a relatively high priority to the open diffusion of research results. A slightly different picture is drawn when considering reputational reward in science (see Figure 5.2). The shares of scientists who agree/strongly agree or disagree/ strongly disagree with the statement that commercialization of research

Table 5.1   Correlation matrix

	C1	C2	C3	C4
Patenting experience (C1)	1.0000			
Cooperation experience (C2)	0.3072*	1.0000		
Reputational reward from commercialization (C3)	0.0842*	0.1017*	1.0000	
Open science identity (C4)	−0.1464*	−0.1654*	−0.1479*	1.000

Note: The total sample comprises 1,059 researchers. The asterisk* denotes significance of pairwise correlation at the 1 percent level.

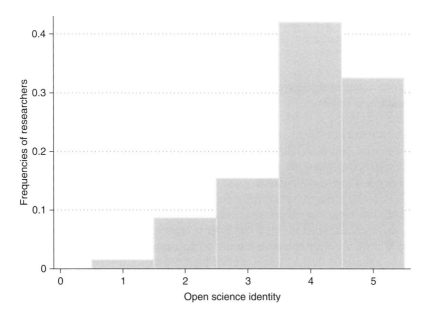

Figure 5.1   Distribution of open science identity

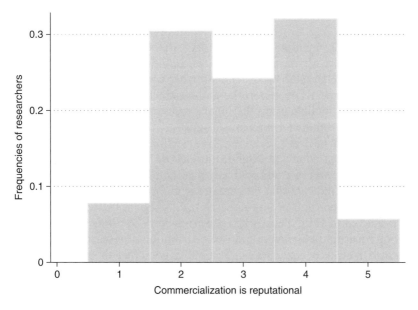

Figure 5.2   Distribution of perceived reputational reward from commercialization

results increases academic reputation are almost identical. On average, the level of agreement is lower compared to the agreement that research results should be freely available.

Determinants of the Perceived Value of Open Science and Commercialization

Determinants of scientists' perceived value of freely distributing research results and commercialization efforts are analyzed with the help of two different techniques. First, ordered probit regressions are applied using the ordinal measures regarding the degree of agreement to the perceived values as dependent variables. Second, the latter ordinal variables are reduced to binary variables indicating whether or not a scientist agreed or strongly agreed with the two statements (see Section 3). This differentiation allows a comprehensive picture to be drawn of which determinants shape scientists' likelihood to accord high relevance to the two academic values.

In Table 5.2, the results of the ordered regression models on perceived open science identity are reported. Columns (1) and (2) report the ordered probit regressions using the ordinal (5-point Likert-type) measure *open science identity* as the dependent variable. Column (1) reports the baseline model which includes only institute mean open science identity, institute age, scientists' age as well as commercialization experience via research cooperation or patenting as explanatory variables. Column (2) reports an extended model which also includes research field, research position and idiosyncratic characteristics such as further controls. Similarly, columns (3) and (4), respectively, report the probit estimation results of the baseline and extended models using the binary measure of open science identity which takes a value of 1 if scientists agree or strongly agree that research results should be freely available (see Section 3 for details). Marginal effects of the baseline and extended models on this probit analysis, given in columns (3) and (4), are provided, in columns (5) and (6), respectively.

The results indicate that peer influence has a strong and robust impact on scientists' perception that research results should be freely available – as predicted in H1a. Thus, when scientists work in an institution with a strong focus on publication and free distribution of research results, they are also likely to perceive science as a public good that should be available to everyone. The marginal effect in the extended model is significant and takes a value of 0.140, which means that the likelihood that a scientist agrees or strongly agrees with the open science statement increases by 14 percentage points when the institute mean value increases by 1 point. However, the institutional impact is not dependent on institute maturity,

Table 5.2   Ordered probit and probit analysis of scientists' open science identity

	(1)	(2)	(3)	(4)	(5)	(6)
	Ordered probit analysis		Probit analysis (D)		Marginal effects (D)	
	Baseline	Extended	Baseline	Extended	Baseline	Extended
Organizational influence						
Mean open science identity at institute	0.436***	0.349***	0.577***	0.461***	0.179***	0.140***
	(0.094)	(0.112)	(0.125)	(0.165)	(0.039)	(0.499)
Institute age	0.000	0.000	0.001	0.001	0.001	0.001
	(0.001)	(0.001)	(0.001)	(0.001)	(0.001)	(0.001)
Age and commercialization experience						
Age	0.017***	0.020***	0.012**	0.023***	0.004**	0.007***
	(0.004)	(0.005)	(0.005)	(0.008)	(0.002)	(0.002)
Patenting experience	-0.342***	-0.307***	-0.338***	-0.277**	-0.112***	-0.089**
	(0.088)	(0.098)	(0.108)	(0.116)	(0.038)	(0.039)
Cooperation experience	-0.338***	-0.308***	-0.523***	-0.484***	-0.167***	-0.151***
	(0.073)	(0.073)	(0.092)	(0.106)	(0.030)	(0.033)
Research field of doctorate degree						
Chemistry		0.037		0.085		0.025
		(0.111)		(0.185)		(0.054)
Physics		0.280***		0.401***		0.114***
		(0.083)		(0.141)		(0.039)
Economics/management/law		0.198		0.147		0.042
		(0.267)		(0.215)		(0.058)

Table 5.2 (continued)

	(1)	(2)	(3)	(4)	(5)	(6)
	Ordered probit analysis		Probit analysis (D)		Marginal effects (D)	
	Baseline	Extended	Baseline	Extended	Baseline	Extended
Research field of doctorate degree						
Social sciences		0.080		−0.218		−0.071
		(0.228)		(0.389)		(0.135)
Engineering		−0.075		−0.010		−0.003
		(0.139)		(0.231)		(0.071)
Mathematics/computer		0.659***		0.773***		0.172***
science		(0.191)		(0.286)		(0.042)
Medicine		0.333**		0.467***		0.119***
		(0.153)		(0.178)		(0.035)
Earth sciences		0.162		0.436		0.111
		(0.193)		(0.387)		(0.081)
Biology (reference category)		–		–		–
Research position						
Group leader		−0.034		−0.103		−0.032
		(0.095)		(0.120)		(0.037)
Professor		−0.551**		−0.832**		−0.306**
		(0.229)		(0.331)		(0.130)
Director		−0.028		−0.356		−0.120
		(0.203)		(0.251)		(0.091)
Postdoctoral researcher (reference category)		–		–		–

Idiosyncratic characteristics					
Work experience in industry	−0.118		−0.315**		−0.103**
	(0.102)		(0.155)		(0.054)
Gender (1 = female)	−0.127		−0.062		−0.019
	(0.092)		(0.121)		(0.038)
German citizenship	−0.117		−0.218**		−0.066**
	(0.098)		(0.108)		(0.031)
Risk attitude	0.010		0.007		0.002
	(0.021)		(0.031)		(0.009)
N	1,059	1,059	1,059	1,059	1,059
McFadden's R^2	0.030	0.044	0.069	0.102	0.069	0.102
Log-likelihood	−1,327.9749	−1,309.9707	−560.56527	−540.59271	−560.56	−540.59
Wald-Chi²	$\chi^2(5)$ 83.34***	$\chi^2(20)$ 168.05***	$\chi^2(5)$ 83.43***	$\chi^2(20)$ 193.71***	$\chi^2(5)$ 83.43***	$\chi^2(20)$ 193.71***

Note: Robust standard errors which are adjusted for clusters (institutes) are reported in parentheses. *, ** and *** denote significance at the 10, 5 and 1 percent levels, respectively.

contradicting the prediction derived in hypothesis H2a. The variable capturing institute age is insignificant in all models. By contrast, scientists' age is significantly and positively related to scientists' perception that research results should be freely available. This result indicates that the norm of open science is diminishing with younger scientists and researchers devoting significantly less relevance to free availability of research results than their older colleagues. This evidence suggests that hypothesis H3a cannot be rejected.

By analogy to the analysis of open science identity, determinants of scientists' perception that academic reputation depends upon successful commercialization of research results are analyzed. In Table 5.3, the results of ordered probit and probit regression models of scientists' perceived reputational reward from commercializing research are reported. Again, columns (1) and (2) denote the analysis of ordered probit models utilizing the ordinal variable *reputational reward from commercialization* as the dependent variable. As mentioned in Section 3, this variable is reduced to a binary variable indicating, by a value of 1, strong agreement with reputational reward associated with commercialization. This binary variable is used as the dependent variable in the probit regressions given in columns (3) and (4), Furthermore, as in the analysis of open science identity, both baseline models and extended models are provided. Again, in columns (5) and (6) marginal effects of the baseline and extended model of the probit regressions are also provided in order to ease interpretation.

The results indicate similar evidence as the examination of open science identity. Mean perceptions of peers have a strong and significant positive relationship to scientists' individual perceptions. The more importance institute peers attach to commercialization efforts as a tool to gain academic reputation, the more likely it is that individual scientists adopt a similar view and also attach great importance to this instrument of obtaining recognition. The marginal effect in the extended model is significant and takes a value of 0.164, which means that the likelihood that a scientist agrees or strongly agrees with the statement that commercialization increases the academic reputation of a scientist increases by 16.4 percentage points when the institute mean value increases by 1 point. Thus, hypothesis H1b cannot be rejected. The impact of peers seems to be a key driver of academic values and norms. Institute maturity has no effect on scientists' perception of reputational reward from commercialization. I interpret this finding as an indication that all research institutions adapt to the new challenges that scientific organizations are facing. However, I acknowledge that the limited variance may also stem from the common institutional framework of the MPS.

Table 5.3   Ordered probit and probit analysis of scientists' perceived reputational reward from commercializing research

	(1)	(2)	(3)	(4)	(5)	(6)
	Ordered probit analysis		Probit analysis (D)		Marginal effects (D)	
	Baseline	Extended	Baseline	Extended	Baseline	Extended
Organizational influence						
Institute mean of perceived reputational reward from commercialization	0.550***	0.475***	0.491***	0.435***	0.186***	0.164***
	(0.076)	(0.088)	(0.096)	(0.115)	(0.036)	(0.043)
Institute age	0.000	0.000	0.001	0.000	0.001	0.000
	(0.001)	(0.001)	(0.001)	(0.001)	(0.001)	(0.000)
Age and commercialization experience						
Age	−0.008**	−0.001	−0.009*	0.001	−0.003*	0.000
	(0.004)	(0.004)	(0.004)	(0.006)	(0.002)	(0.00w)
Patenting experience	0.119	0.122	0.052	0.077	0.020	0.029
	(0.088)	(0.089)	(0.106)	(0.095)	(0.041)	(0.036)
Cooperation experience	0.129	0.124	0.134	0.155	0.051	0.059
	(0.072)	(0.084)	(0.087)	(0.106)	(0.033)	(0.040)
Research field of doctorate						
Chemistry		0.079		0.135		0.052
		(0.089)		(0.100)		(0.038)
Physics		−0.102		0.040		0.015
		(0.072)		(0.097)		(0.037)
Economics/management/ law		−0.314*		−0.089		−0.032
		(0.175)		(0.326)		(0.119)

93

Table 5.3 (continued)

	(1)	(2)	(3)	(4)	(5)	(6)
	Ordered probit analysis		Probit analysis (D)		Marginal effects (D)	
	Baseline	Extended	Baseline	Extended	Baseline	Extended
Research field of doctorate						
Social sciences		-0.245		-0.465		-0.158
		(0.162)		(0.319)		(0.094)
Engineering		0.293		-0.010		0.072
		(0.189)		(0.231)		(0.087)
Mathematics/computer science		-0.165		-0.326		-0.114
		(0.199)		(0.323)		(0.105)
Medicine		0.044		0.359		0.140
		(0.259)		(0.289)		(0.115)
Earth sciences		0.163		0.365*		0.143*
		(0.192)		(0.202)		(0.081)
Biology (reference category)		—		—		—
Research position						
Group leader		-0.205*		-0.225*		-0.083*
		(0.107)		(0.123)		(0.044)
Professor		0.031		0.318		0.124
		(0.384)		(0.298)		(0.118)
Director		-0.209		-0.233		-0.084
		(0.169)		(0.249)		(0.085)
Postdoctoral researcher (reference category)		—		—		—

94

Idiosyncratic characteristics						
Work experience in industry		0.079		0.147		0.056
		(0.088)		(0.101)		(0.039)
Gender (1 = female)		−0.005		0.121		0.046
		(0.090)		(0.110)		(0.042)
German citizenship		−0.027		−0.278***		−0.105***
		(0.078)		(0.093)		(0.035)
Risk attitude		0.018		−0.012		−0.004
		(0.021)		(0.025)		(0.009)
N	1,059	1,059	1,059	1,059	1,059	1,059
McFadden's R^2	0.026	0.033	0.030	0.057	0.030	0.057
Log-likelihood	−1,476.3101	−1,465.7319	−680.8176	−661.38469	−680.81	−661.38
Wald-Chi²	$\chi^2(5)$	$\chi^2(20)$	$\chi^2(5)$	$\chi^2(20)$	$\chi^2(5)$	$\chi^2(20)$
	77.43***	317.09***	41.46***	118.13***	41.46***	118.13***

Note: Robust standard errors which are adjusted for clusters (institutes) are reported in parentheses. *, ** and *** denote significance at the 10, 5 and 1 percent levels, respectively.

Research agenda and relevance of open science and commercialization efforts are not dependent on institute maturity, such that hypothesis H2b is to be rejected. The relationship between scientists' age and their perception that commercialization is related to academic reputation is ambiguous. While the baseline models indicate (weak) evidence that older scientists agree to a lesser extent that reputation depends on commercialization efforts, this effect becomes insignificant when including research field and research position as further control variables. However, the vanishing effect seems to stem from the strong correlation of age and research position. Thus, I interpret the findings as evidence that scientists' age has a weakly significant, yet minor influence on the perception that reputation is driven by commercialization, which was hypothesized in H3b.

5   CONCLUSION

The empirical results presented in this study yield four noteworthy results. First, peer influence is a key determinant shaping academic norms and values. Both scientists' perception that research results should be freely disseminated and that academic reputation depends upon commercialization success are critically influenced by the perceptions of institute peers. This evidence indicates that 'social imprint' is a key determinant shaping academic values of individual scientists. Second, older scientists place stronger emphasis on free dissemination of research results. Thus, the norm of open science may increasingly diminish in the next generations of academics – if the process of less emphasis on open science continues. Third, while personal age of a scientist is positively related to the norm of open science, the maturity of institutions is not found to have a relation to academic values. Contradicting the predicted hypotheses, older institutions do not place greater emphasis on open science and less emphasis on commercialization. I conclude that the transformation process in higher education and research institutions affects all institutions to a similar extent such that institutes have to adapt their research agenda, independent of their institute history. Fourth, I detect hardly any significant differences in the relevance of commercialization activities according to research field. In the analysis presented in columns (2) and (4) of Table 5.3 different research fields are used as measures explaining different perceived reputational reward from commercialization. Using biology as the reference category I find no significant difference to other research fields on the 5 percent level. This result suggests that knowledge transfer to the private sector increases academic reputation to a similar extent across research fields.

These insights complement the growing body of analysis on the transformation of scientific values and norms and may have important implications for academic administrators, deans, and policy makers. While open science identity is found to be (still) strongly prevalent among scientists, this may change in the coming decades as younger scientists place less emphasis on free availability of research results. Further, academic values are heavily affected by peer influence. Thus, academic values appear to be self-inflicted on the organizational level. Deans and heads of department or institutions, therefore, seem to have a strong influence on academic norms since they can influence the research agenda and team composition in academic institutions. From a policy perspective, it seems as if rewards for commercialization activities may lead to an increased emphasis on knowledge transfer in academic institutions. Thus, by honoring the successful commercialization of research results, leaders of scientific institutions and policy makers may direct academic institutions toward more involvement in knowledge transfer activities by researchers – if desired.

REFERENCES

Azoulay, P., W. Ding and T. Stuart (2007), 'The determinants of faculty patenting behavior: demographics or opportunities?', *Journal of Economic Behavior and Organization*, **63** (4): 599–623.

Buenstorf, G. (2009), 'Is commercialization good or bad for science? Individual-level evidence from the Max Planck Society', *Research Policy*, **38** (2): 281–92.

Cohen, W.M., R. Florida, L. Randazzese and J. Walsh (1998), 'Industry and the academy: uneasy partners in the cause of technology advance', in R. Noll (ed.), *Challenge to the Research University*, Washington, DC: Brookings Institution, pp. 171–200.

Colyvas, J. and W.W. Powell (2007), 'From vulnerable to venerated: the institutionalization of academic entrepreneurship in the life sciences', *Research in the Sociology of Organizations*, **25**: 219–59.

Dasgupta, P. and P. David (1994), 'Toward a new economics of science', *Research Policy*, **23** (5): 487–521.

Di Gregorio, D. and S. Shane (2003), 'Why do some universities generate more start-ups than others?', *Research Policy*, **32** (2): 209–27.

Dohmen, T., A. Falk, D. Huffman, U. Sunde, J. Schrupp and G.G. Wagner (2005), 'Individual risk attitudes: new evidence from a large, representative, experimentally-validated survey', DIW discussion paper 511, accessed at http://193.174.141.131/documents/publikationen/73/43553/dp511.pdf.

Etzkowitz, H. (1989), 'Entrepreneurial science and the academy: a case of the transformation of norms', *Social Problems*, **36** (1): 14–29.

Gittelman, M. (1999), 'Knowledge as property: innovation in biotechnology in the United States and in France', in *Academy of Management Proceedings*, IM: L1–L6.

Glenna, L.L., W.B. Lacy, R. Welsh and D. Biscotti (2007), 'University administrators, agricultural biotechnology and academic capitalism', *Sociological Quarterly*, **48**: 141–63.

Hackett, E.J. (1990), 'Science as a vocation in the 1990s: the changing organizational culture of academic science', *Journal of Higher Education*, **61**: 241–79.

Henderson, R.M., A.B. Jaffe and M. Trajtenberg (1998), 'Universities as a source of commercial technology: a detailed analysis of university patenting 1965–1988', *Review of Economics and Statistics*, **80** (1): 119–27.

Hong, W. and J. Walsh (2009), 'For money or glory? Commercialization, competition, and secrecy in the entrepreneurial university', *Sociological Quarterly*, **50** (1): 145–71.

Jaffe, A.B. (1989), 'Real effects of academic research', *American Economic Review*, **79** (5): 957–70.

Jaffe, A.B. and J. Lerner (2001), 'Reinventing public R&D: patent policy and the commercialization of national laboratory technologies', *Rand Journal of Economics*, **32** (1): 167–98.

Jensen, R. and M.C. Thursby (2001), 'Proofs and prototypes for sale: the licensing of university inventions', *American Economic Review*, **91** (1): 240–59.

Krabel, S. and P. Mueller (2009), 'What drives scientists to start their own company? An empirical investigation of Max Planck Society scientists', *Research Policy*, **38** (6): 947–56.

Link, A.N. and D.S. Siegel (2007), *Innovation, Entrepreneurship, and Technological Change*, Oxford and New York: Oxford University Press.

Lissoni, F., P. Llerena, M. McKelvey and B. Sanditov (2007), 'Academic patenting in Europe: new evidence from the KEINS database', CESPRI working paper no. 202, Milan, June.

Lowe, R. and C. Gonzalez-Brambila (2007), 'Faculty entrepreneurs and research productivity', *Journal of Technology Transfer*, **32** (3): 173–94.

Mansfield, E. (1995), 'Academic research underlying industrial innovation', *Review of Economics and Statistics*, **77** (1): 55–65.

Max Planck Society (2009), *Annual Report 2008*, Munich.

Max Planck Society (2010), *Annual Report 2009*, Munich.

Merton, R. (1957), 'Priorities in scientific discovery: a chapter in the sociology of science', *American Sociological Review*, **22** (6): 635–59.

Merton, R.K. (1973), 'The normative structure of science', in *The Sociology of Science*, Chicago, IL: University of Chicago Press, pp. 267–78.

Mowery, D.C., R.N. Nelson, B.N. Sampat and A.A. Ziedonis (2001), 'The growth of patenting and licensing by U.S. universities: an assessment of the effects of the Bayh–Dole Act of 1980', *Research Policy*, **30** (1): 99–119.

Owen-Smith, J. and W. Powell (2001), 'Careers and contradictions: faculty responses to the transformation of knowledge and its uses in the life sciences', *Research in the Sociology of Work*, **10**: 109–40.

Owen-Smith, J. and W. Powell (2004), 'Careers and contradictions: faculty responses to the transformation of knowledge and its uses in the life sciences', *Sociologie du travail*, **46** (3): 347–77.

Powers, J.B. and P.P. McDougall (2005), 'University start-up formation and technology licensing with firms that go public: a resource-based view of academic entrepreneurship', *Journal of Business Venturing*, **20** (3): 291–311.

Roach, M. and H. Sauermann (2010), 'A taste for science? PhD scientists' academic orientation and self-selection into research careers with industry', *Research Policy*, **39** (3), 422–34.

Shane, S. (2004), *Academic Entrepreneurship: University Spinoffs and Wealth Creation*, Cheltenham, UK and Northampton, MA, USA: Edward Elgar.

Slaughter, S. and L. Leslie (1997), *Academic Capitalism: Politics, Policies, and the Entrepreneurial University*, Baltimore, MD and London: Johns Hopkins University Press.

Stephan, P. (1996), 'The economics of science', *Journal of Economic Literature*, **34** (3): 1199–235.

Stephan, P. and S. Levin (1991), 'Research productivity over the life cycle: evidence for academic scientists', *American Economic Review*, **81** (1): 114–32.

Tartari, V., A. Salter, M. Perkmann and P. d'Este (2010), 'Come engage with me: behavioral and attitudinal peer effects on academics' engagement with industry', paper presented at the Druid Winter Conference, Copenhagen, 22 January.

Thursby, J.G. and M.C. Thursby (2002), 'Who is selling the ivory tower? Sources of growth in university licensing', *Management Science*, **48** (1): 90–104.

Thursby, J.G. and M.C. Thursby (2003), 'Are faculty critical? Their role in university–industry licensing', NBER working paper no. 9991, Cambridge, MA.

Wagner, G.G., J. Frick and J. Schrupp (2007), 'Socio-economic panel', accessed 19 July 2011 at www.diw.de/documents/dokumentenarchiv/17/56579/personen 2007.pdf.

PART II

The evolution of firms

6. Capturing firm behavior in agent-based models of industry evolution and macroeconomic dynamics

Herbert Dawid and Philipp Harting*

1 INTRODUCTION

The description of the dynamics emerging from the interaction of different types of economic actors, who independently make decisions and take actions, is a challenging task underlying any analysis of market dynamics, industry evolution or macroeconomic dynamics. This task has been tackled using a number of different approaches. In the area of evolutionary economics, the use of agent-based simulation models has traditionally been an important tool and one that continues to attract an increasing amount of research. Starting with the pioneering work of Nelson and Winter (1982), various aspects of industry dynamics have been explored using simulation methods both in rather generic industry frameworks and in specific application areas taking into account characteristic features of the considered industry (see, for example, surveys in Dawid, 2006 or Safarzynska and van den Bergh, 2010). Recently, substantial effort has also been invested in the development of agent-based closed macroeconomic models that capture the interplay of different markets and sectors in the economy while at the same time providing an explicit representation of behavior of different types of potentially heterogeneous actors and the institutions governing their (local) interaction patterns (for example, Silverberg and Verspagen, 1993; Delli Gatti et al., 2005; Dawid et al., 2009; or Dosi et al., 2010). In the tradition of evolutionary economics, this kind of work is based on the assertion that economic systems generically are not in equilibrium and aims to explore properties that emerge from certain assumptions about micro behavior and micro structure.

In contrast to dynamic equilibrium models, where it is assumed that the behavior of all actors is determined by maximization of the own (intertemporal) objective function using correct expectations about the behavior of the other actors, agent-based simulation models need to provide explicit constructive rules that describe how different agents take different decisions. The need to provide such rules is based not only on the basic conviction underlying these models, that in most economic settings actual behavior of decision makers is far away from intertemporally optimal behavior under rational expectations, but also on the fact that in most models incorporating heterogeneity among agents and explicit interaction protocols (for example, market rules), the characterization of dynamic equilibria is outside the scope of analytical and numerical analysis. Given that need to specify explicit rules for all decisions taken by all actors in an agent-based model, the determination and motivation of the implemented rules becomes a major modeling issue. The 'wilderness of bounded rationality' (Sims, 1980) is a serious concern since a large number of different approaches to model boundedly rational behavior and its adaptation have been put forward in the literature, and at this point there is little indication for the emergence of a widely accepted consensus that provides empirically or theoretically well-founded concepts for tackling this issue (see, for example, Hommes, 2009). Providing such concepts, however, seems important for several reasons. First and foremost, it would add to the credibility of agent-based models and the normative implications derived from such models in the areas of firm strategy, market design or economic policy. Second, the comparison between results derived in different models capturing different economic settings is facilitated if these models share a common approach to modeling certain (standard) decision processes, such as the consumption choice of households or pricing and investment of firms. Third, if the structure of the considered rules for a given type of decision can be restricted, for example to a parametrized family of rules, the test for robustness of simulation results becomes much easier, since it involves only the consideration of parameter variations rather than that of structural changes in the decision rule.

The most suitable approach to providing empirical or theoretical foundations for certain types of rules depends strongly on the type of agent that is to be modeled. Describing the decision rule of an individual choosing a consumption good is very different from capturing the rule determining the interest rate decisions of a central bank. In fact, the interest rate decision of a central bank is one of the few types of decision where there indeed seems to be some consensus about the structure of the corresponding decision rule within the agent-based models that include a central bank. Since central banks have an interest in making their decision processes transparent and predictable, there is something similar to publicly documented decision rules (such as the Taylor rule) which can easily be implemented in an agent-based model. If we consider decisions taken by individuals rather than an institution such as a central bank, such documentation of the rules or processes leading to a decision is missing. An obvious candidate to obtain empirically founded insights into the decision processes of individuals in different economic frameworks is the consideration of experimental evidence. The fast-growing literature in experimental and behavioral economics provides a rich basis to develop empirically grounded representations of individual decisions in agent-based models. There is quite a bit of work linking experimental with agent-based work (see, for example, the survey in Duffy, 2006) and recently attempts have been made to design individual decision and learning rules as well as expectation rules in agent-based models in a way such that they closely resemble experimental evidence (for example, Arifovic and Ledyard, 2008; Hommes, 2009).

The focus of this chapter is on the representation of firm decisions in agent-based models. Most decisions of firms that are typically considered in agent-based models are taken according to well-structured processes and are only to a small extent at the discretion of individual decision makers. Hence, evidence from laboratory experiments might be of limited use when developing models of firms' decision rules.[1] The fact that firms in many domains indeed follow well-established routines or heuristics has been highlighted in the literature on evolutionary theory (Nelson and Winter, 1982; Nelson, 2005), but is also evident from considering the management literature. For many decision problems relevant for a firm, standard decision heuristics have been developed in the corresponding literature in management science and operations research. They are presented in the main textbooks for business studies and have been at least partly implemented in decision support software available to companies. Hence, for many decision problems of firms there exist well-documented algorithms that determine or at least strongly influence the way the corresponding decisions are taken in a large percentage of firms. Paying attention to such decision algorithms and trying to implement them in an agent-based framework should provide additional empirical grounding for the models and also lead to a stronger standardization of the representation of firms' decisions.

The purpose of this chapter is to highlight how such an approach, which we call the 'management science approach', can be used in different economic settings to derive descriptive and in particular normative insights into firm behavior and policy design. Prior to the treatment of the management science approach in the framework of a macroeconomic model (Section 3), we shall give a brief discussion and categorization of the approaches to the modeling of firm decisions that are present in the literature (Section 2). A concluding discussion is given in Section 4.

2   APPROACHES TO MODELING FIRM DECISIONS IN ACE: A BRIEF SURVEY

To put the different approaches for modeling firm decision processes that have been put forward in the agent-based literature into perspective, it might be useful to realize that the role of firms and their decision processes depends crucially on the research agenda underlying the study under consideration. At least three different branches of the literature that have attracted considerable attention can be distinguished in this respect.

First, papers that deal with the effects of policy interventions or changes in market characteristics on market outcomes, industry dynamics or growth (for example, Nelson and Winter, 1982; Winter, 1984; Malerba et al., 2001; Dawid et al., 2008, 2009; Dosi et al., 2010; Li et al., 2010). Here the focus is not on the firms' behavior, but on the effects of certain changes in the economic environment *given* the decision rules (and maybe their adjustment dynamics) of the firms. Obviously, different types of decision rules for firms might, in principle, generate quite different effects of these changes in the economic environment. Therefore, although the exact form of the decision rules used might not be of major importance, the validity of the derived market design or policy conclusions is strongly affected by the empirical foundation of the considered rules and the robustness of the qualitative conclusions with respect to changes of the rules within an (empirically) reasonable range. The largest part of the ACE literature where firm behavior plays some role falls into this category.

Second, there is some literature exploring the characteristics of firm strategies that evolve in particular market frameworks (for example, Midgley et al., 1997; Dosi et al., 1999; Dawid and Reimann, 2004, 2011). Here the focus is on the firm strategy and, depending on the way decision rules and their updating are modeled, the structure of the decision rule might be quite flexible without requiring strong assumptions about its characteristics (see, for example, the brief discussion of Dosi et al., 1999, below). However, to a certain degree this just transfers the problem of the empirical or theoretical foundation to the level of the rule-adjustment process. The properties of the evolved strategies in general depend on the type of adjustment process considered, and any conclusions drawn about properties of (long-run) strategies therefore rest on the validity of the underlying adjustment process or the robustness of these properties with respect to changes in this process.

Finally, a third stream of literature has treated the question under which kind of assumptions about market environment and learning behavior *ex ante* uncoordinated firms can in the long run coordinate their behavior and how far this coordinated behavior resembles Nash or Walras equilibria (for example, Arifovic, 1994; Price, 1997; Dawid and Kopel, 1998; Vriend, 2000; Arifovic and Maschek, 2008). It turns out that even in a given standard market environment, such as a Cournot oligopoly, convergence of behavior and also the equilibrium selection in the case of convergence depends crucially on the way firm strategies are represented (Dawid and Kopel, 1998) or updated (Vriend, 2000; Arifovic and Maschek, 2008).

Within these different branches of literature quite a wide range of approaches for representation, design and updating of firms' behavioral rules have been used. In order to give a somewhat systematic overview we have tried to categorize these approaches, without, however, claiming that this listing is exhaustive or the categorization is in any way generic:

- *Fixed rules with heuristic basis* Perhaps the most common way firms' decision behavior is represented in ACE models is the use of relatively simple fixed decision rules that are motivated by (sometimes anecdotal) empirical arguments or plausibility considerations. Examples include the original Nelson and Winter model of Schumpeterian competition where innovation and imitation expenses as well as investments in physical capital are determined by simple closed-form functions that stay constant over time, and the output decision is made using the assumption that capacities are always fully exploited (see Nelson and Winter, 1982). Frequently used simple decision rules with empirical foundations are fixed markup pricing rules and research and development (R&D) rules assuming constant R&D intensities of firms (see, for example, Dosi et al., 2003).

- *Adaptation of actions* In this approach the behavior of a firm is updated over time due to (typically evolutionary) learning, where the object that is adapted over time is the action itself (for example, price, quantity) rather than some rule determining the action (for example, Arifovic, 1994; Vriend, 2000). Since the economic environment in models of this type is often assumed to be static, the fact that firms' *actions* are updated over time due to processes such as imitation or reinforcement could be interpreted as a short-cut for assuming that the decision rules determining the actions are adjusted in such a way and then applied to more or less static input data. Another underlying assumption could be that firms do not follow any structured decision rules to come up with this decision, but evaluate their different action choices in each period entirely based on past performance of different choices by the firm itself and its competitors. How reasonable such an interpretation is seems to depend strongly on the kind of decision that is considered. In particular for standard operational decisions, such as production decisions, pricing, and investment, this interpretation, however, seems to be rather far-fetched.

- *Adaptation of rules*   Decisions of firms are taken according to rules that change over time. Either the structure of the rules is fixed and rule parameters are adjusted over time (for example, Winter, 1984; Yildizoglu, 2002) or the representation of the rule is so flexible that its whole structure (including the set of variables that is taken into account) can evolve over time. A nice example in this respect is Dosi et al. (1999), where the rules determining the pricing decisions of firms in an oligopoly are represented as genetic programming trees and are updated by standard genetic programming operators. Potential input data for the rules consist of past observations of all prices, aggregate demand quantity, own costs and market share. It is shown that the rules that emerge in the long run lead to trajectories where the price a firm charges is moving almost in parallel to the costs. This means that although a large variety of pricing-rule structures would be available to the firm, in the long run a pricing rule very close to a markup rule with constant markup is adopted by the firms. Other examples of the emergence of firms' decision rules in large rule spaces are Marks (1992) and Midgley et al. (1997).

3   A MANAGEMENT SCIENCE APPROACH TO MODEL FIRMS' DECISION MAKING

Considering the brief literature survey in the previous section, several observations can be made. First, as discussed earlier, only a small fraction of work in this area refers to actual firms' decision processes when motivating the employed modeling approach. Second, typically decision rules are represented by closed-form functions of certain input variables, but there is very little consideration of actual processes or algorithms that are used to come up with certain decisions, although in principle agent-based models would allow the capture of such decision structures. Third, in the agent-based literature, firms typically do not engage in any kind of explicit optimization of an objective function. The insight that determining equilibrium behavior in such models is typically infeasible and that firms act boundedly rational would not necessarily imply such an absence of optimization. In related literature (see, for example, Day, 1999) models have been suggested where decision makers build simplified models of their economic environment and then choose their action in a way to maximize their objective within their simplified internal model. Also many heuristic decision rules for managerial decisions result from optimization in relatively simple models that abstract from many complex aspects of the firm's decision problem.

The management science approach, which we shall illustrate in this section, aims at implementing relatively simple decision rules that match standard procedures of real-world firms as described in the corresponding management literature. There is a rich literature on (heuristic) managerial decision rules in many areas of management science. This includes pricing (see, for example, Nagle and Hogan, 2006), production planning (see, for example, Silver et al., 1998) or market selection (see, for example, Wind and Mahajan, 1981; Kotler and Keller, 2009). Although it certainly cannot be assumed that all firms in an economy rely on such standard managerial heuristics, capturing the main features of these heuristics when modeling the firm adds a strong empirical micro foundation to the agent-based model.

To be more specific about the management science approach, let us consider the modeling of firm decisions in a large agent-based macroeconomic model that was initially developed in the European project EURACE and later extended (see Deissenberg et al., 2008; Dawid et al., 2009, 2010 for treatments of previous versions of the model). We only sketch some main features of the model here that allow the firm decisions we shall focus on to be put into perspective. A more extensive description of the model is given in Appendix 6A. The model describes an economy containing labor, consumption goods, capital goods, and financial and credit markets in a regional context. Each agent – firms, households and banks – is located in one of the regions. The spatial extensions of the markets differ. The capital goods market is global, meaning that firms in all regions buy from the same global capital goods producer and therefore have access to the same technology. On the consumption goods market, demand is determined locally in the sense that all consumers buy at regional markets, denoted as 'malls', that are located in their region, but supply is global because every firm might sell its products in all regional markets of the economy. Labor markets are characterized by spatial frictions determined by commuting costs that arise if workers accept jobs outside their own region. The basic time unit in the model is one day, where many decisions, such as production choice or hiring of firms, are taken monthly.

In what follows we shall concentrate on decisions of consumption goods producers in this model. These firms use a vintage capital stock and labor to produce the consumption goods on a monthly basis. The consumption goods are then distributed to the different regions this producer serves. For simplicity it is assumed that all producers offer their products in all regions. Each producer keeps a stock of its products at each of the regional malls and offers the goods at a posted price that is updated once a month at the point in time when the stock is replenished.

All sales of consumption goods take place at the malls. Each household determines once a month the budget which it will spend for consumption based on its income and its assets carried over from the previous period. Once a week the household then visits the (regional) mall to purchase consumption goods. When visiting the mall each consumer collects information about the range of goods provided and about the prices and inventories of the different goods. In the marketing literature it is standard to describe individual consumption decisions using logit models. These models represent the stochastic influence of factors not explicitly modeled on consumption decisions and the power of these models to explain real market data has been well documented (see, for example, Guadagni and Little, 1983). Therefore, we rely on a model of that kind and assume that a consumer's decision regarding which goods to buy is random, where purchasing probabilities are based on the values the household attaches to the different choices the consumer is aware of. In particular, these values are influenced by the prices at which the different producers offer their goods. If possible, each household spends its entire planned weekly consumption budget at the mall. If the stock of a certain producer at the mall is empty when the household visits the mall, then this product is excluded from the consumer's consideration, which means that the producer is losing potential sales. The introduction of the regional malls is supposed to capture in a simple way the interaction on regionally separated consumption goods markets with search frictions, storage of goods and potential rationing on both market sides.

Overall, a consumption goods producer has to make a large number of decisions affecting different markets, but focusing on the mall transactions this boils down to two major decisions. First, which quantities should be delivered to each mall in a given period and, based on this, how much should be produced in a given month. Second, which price should be posted at the malls in a given period. We shall discuss several aspects of these two decisions in the remainder of this section.

Let us first consider the monthly quantity decision of a consumption goods producer. On a given day of the month (which might differ between different producers), the firm receives messages from all the malls it serves reporting the current stock levels. Based on this information the firm calculates its sales at each mall every month. Due to the fluctuations in consumption budgets of households and the stochastic aspects of the product choice decisions, sales at the malls fluctuate in a non-deterministic way. Furthermore, it is costly for a producer to keep the stock at a mall so low that it is fully sold during the month, because households arriving after the stock has been depleted will buy from competitors rather than put off their consumption, and therefore potential sales are lost. This means that the producer in our agent-based economy faces for each of the malls a production planning problem with stochastic demand and out-of-stock costs, where the delivery intervals are given and fixed. Such problems have been extensively treated in the operations management literature as 'news-vendor problems'. Procedures, how to treat such problems, are presented in most standard textbooks in this area. Although these procedures are based on optimal solutions to certain optimization problems, they are heuristics in the sense that the underlying optimization problem is a sim-plified representation of the actual problem abstracting from aspects such as competition or intertemporal effects. Furthermore, they are relatively easy to implement and therefore widely applicable. A standard approach for firms to deal with newsvendor problems of this type is the use of a policy where the firm replenishes its stock in each period up to a given level Y. In order to determine Y the firm estimates the demand distribution for the following period and then chooses Y in a way that the stock-out prob-ability under the estimated demand distribution matches a certain target value. This target value depends on inventory and stock-out costs and also crucially on the risk attitude of the firm.

Although this decision heuristic cannot be represented in a single closed-form expression, it is straightforward to implement it in an agent-based model. In the EURACE model, firms follow this heuristic, where the stock-out probability used by the firm is considered as an important strategy parameter. Below we shall consider effects of changes in this parameter on the dynamics of produced output on the aggregate level. The actual implementation of the rule in the model then proceeds as follows. Let vector $\{\hat{D}_{i,r,t-\tau}, \ldots, \hat{D}_{i,r,t-1}\}$ denote the estimated demands[2] for the good of firm i reported by mall r during the last τ periods. Furthermore, $SL_{i,r,t}$ is the firm's current mall stock on the day in period t when the stock is checked. Following the procedure described above, the firm chooses its desired replenishment quantity for region r according to the following rule:

$$\tilde{D}_{i,r,t} = \begin{cases} 0 & SL_{i,r,t} \geq Y_{i,r,t}, \\ Y_{i,r,t} - SL_{i,r,t} & \text{else,} \end{cases}$$

where $Y_{i,r,t}$ is chosen such that the firm expects to be able to satisfy the market demand with some probability $1 - \chi$. Again following standard procedures described in the managerial literature, demand distribution in the following period is estimated using a linear regression based on previous demands. Put formally,

$$Y_{i,r,t} = \hat{a}_{i,r,t} + \tau \cdot \hat{b}_{i,r,t} + \bar{q}_{1-\chi} \cdot \sqrt{\hat{\sigma}^2_{i,r,t}},$$

where $\bar{q}_{1-\chi}$ is the $1 - \chi$ quantile of the standard normal distribution and the regression coefficients $\hat{a}_{i,r,t}$ and $\hat{b}_{i,r,t}$ as well as the variance $\hat{\sigma}^2_{i,r,t}$ are estimated using standard linear regression methods.

The sum of the orders received by all malls becomes:

$$\tilde{D}_{i,t} = \sum_{r=1}^{R} \tilde{D}_{i,r,t}.$$

In principle this should be the production quantity of the firm, but to capture rigidities in production plan adjustments the consumption good producer shows some inertia in adapting the actual production quantity to the quantity requested by the malls. In particular, we have:

$$\tilde{Q}_{i,t} = \xi \tilde{D}_{i,t} + (1 - \xi)\frac{1}{T}\sum_{k=t-T}^{t-1} \tilde{Q}_{i,k},$$

where $\tilde{Q}_{i,t}$ is the planned production quantity of firm i in period t. As discussed in more detail in Appendix 6A, the realized production volume $Q_{i,t}$ can deviate from the planned output $\tilde{Q}_{i,t}$ due to rationing on the factor markets. The quantities actually delivered to the malls, $D_{i,r,t}$, are adjusted proportionally to the intended quantities $\tilde{D}_{i,r,t}$ so that:

$$D_{i,r,t} = \frac{\tilde{D}_{i,r,t}}{\tilde{D}_{i,t}}Q_t.$$

Production times of consumption goods are not explicitly taken into account and the produced quantities are delivered on the same day as production. The local stock levels at the malls are updated accordingly.

This representation of the quantity decision of firms is not only based on a clear empirical basis, but also leads within the EURACE model to realistic properties of time series on the macro level (see Dawid et al., 2008, 2009). Several parameters govern the procedure, in particular, the number of past observations used to estimate the demand distribution (τ) and, more importantly, the stock-out probability parameter χ. Although empirical evidence allows values of this parameter to be restricted to some plausible range, an important consideration is how far conclusions drawn from the model are robust with respect to changes of the parameter within this range. The main purpose of the EURACE model is to allow the analysis of effects of different policy measures, such as innovation policies or labor market policies, on the dynamics of the economy as a whole and of different sectors. Hence, the effects of changes of the stock-out parameter χ on aggregate variables of the economy are of main interest. In Figure 6.1 we show

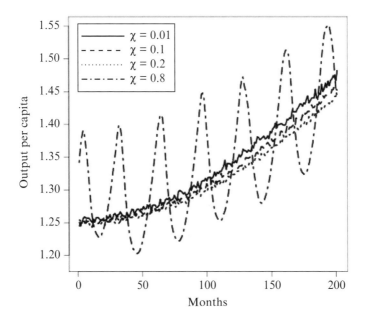

Figure 6.1   Dynamics of per capita output averaged over 10 runs for different values of the stock-out probability

the effect of changes of χ on per capita output of the economy. The different time series depict averages over 10 runs carried out for the corresponding stock-out probabilities. The figure clearly shows that, although the aggressiveness of firms with respect to their production planning somehow influences the total output in the economy, qualitative changes in the dynamics appear only for an extreme stock-out probability of 80 percent.

Let us now turn to the pricing decision of the firm. As discussed earlier, a very popular approach to capture price determination in agent-based models is the use of markup pricing, where typically the markup is assumed to be constant over time. Although there is extensive empirical evidence for widespread use of markup pricing in the real world, it is much less clear what determines the size of the markup chosen by a firm. The size of the markup chosen by the firms not only effects the performance of the individual firms, but, as can be seen in Figure 6.2, also strongly influences the level of the overall output in the economy. The figure demonstrates that an increase of the markup by all consumption good producers from 5 to 20 percent reduces the per capita output by about 20 percent. This strong effect is quite surprising because the closed EURACE model takes into account that firm profits that might

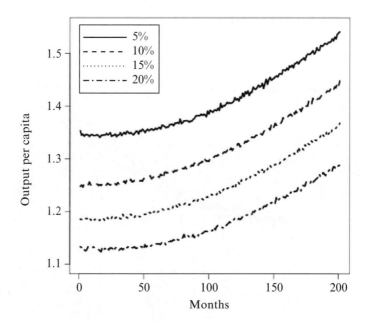

Figure 6.2   Dynamics of per capita output averaged over 10 runs for different values of the markup

be generated by large markups are to a large extent channeled back to households, and thus to consumption, through firms' dividend payments.

These observations suggest that a careful analysis of empirically meaningful markup values and of the way the markup level is set can be an important factor in providing confidence in the conclusions drawn from simulation results. As is also well known from microeconomic theory, the two crucial factors determining the price a firm should charge are (marginal) costs and the elasticity of the demand for the product of this firm with respect to its price. In particular, the elasticity of the firm's individual demand is, however, typically unknown to a firm operating in a dynamic complex environment and therefore can only be estimated. In the management literature, heuristic procedures are proposed that would in the ideal world of oligopolies with full information about demand and cost lead to standard elasticity-based pricing, but are also applicable in more messy environments where the actual demand structure is unknown to the firm. We adopt here a simple heuristic of this kind that can be summarized as follows if it is applied to the EURACE economy (see, for example, Nagle and Hogan, 2006, p. 136). For each considered price change:

1. determine the effects of changes in sales on production costs;
2. evaluate buyers' price sensitivity and determine a sales distribution after the price change;
3. calculate profit implications for various probable sales changes; and
4. accept or reject the proposed price change based on these considerations.

Step 4 of this procedure of course depends strongly on the objective of the firm. In our implementation of this procedure we assume that the firm maximizes expected profits and therefore compares the expected profit implications of the different price changes it considers. The main challenge of this procedure lies in step 2, where the firm has to determine the expected change in its sales for different potential price changes. To address this challenge we again rely on a procedure put forward in the relevant literature, 'namely simulated purchase surveys' (for example, see ibid., p. 300). Such surveys are performed by presenting consumers with a sample of products of the firm under consideration and its competitors together with prices, and asking the consumers which product they would choose. Based on the results of these surveys, the sensitivity of buyers with respect to price changes can be estimated.

To implement this procedure in our model we assume that each firm carries out market research and updates its prices once a year. From the household population it draws a sample where the sample size n_S has to be sufficiently large in order to obtain significant results. Therefore, the firm contacts randomly chosen households by sending an interview request. Contacted households decide whether they are willing to attend an interview based on a random process. If firms are not able to achieve the planned number of interviews n_S on their activation day, they repeat the recruiting procedure on the following days until the desired number is reached. Attending households receive a questionnaire containing a set of prices and goods where both the good of the firm and those of the competitors are included. The households are asked whether they would buy the firm's good at one of these prices or if they would decide on a different good offered at its original price. The simulated purchasing decision is based on the same logit model that households use for their real purchasing decision. Based on these answers the firm determines the expected change in sales coming with each of the considered price changes and calculates the corresponding profit implications, taking into account the cost effects of the change in sales. Among all considered price changes the one with the highest expected profit is then chosen.

In Figure 6.3 we show the dynamics of the resulting markups of firms for a single run. The solid line depicts the population mean, the dashed

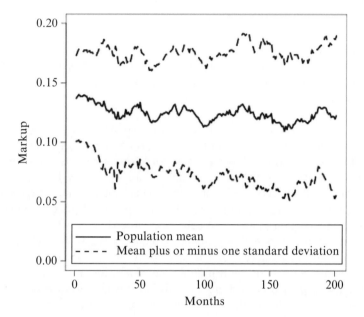

*Figure 6.3   Dynamics of the markup charged by firms in a single
              simulation run*

lines indicate the band of plus/minus one standard deviation. The population mean is quite stable over time, fluctuating slightly in a range between
10 and 15 percent. The heterogeneity within the population is, however,
substantial and also persistent, as can be seen from the standard deviation
band. So it can be concluded that the standard setting with a fixed markup
of 10 percent for all firms is close to what would emerge from this endogenous markup rule but misses the persistent heterogeneity of markups in
the firm population. To what extent the consideration of such persistent
heterogeneity in firm behavior would affect qualitative properties of the
aggregate dynamics or of policy effects depends on the particular research
issue and cannot be discussed here.

   Having discussed an empirically founded way to model the quantity and
pricing decisions in terms of parametrized families to decision heuristics
and examined some robustness properties of the results with respect to
changes in the parameters of the heuristic, we now briefly discuss another
important issue of the description of the firm behavior in agent-based
models, namely the synchronization, or lack thereof, of the points in time
when different firms in the economy make their decisions. In the majority of agent-based models, as in almost all models examining market

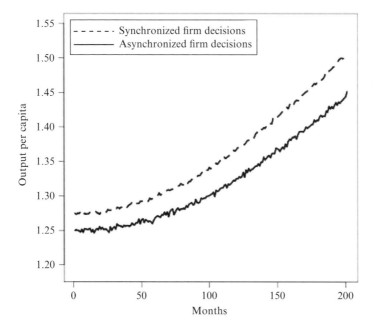

Figure 6.4   Dynamics of per capita output averaged over 10 runs

or industry dynamics, the time structure consisting of discrete periods without any further fragmentation implies complete synchronization of the decisions of firms. It is well known that such synchronization is prone to producing overshooting phenomena, and for many firm decisions such strong synchronization cannot be observed in reality. The EURACE model allows one to study how the assumption that the points in time when firms act are fully synchronized influences the dynamics of the model. As briefly discussed above, in the EURACE model the basic time unit is a day, but many decisions are taken once a week, once a month or once a quarter. The quantity and pricing decisions of firms are taken once a month, which means that each firm has one fixed day of the month when it applies the procedures described above to determine these values. In the standard setting it is assumed that each firm chooses its 'day to act' randomly and hence the decisions of the different firms are distributed over time, but full synchronization can be achieved by assigning identical days to act to all firms. Figure 6.4 shows that synchronization of firm decisions does indeed have a nonnegligible effect on the emerging dynamics. Rather surprisingly, the effect of synchronization is positive, leading to an increase in per capita output of almost 5 percent. Actually, the effect of the synchronization of the firms is larger than the effect of a decrease in the stock-out probability from χ = 0.2 to χ = 0.01 by all firms. This highlights that the usual assumption of synchronization of firms' action in ACE models should be treated with caution and if possible robustness considerations should be made not only with respect to parameter variations but also with respect to the schedule of events in a period. The actual mechanisms and causal chains leading to the positive effect of synchronization could be identified by examining the interrelated dynamics of different micro variables; see Dawid et al. (2009, 2010) for examples of extensive examinations of the economic mechanisms on the micro level that give rise to certain macro-level effects of different economic policy measures. Although certainly interesting, we abstain here from presenting such a detailed analysis of the effect of synchronization in our model. Rather we want to stress the general point that the assumption of synchronized actions often does have substantial implications.

4   CONCLUSIONS

In this chapter we have argued that in agent-based models of industry and macro dynamics, relatively little attention has been paid to the way in which decision-making processes of firms are modeled. While in recent literature the effort to provide empirical and experimental foundations for the description of decisions by *individuals* in agent-based models has increased, a clear conceptual basis for the choice of firms' decision rules in such models is often missing. A potentially fruitful approach seems to be the management science approach where decision heuristics that are well documented in the relevant managerial literature are implemented in the agent-based model in order to capture the decision processes of the firms. Here this approach has been illustrated in the framework of an agent-based macro model where the focus of the analysis lies on understanding the dynamics on the aggregate level and the effects of policy interventions. However, it should be pointed out that the management science approach has also been applied with success in quite different contexts and with a quite different focus. In Dawid and Reimann (2004) a normative analysis from the perspective of the firm was carried out using this approach. In particular they used parametrized families of decision rules taken from the managerial literature to examine how the optimal firm strategy with respect to product range expansion and market selection depends on the properties of the industry environment and the strategies adopted by the competitors. This study shows that the management science approach also has potential as a tool to carry out strategic analysis from a firm perspective using agent-based modeling.

Obviously, more work is needed to increase the appeal of the approach. Standard decision heuristics for different types of firm decisions relevant in ACE models will have to be collected and empirical evidence about which published decision heuristics are indeed applied by a majority of the firms should be provided. Even if such empirical studies showed that the percentage of firms following standard managerial heuristics is relatively small, such research contributing to the development of an empirically founded systematic approach for the modeling of firm decisions in ACE models would be most welcome.

NOTES

* Most of the work discussed in this chapter was carried out in cooperation with Michael Neugart and Simon Gemkow. The EURACE project (EU IST FP6 STREP grant 035086) was carried out by a consortium led by S. Cincotti (University of Genova), H. Dawid (University of Bielefeld), C. Deissenberg (Université de la Méditerrané), K. Erkan (TUBITAK National Research Institute of Electronics and Cryptology), M. Gallegati (Università Politecnica delle Marche), M. Holcombe (University of Sheffield), M. Marchesi (Università di Cagliari), and C. Greenough (STFC – Rutherford Appleton Laboratory).

1. It should be noted that we do not deal here with issues of the organization of the firm, including the organization of certain decision processes. Experimental, evolutionary, and agent-based research has been very active in this area (see, for example, Chang and Harrington, 2006), but at this point in agent-based computational economics (ACE) models of industry and macro dynamics, the inner structure of firms has not been explicitly represented.

2. This quantity is identical to actual sales in all periods where the stock was not emptied during the month. In periods where the product of the firm was sold out at this mall the estimated demand is larger than the actual sales.

REFERENCES

Arifovic, J. (1994), 'Genetic algorithm learning and the cobweb model', *Journal of Economic Dynamics and Control*, **18**, 3–28.

Arifovic, J. and J. Ledyard (2008), 'A behavioral model for mechanism design: individual evolutionary learning', Simon Fraser University working paper, Burnaby, BC.

Arifovic, J. and M. Maschek (2008), 'Revisiting individual evolutionary learning in the cobweb model – an illustration of the virtual spite effect', *Computational Economics*, **28**, 333–54.

Chang, M. and J. Harrington (2006), 'Agent-based models of organizations', in L. Tesfatsion and K. Judd (eds), *Handbook of Computational Economics*, Vol. II, Amsterdam: North-Holland, pp. 1273–337.

Dawid, H. (2006), 'Agent-based models of innovation and technological change', in L. Tesfatsion and K. Judd (eds), *Handbook of Computational Economics*, Vol. II, Amsterdam: North-Holland, pp. 1235–72.

Dawid, H., S. Gemkow, P. Harting and M. Neugart (2009), 'On the effects of skill upgrading in the presence of spatial labor market frictions: an agent-based analysis of spatial policy design', *Journal of Artifical Societies and Social Simulation*, **12**, 5.

Dawid, H., S. Gemkow, P. Harting and M. Neugart (2010), 'Labor market integration policies and the convergence of regions', Bielefeld University working paper.

Dawid, H., S. Gemkow, P. Harting, M. Neugart, K. Kabus and K. Wersching (2008), 'Skills, innovation and growth: an agent-based policy analysis', *Jahrbücher für Nationalökonomie und Statistik/Journal of Economics and Statistics*, **228**, 251–75.

Dawid, H. and M. Kopel (1998), 'The appropriate design of a genetic algorithm in economic applications exemplified by a model of the cobweb type', *Journal of Evolutionary Economics*, **8**, 297–315.

Dawid, H. and M. Reimann (2004), 'Evaluating market attractiveness: individual incentives vs. industry profitability', *Computational Economics*, **24**, 321–55.

Dawid, H. and M. Reimann (2011), 'Diversification: a road to inefficiency in product innovations?', *Journal of Evolutionary Economics*, **21** (2), 191–229.

Day, R. (1999), *Complex Ecoonomic Dynamics*, Vol. II, Cambridge, MA: MIT Press.

Deissenberg, C., S. van der Hoog and H. Dawid (2008), 'EURACE: a massively parallel agent-based model of the European economy', *Applied Mathematics and Computation*, **204**, 541–52.

Delli Gatti, D., C. Guilmi, E. Gaffeo, G. Giulioni, M. Gallegati and A. Palestrini (2005), 'A new approach to business fluctuations: heterogeneous interacting agents, scaling laws and financial fragility', *Journal of Economic Behavior and Organization*, **56**, 489–512.

Dosi, G., G. Fagiolo and A. Roventini (2010), 'Schumpeter meeting Keynes: a policy-friendly model of endogenous growth and business cycles', *Journal of Economic Dynamics and Control*, **34**, 1748–67.

Dosi, G., L. Marengo, A. Bassanini and M. Valente (1999), 'Norms as emergent properties of adaptive learning: the case of economic routines', *Journal of Evolutionary Economics*, **9**, 5–26.

Dosi, G., L. Marengo and G. Fagiolo (2003), 'Learning in evolutionary environments', in K. Dopfer (ed.), *The Evolutionary Foundations of Economics*, Cambridge: Cambridge University Press, pp. 255–338.

Duffy, J. (2006), 'Agent-based models and human subject experiments', in L. Tesfatsion and K. Judd (eds), *Handbook of Computational Economics*, Vol. II, Amsterdam: North-Holland, pp. 949–1011.

Guadagni, P. and J. Little (1983), 'A logit model of brand choice calibrated on scanner data', *Marketing Science*, **2**, 203–38.

Hommes, C. (2009), 'The heterogeneous expectations hypothesis: some evidence from the lab', CeNDEF working paper, Amsterdam.

Kotler, P. and K. Keller (2009), *Marketing Management*, 9th edn, Englewood Cliffs, NJ: Prentice-Hall.

Li, H., J. Sun and L. Tesfatsion (2010), 'Testing institutional arrangements via agent-based modeling: a U.S. electricity market application', in H. Dawid and W. Semmler (eds), *Computational Methods in Economic Dynamics*, New York: Springer, pp. 135–58.

Malerba, F., R. Nelson, L. Orsenigo and S. Winter (2001), 'Competition and industrial policies in a "history-friendly" model of the evolution of the computer industry', *International Journal of Industrial Organization*, **19**, 635–64.

Marks, R. (1992), 'Breeding hybrid strategies: optimal behavior for oligopolists', *Journal of Evolutionary Economics*, **2**, 17–38.

Midgley, D., R. Marks and L. Cooper (1997), 'Breeding competitive strategies', *Management Science*, **43**, 257–75.

Nagle, T. and J. Hogan (2006), *The Strategy and Tactics of Pricing: A Guide to Growing More Profitably*, Englewood Cliffs, NJ: Pearson Prentice-Hall.

Nelson, R. (2005), 'Recent evolutionary theorizing about economic change', *Journal of Economic Literature*, **33**, 48–90.

Nelson, R.R. and S.G. Winter (1982), *An Evolutionary Theory of Economic Change*, Cambridge, MA and London: Harvard University Press.

Price, T. (1997), 'Using co-evolutionary programming to simulate strategic behavior in markets', *Journal of Evolutionary Economics*, **7**, 219–54.

Safarzynska, K. and J. van den Bergh (2010), 'Evolutionary models in economics: a survey of methods and building blocks', *Journal of Evolutionary Economics*, **20**, 329–73.

Silver, E., D. Pyke and R. Peterson (1998), *Inventory Management and Production Planning and Scheduling*, Chichester: John Wiley.

Silverberg, G. and B. Verspagen (1993), 'Collective learning, innovation and growth in a boundedly rational, evolutionary world', *Journal of Evolutionary Economics*, **4**, 207–26.

Sims, C. (1980), 'Macroeconomics and reality', *Econometrica*, **48** (1), 1–48.

Vriend, N. (2000), 'An illustration of the essential difference between individual and social learning, and its consequences for computational analyses', *Journal of Economic Dynamics and Control*, **24**, 1–19.

Wind, J. and V. Mahajan (1981), 'Designing product and business portfolios', *Harvard Business Review*, **59** (1), 155–65.

Winter, S. (1984), 'Schumpeterian competition in alternative technological regimes', *Journal of Economic Behavior and Organization*, **5**, 287–320.

Yildizoglu, M. (2002), 'Competing R&D strategies in an evolutionary industry model', *Computational Economics*, **19**, 51–65.

APPENDIX 6A DETAILED DESCRIPTION OF THE (EXTENDED VERSION OF THE) EURACE MODEL

Although some parts of the model have been described in detail in the body of the chapter, we have repeated them here for easier readability of the entire model description.

Overall Structure

The model describes an economy containing labor, consumption goods, capital goods, financial and credit markets in a regional context. Each agent (firms, households and banks) is located in one of the regions.

Table 6A.1   Parameter settings

Description	Parameter	Value
Number of households		1,600
Number of firms		80
Number of regions	R	1
Depreciation rate of capital (monthly)	δ	0.01
Monthly discount factor	ρ	0.95
Production smoothing	ξ	0.50
Stock-out probability (default value)	χ	0.20
Markup factor (default value)	$\dfrac{1}{\lvert \varepsilon_i^e \rvert - 1}$	0.10
Wage update	φ_i	0.01
Reservation wage update	ψ_k	0.02
Intensity of choice by consumers	λ_k^{cons}	7

Capital goods are provided with infinite supply at exogenously given prices. The quality of the capital goods improves over time where technological change is driven by a stochastic (innovation) process. Firms in the consumption goods sector use capital goods combined with labor input to produce consumption goods. The labor market is populated with workers that have a finite number of general skill levels and acquire specific skills on the job which they need to fully exploit the technological advantages of the capital goods employed in the production process. Consumption goods are sold at malls. Malls are treated as local market platforms where firms store and offer their products and consumers come to buy goods at posted prices.

The spatial extensions of the markets differ. The capital goods market is global, meaning that firms in all regions buy from the same global capital good producer and therefore have access to the same technology. On the consumption goods market, demand is determined locally in the sense that all consumers buy at the local mall located in their region, but supply is global because every firm might sell its products in all regional markets of the economy. Labor markets are characterized by spatial frictions determined by commuting costs that arise if workers accept jobs outside their own region. The basic time unit in the model is one day, where many decisions, such as production choice or hiring of firms, are taken monthly and others, such as consumption decisions of households, are taken weekly.

Table 6A.1 summarizes the setup of the model by showing the values of the most important model parameters.

Consumption Goods Producer

Quantity choice and factor demand

For a detailed description of the quantity choice, the reader is referred to Section 3.

Consumption goods producers need physical capital and labor to produce the consumption goods. A firm i has a capital stock $K_{i,t}$ that is composed of different vintages of the production technology $\mathbb{V} = \{V\}_1^{V\,\text{max}}$,

$$K_{i,t} = \sum_{V=1}^{V\,\text{max}} K_{i,t}^V. \qquad (6A.1)$$

The accumulation of physical capital by a consumption goods producer follows:

$$K_{i,t+1} = \sum_{V=1}^{V\,\text{max}} (1-\delta) K_{i,t}^V + \sum_{V=1}^{V\,\text{max}} I_{i,t}^V, \qquad (6A.2)$$

where δ is the depreciation rate and $I_{i,t}^V \geq 0$ is the gross investment in vintage V.

Every worker w has a level of general skills $b_w^{gen} \in \{1, \ldots, b_{max}^{gen}\}$ and a level of specific skills $b_{w,t}$. The specific skills of worker w indicate how efficiently the corresponding technology is exploited by the individual worker. Building up those specific skills depends on collecting experience by using the technology in the production process. The specific skills are updated once in each production cycle of one month. Further, we assume that updating takes place at the end of the cycle.

A crucial assumption is the positive relationship between the general skills b_w^{gen} of a worker and his/her ability to utilize his/her experiences. Taking the relevance of the general skill level into account, the specific skills of a worker w are assumed to evolve according to:

$$b_{w,t+1} = b_{w,t} + \chi(b_w^{gen}) \cdot \text{max}\,[A_{i,t} - b_{w,t}, 0], \qquad (6A.3)$$

where we denote with $A_{i,t}$ the average quality of the capital stock over all vintages. The function χ is increasing in the general skill level of the worker.

The production technology in the consumption goods sector is represented by a Leontief-type production function with complementarities between the qualities of the different vintages of the capital goods and the specific skill level of employees for using these types of technologies. Vintages are deployed for production in descending order by using the best vintage first. For each vintage the effective productivity is determined by the minimum of its productivity and the average level of relevant specific skills of the workers. Accordingly, output for a consumption goods producer is given by:

$$Q_{i,t} = \sum_{V=1}^{V\max} \min \left\{ K_{i,t}^V, \max\left[0, L_{i,t} - \sum_{k=V+1}^{V\max} K_{i,t}^k \right] \right\} \cdot \min [A^V, B_{i,t}], \quad (6A.4)$$

where A^V is the productivity of vintage V and $B_{i,t}$ denotes the average specific skill level in firms.

Let $\tilde{Q}_{i,t}$ be the planned production quantity of firm i in t and $\hat{Q}_{i,t}$ the feasible output that can be produced with the current capital stock. This potential output is computed according to:

$$\hat{Q}_{i,t} = \sum_{V=1}^{V\max} (1 - \delta) K_{i,t}^V \cdot \min [A^V, B_{i,t}]. \quad (6A.5)$$

Two cases have to be considered for the factor demand determination:

1. If $\hat{Q}_{i,t} \geq \tilde{Q}_{i,t}$: In that case the desired output can be produced with the current capital stock and no additional investments are necessary. We have $I_{i,t} = 0$ and the labor input is computed by taking the labor productivity of the last month into account:

$$\tilde{L}_{i,t} = \tilde{Q}_{i,t} \cdot \frac{L_{i,t-1}}{Q_{i,t-1}}. \quad (6A.6)$$

2. If $\hat{Q}_{i,t} < \tilde{Q}_{i,t}$: Here we have positive investments $I_{i,t} > 0$; the amount depends on the outcome of the vintage choice (see next subsection). If V is the selected vintage, the investment volume is:

$$I_{i,t} = \frac{\tilde{Q}_{i,t} - \hat{Q}_{i,t}}{\min [A^V, B_{i,t}]} \quad (6A.7)$$

and the labor demand:

$$\tilde{L}_{i,t} = K_{i,t-1}(1 - \delta) + I_{i,t}. \quad (6A.8)$$

Vintage choice

The consumption goods firm can choose from a set of vintages $\mathbb{V} = \{V\}_1^{V\max}$ which differ regarding their productivity A^V. The decision regarding in which vintage to invest depends on a comparison of the effective productivities and the corresponding prices. For this consideration the complementarity between specific skills and technology, $\min[A^V, B_{i,t}]$, plays an important role: due to the inertia of the specific skill adaptation, the advantage of a better vintage with $A^V > B_{i,t}$ cannot be fully taken into account immediately, but the productivity gap is closed over time. To account for this updating process the firm computes a discounted sum of estimated effective productivities over a fixed time horizon S. Therefore the specific skill evolution has to be estimated for each time step within this period $[t, t + S]$ by using equation (6A.3) with as parameters the firm's mean general skill level $B_{i,t}^{gen}$ and mean specific skill level $B_{i,t}$. Formally, we have:

$$\check{A}_{i,t}^{Eff}(V) = \sum_{s=0}^{S}\left(\frac{1}{1+\rho}\right)^{s} \min\,[A^V, \widetilde{B}_{i,t+s}(A^V)],\qquad(6A.9)$$

where ρ is the discount rate and the estimated adaptation follows:

$$\widetilde{B}_{i,t+s} = \widetilde{B}_{i,t+s-1} + \chi(B_{i,t}^{gen})\cdot\max\,[A^V - \widetilde{B}_{i,t+s-1}, 0].\qquad(6A.10)$$

A logit model is applied for the vintage choice. The decision is random where the probabilities depend on the ratios of effective productivity and prices $\check{A}_{i,t}^{Eff}(V)/p_t^V$. The higher the ratio is for a certain vintage the higher is the probability to buy it. Formally, we have for vintage V:

$$Prob_{i,V,t} = \frac{\exp\left\{\gamma\log\left[\dfrac{\check{A}_{i,t}^{Eff}(V)}{p_t^V}\right]\right\}}{\sum_{v\in\mathbb{V}}\exp\left\{\gamma\log\left[\dfrac{\check{A}_{i,t}^{Eff}(v)}{p_t^v}\right]\right\}}.\qquad(6A.11)$$

Financial management

If a firm does not have sufficient internal financial resources to cover all expenses related to production, it has the opportunity to raise external financing on the credit market. Banks accept credit requests by taking into account individual risks of the applicant and risks of their loan portfolio according to some stylized Basel II standards. If the credit request is refused or not fully accepted, the firm has to reduce its planned production quantity as long as the planned expenditures can be financed.

The wage bill of the full month as well as capital investments are paid on the day when the firm starts production.

The monthly realized profit of a consumption goods producer is the difference between sales revenues achieved in the malls and production costs (that is, labor costs and discounted capital costs) in the period just ended. In the case of positive profits, the firm pays dividends to its shareholders and the remaining funds or losses are entered on a payment account $Acc_{i,t}$. We assume that all households hold equal shares in all consumption goods producers, consequently the dividends are equally distributed to the households.

Besides the expenditures for production, that is, labor costs and investments, the firm also has financial obligations such as taxes on profits, installment and interest payments. If the firm is not able to pay these financial commitments it goes out of business. It also goes bankrupt if the firm's equity becomes negative. In the case of bankruptcy, it fires all its employees, writes off a fraction of its debt and stays idle for a certain period before it becomes active again.

Pricing

The managerial pricing rule corresponds to standard markup pricing. The firms set the price according to:

$$p_{i,t} = c_{i,t} \cdot (1 + \mu), \qquad (6A.12)$$

where $\bar{c}_{i,t}$ denotes unit costs in production of firm i in the current period and μ the exogenously given markup. Once the firm has determined the updated prices $p_{i,r,t}$ for all regions r where it offers its goods, the new prices are sent to the regional malls and posted there for the following period.

Investment Goods Producer

The capital goods sector is represented by a single capital goods-producing firm. The capital good is heterogeneous and consists of different vintages varying in their technological productivities. The vintages of the capital goods are offered with infinite supply.

The quality of the best-practice technology increases over time due to a stochastic process. Every period the quality is increased with probability $\gamma^{inv} \in (0, 1)$ where with probability $(1 - \gamma^{inv})$ there is no change in quality. In the case of an increase, the quality of the best-practice technology changes by a fixed percentage Δq^{inv}; this newly developed technology is added as a new vintage to the range of offered vintages without replacing an old one.

The investment goods producer is modeled as a passive agent, meaning that although producing goods, the firm does not deploy any input factors for production and consequently does not bear any production costs. Revenues accruing to the capital goods producer are channeled back into the economy by distributing them in equal shares among all households in order to close the model.

The pricing of capital goods is based on a combination of two pricing methods. Even if the capital good firm produces at no cost, capital goods pricing is connected to the labor cost trend in the economy. In our model the development of wages is mainly driven by the progress of workers' productivity B^{Eco}. Thus, a cost-based price component, which is assumed to be equal for all vintages, evolves over time according to:

$$p_t^{Cost} = \frac{B_t^{Eco} - B_{t-1}^{Eco}}{B_{t-1}^{Eco}} \cdot p_{t-1}^{Cost}. \tag{6A.13}$$

The second price component is value-based pricing. The value that a vintage has for the buyer can be derived from its effective productivity in the production process of a consumption goods firm. For its determination the investment goods firm replicates the way consumption good producers compute the discounted effective productivity gains. It computes these values for an average firm, that is, a firm that has economy-wide averages for the general skills B_{Eco}^{gen} and specific skills B_t^{Eco}. For the average firm the discounted sum for vintage V over a time horizon S is denoted by:

$$\check{A}_t^{Eff}(V) = \sum_{s=0}^{S} \left(\frac{1}{1+\rho}\right)^s \min[A^V, \widetilde{B}_{t+s}^{Eco}(A^V, b_{Eco}^{gen})]. \tag{6A.14}$$

The relative difference of V to a benchmark vintage is used to compute the value-based price component $p_{V,t}^{Value}$, where the benchmark is the best-practice *Vmax* of the previous period $t-1$:

$$p_{V,t}^{Value} = p_{t-1}^{V\max} \frac{\check{A}_t^{Eff}(V)}{\check{A}_{t-1}^{Eff}(V\max)}. \tag{6A.15}$$

Finally, the price of the vintage is a linear combination of p_t^{Cost} and $p_{V,t}^{Value}$ with weight θ,

$$p_t^V = \theta \cdot p_t^{Cost} + (1-\theta) p_{V,t}^{Value}. \tag{6A.16}$$

Households' Consumption

Once a month, households receive their income. Depending on the available cash, that is the current income from factor markets (that is, labor income and dividends distributed by capital and consumption goods producers) plus assets carried over from the previous period, the household sets the budget which it will spend for consumption and consequently determines the remaining part which is saved. On a weekly basis, sampling prices at the (regional) mall the consumer decides which goods to buy.

The savings decision

At the beginning of period t, a consumer k decides on the budget $B_{k,t}^{cons}$ that he/she plans to spend. In period t the agent receives an income $I_{k,t}$, and has a total wealth $W_{k,t}$, consisting of money holdings and asset wealth in firm shares.

The consumer sets his/her consumption according to the following consumption rule:

$$B_{k,t}^{cons} = I_{k,t}^{Mean} + \kappa \cdot (W_{k,t} - \Phi \cdot I_{k,t}^{Mean}), \qquad (6A.17)$$

where $I_{k,t}^{Mean}$ is the mean individual income of an agent over the last T periods and the parameter Φ is the target wealth/income ratio. The intuition is that as long as household wealth matches the target level, the consumption budget $B_{k,t}^{cons}$ corresponds to household's mean income $I_{k,t}^{Mean}$. If it does not match, the budget has to deviate from the mean income so that the actual wealth can converge to the target level. Parameter κ indicates how sensitively the consumption reacts to deviations of the actual wealth/income ration to the target level.

Each consumer goes shopping once a week, but different households go on different days. The monthly budget is equally split over the four weeks. Parts of the weekly budget that are not spent in a given week are rolled over to the consumption budget of the following week. This yields a weekly consumption budget $B_{k,week_t}^{cons}$ for each week in period t.

Selection of consumption goods

Consumers collect information about the range of goods provided. They receive information about prices and inventories. In the marketing literature it is standard to describe individual consumption decisions using logit models. We assume that a consumer's decision regarding which good to buy is random, where purchasing probabilities are based on the values he/she attaches to the different choices he/she is aware of. Denote by $G_{k,week_t}$ the set of producers whose goods consumer k has sampled in week $week_t$ of period t and where a positive stock is available at the attended mall. Since in our setup there are no quality differences between consumer goods and we also do not explicitly take account of horizontal product differentiation, choice probabilities depend solely on prices. The value of consumption good $i \in G_{k,week_t}$ is then simply given by:

$$v_k(p_{i,t}) = - \ln(p_{i,t}). \qquad (6A.18)$$

The consumer selects one good $i \in G_{k,week_t}$, where the selection probability for i reads:

$$Prob_{k,i,t} = \frac{Exp[\lambda_k^{cons} v_k (p_{i,t})]}{\sum_{i' \in G_{k,week_t}} Exp[\lambda_k^{cons} v_k (p_{i',t})]}. \tag{6A.19}$$

Thus, consumers prefer cheaper products and the intensity of competition in the market is parameterized by λ_k^{cons}. Once consumers have selected a good, they spend their entire budget $B_{k,week_t}^{cons}$ for that good if the stock at the mall is sufficiently large. In the case that consumers cannot spend all their budget the product selected first, they spend as much as possible, remove that product from the list $G_{k,week_t}$, update the logit values and select another product to spend the remaining consumption budget there. If consumers are rationed again, they spend as much as possible on the second selected product, roll over the remaining budget to the following week and finish the visit to the mall.

Labor Market

Labor demand
Labor demand is determined in the consumption goods market. If the firms plan to extend the production, they post vacancies and corresponding wage offers. The wage offers $w_{i,t,g}^O$ for each general skill group g stay unchanged as long as the firm can fill its vacancies, otherwise the firm updates the wage offer by a parameterized fraction. In the case of downsizing the incumbent workforce, the firm dismisses workers with lowest general skill levels first.

Labor supply
Labor supply is generated by the unemployed. An unemployed k takes only the posted wage offer into consideration and compares it with his/her reservation wage $w_{k,t}^R$. Workers will not apply at a firm that makes a wage offer which is lower than their reservation wage. The level of the reservation wage is determined by the current wage if the workers are employed, and in the case of the unemployed by their adjusted past wage. Unemployed workers will thus reduce their reservation wage with the duration of unemployment. When workers apply, they send information about their general as well as their specific skill level to the firm.

Matching algorithm
According to the procedures described in the previous subsections, consumption good producers review once a month whether to post vacancies for production workers. Job seekers check for vacancies. The matching between vacancies and job seekers works in the following way:

- *Step 1*   The firms post vacancies including wage offers.
- *Step 2*   Job seekers extract from the list of vacancies those postings to which they fit in terms of their reservation wage. They rank the suitable vacancies and then send an exogenously determined number of applications to randomly chosen firms.
- *Step 3*   If the number of applicants is smaller or equal to the number of vacancies, the firms send job offers to every applicant. If the number of applicants is higher than the number of vacancies, firms send job offers to as many applicants as they have vacancies to fill. Applicants with higher general skill levels b_w^{gen} are more likely to receive a job offer.
- *Step 4*   Workers rank the incoming job offers according to the wages net of commuting costs (*comm* > 0) that may arise if they were to accept a job in the region where they do not live. Each worker accepts the highest-ranked job offer at the advertised wage rate. After acceptance a worker refuses all other job offers and outstanding applications.
- *Step 5*   Vacancies' lists are adjusted for filled jobs and the labor force is adjusted for new employees.
- *Step 6*   If the number of untitled vacancies exceeds some threshold $\bar{v} > 0$ the firm raises the base wage offer which is paid per unit of specific skills by a fraction φ_i such that $w_{i,t+1}^b = (1 + \varphi_i)w_{i,t}^O$. If unemployed job seekers do not find a job, they reduce their reservation wage by a fraction ψ_k, that is $w_{k,t+1}^R = (1 - \psi_k)w_{k,t}^R$. There exists a lower bound to the reservation wage w_{min}^R which may be a function of unemployment benefits, opportunities for black market activity or the value of leisure. If workers find a job, their new reservation wage is the actual wage, that is, $w_{k,t}^R = w_{i,t}$. Go to step 1.

This cycle is aborted after two iterations even if not all firms may have satisfied their demand for labor. As indicated above, this might lead to rationing of firms on the labor market and therefore to deviations of actual output quantities from the planned quantities. In such a case, the quantities delivered by the consumption good producer to the malls it serves are reduced proportionally. This results in lower stock levels and therefore increases the expected planned production quantities in the following period.

7. The emergence of clan control in a science-based firm: the case of Carl Zeiss

Markus C. Becker*

1 INTRODUCTION

One of the essential challenges for an organization is to ensure that its members act in ways that meet the organization's objectives. This is the challenge of organizational control (Ouchi 1980; see also Otley, 2003). To attain it, organizations employ processes and mechanisms by which managers direct attention, motivate, and encourage organizational members to act to meet the firm's objectives (Ouchi, 1977, 1979; Cardinal, 2001; Kirsch et al., 2010).

The study of organizational control has a long tradition (Cyert and March, 1963 [1992]). Yet, scholars who have studied organizational control have concentrated almost exclusively on understanding the characteristics and effects of control in large, mature organizations (Cardinal et al., 2004: 411). They paid little or no attention to 'how [these organizations] came to be that way' (Aldrich, 1999: 1), and virtually ignored the origins and the evolution of organizational control (Cardinal et al., 2004: 411). Studies of the genesis of control configurations during founding are rare (ibid.). Within this research gap, my particular interest is on one form of organizational control: clan control (Ouchi, 1979, 1980). As Ouchi (1979, 1980) has argued, clan control is the appropriate form of control for a research and development (R&D) laboratory (explained below). Yet, providing the prerequisites for clan-based control and supporting its emergence is not trivial, because clan control is challenging (Ouchi, 1979). The question of how top management can support the emergence of clan control is therefore of interest, and not yet fully answered. In this chapter, I ask 'How can the actions of top management contribute to the emergence of clan control?'. I cast light on this question with a case study of an R&D-intensive firm, Carl Zeiss, drawing on the secondary literature on Zeiss.

2   PRIOR LITERATURE

Organizational Control

The notion of organizational control can already be found in the Behavioral Theory of the Firm. Cyert and March (1963 [1992]: 21) identify organizational control as one of the four 'major subtheories of a behavioral theory of the firm'. As Cyert and March (p. 21) explain, a theory of organizational control would 'specify the differences between executive choice in an organization and the decisions actually implemented'. At about the same time, Anthony (1965: 17) defined management control as 'the process by which managers assure that resources are obtained and used, effectively and efficiently, in the accomplishment of the organization's objectives'. He also distinguished management control from strategic planning and from operational control. As Otley et al. (1995) argue, one of the unintended consequences of Anthony's (1965) work was that 'management control research developed in an accounting-based framework' (Berry et al., 2009: 3).

In the organization literature, Ouchi subsequently shaped the notion of organizational control (Ouchi and Maguire, 1975; Ouchi, 1977, 1978, 1979, 1980). In an influential definition, Ouchi identified the challenge of organizational control as ensuring that an organization's members act in ways that meet the organization's objectives (Ouchi, 1980; see also Daft and Macintosh, 1984; Flamholtz et al., 1985; Otley, 2003). Ouchi conceives organizational control as an evaluation process which is based on the monitoring and evaluation of behavior or outputs (Ouchi, 1977: 95). For evaluation, feedback is crucial. Control in organizations can thus be described as a process of monitoring, evaluating, and providing feedback (Ouchi, 1978: 174). The process of control is basically a process of monitoring, comparing with some standard, and then providing selective rewards and adjustments (Ouchi, 1977: 95–6).

Control Mechanisms

To ensure that an organization's members act in ways that meet the organization's objectives, organizations employ processes and mechanisms by which managers direct attention, motivate, and encourage organizational members to act to meet the firm's objectives (Ouchi, 1977, 1979; Cardinal, 2001: 22; Kirsch et al., 2010). These mechanisms and processes draw from three different literature streams (Flamholtz et al., 1985). Scholars taking a sociological perspective emphasize structural mechanisms such as rules, policies, hierarchy of authority (Weber, 1978), or coordinative units (for example, Thompson, 1967). Administrative scholars have a special focus on plans, measurement, supervision, evaluation and feedback (Urwick, 1928). For scholars who draw on psychology, mechanisms such as goal and standard setting, extrinsic or intrinsic rewards, feedback or interpersonal influence (Tannenbaum, 1968) are in the foreground (Flamholtz et al., 1985: 37). Summarizing these different sources of control mechanisms, Flamholtz et al. identify four core control mechanisms: planning, measurement, feedback and evaluation-reward.

An important feature of control mechanisms is what is being measured, what feedback is provided, and what is rewarded in order to influence organizational members' behavior so it meets the firm's objectives. In the organization literature, control is intended to influence three different dimensions, giving rise to three control types: output, process, and social control (Ouchi, 1979; Kirsch, 1996; Cardinal, 2001; Chen et al., 2009). Output control measures and rewards outcomes, process control monitors ongoing behaviors, and social control influences embedded values of the controlee (Chen et al., 2009: 1136). This distinction of control types is widely used in management research (Turner and Makhija, 2006; Chen et al., 2009: 1136).

In the organization literature, Ouchi's (1979, 1980) distinction of three control mechanisms has been highly influential. Ouchi (1979, 1980) identifies markets, bureaucracies and clans, adding the last control mechanism to the well-established mechanisms in the organization and organizational economics literature.

Clan Control

Ouchi identifies the features of clan control by asking when the two control forms, market and bureaucracies, will be limited in their ability to control. Two factors are crucial in this regard. First, the ability to measure individual performance by measuring outputs. Second, the knowledge of the work (or transformation) process. Combining the two criteria identifies four different cases: (a) where it is possible to measure outputs and there is perfect knowledge of the transformation process, behavior or output measurement can be applied; (b) where measuring output is difficult and there is perfect knowledge of the transformation process, behavior has to be measured; (c) with the possibility of measuring outputs and imperfect knowledge of the transformation process, output measurement has to be relied on. In the most difficult case; (d) where measuring output is difficult and there is imperfect knowledge of the transformation process, both behavior and output measurement are problematic (for instance, this is the case in research). The solution of choice for this case is clan control (Ouchi, 1979: 843).

Rather than measure output and provide incentives in order to attain particular output objectives, the lever that clan control uses is the creation of goal congruity between, for instance, employees' and the employer's goals (Ouchi, 1980: 135). Clan control acknowledges that it is difficult either to specify a particular behavior *ex ante*, or to monitor output unambiguously *ex post*. Therefore, it does not put much emphasis on monitoring and performance measurement. Rather, the clan is a form of organization that has particularly strong mechanisms for providing goal congruity. It focuses on reducing goal incongruence in order to make an organization's members act in ways that meet the organization's objectives. Therefore, the clan is the appropriate control mechanism for situations of low goal incongruence and high performance ambiguity (Ouchi, 1979, 1980).

A clan is thus a group of individuals who are dependent on one another, and who display a great deal of goal congruence, shared values and norms, discipline toward their work, and 'solidarity' and 'regularity' in their relations with one another (Ouchi, 1979, 1980; Kirsch et al., 2010: 470). Clans can exercise control over their members. Traditions, implicit knowledge and disciplined work processes help define acceptable behaviors and foster learning (Ouchi, 1979, 1980; Kirsch et al., 2010: 470). A clan mechanism 'attains cooperation by selecting and socializing individuals such that their individual objectives substantially overlap with the organization's objectives' (Ouchi, 1979: 846). Clan control motivates behavior by shared values and norms and a common vision. Individuals attempt to be 'regular' members of a group by behaving in a manner that is consistent with agreed-upon behaviors (Ouchi 1980; Kirsch et al., 2010: 470).

To sum up, goal congruence is the main lever of clan control, rather than performance evaluation. The principal means for bringing about goal congruence are: (i) socialization processes, which effectively eliminate goal incongruence between individuals (Ouchi, 1979: 833), and lead to sharing personal goals that are compatible with the goals of the organization (Ouchi, 1980: 138); (ii) commitment and agreement – agreement between members on what constitutes proper behavior, and a high level of commitment on the part of each individual to those socially prescribed behaviors (Ouchi, 1979: 838); (iii) rituals and ceremonies: engaging in rituals and ceremonies which serve the purpose of rewarding those who display the underlying attitudes and values (ibid.: 844); (iv) stable membership: because attitudes, values, and beliefs are typically acquired more slowly than are manual or cognitive abilities, ceremonial forms of control require the stability of membership which characterizes the clan (ibid.: 844); and (v) traditions, which are implicit rather than explicit rules that govern behavior. Because traditions are not specified, they are not easily accessible, and a new member will not be able to function effectively until he or she has spent a number of years learning them (Ouchi, 1980: 139).

Control in R&D Firms

In terms of organizational control, R&D poses a special challenge. This is because in research and development, knowledge of the transformation process is low – it is not obvious exactly how one has to proceed to, for instance, make a scientific discovery, or even develop a radical innovation. The measurement of research output (such as articles in scholarly journals) and development (such as alternative designs) also has a substantial degree of ambiguity. Therefore, some scholars (Anthony, 1952; Waterhouse and Tiessen, 1978; Gambino and Gartenberg, 1979) argued that control of R&D is exercised primarily by social controls (Rockness and Shields, 1984: 167). Therefore Ouchi's clan control mechanism is particularly suited to R&D firms, because of the high performance ambiguity and the lack of knowledge of transformation processes. In fact, Ouchi (1979: 844) explicitly uses an R&D laboratory as an example of conditions where clan control is to be found. In her investigation of input, behavior and output control in R&D in the pharmaceutical industry, Cardinal (2001) considered all three forms of control: input, behavior, and output control. Her results showed that input, behavior, and output control enhanced radical innovation, and input and output controls enhanced incremental innovation, challenging common beliefs about R&D management at the project level. Namely, Cardinal's results support the idea that incremental and radical innovation should not be managed differently, at least in the pharmaceutical industry.

The Emergence of Clan Control

Studies of organizational control have concentrated almost exclusively on understanding the characteristics and effects of control in large, mature organizations (Cardinal et al., 2004: 411). They paid little or no attention to 'how [these organizations] came to be that way' (Aldrich, 1999: 1), and virtually ignored the origins and evolution of organizational control (Cardinal et al., 2004: 411). Studies of the genesis of control configurations during founding are rare. Barker (1993) analyzed the shift in self-managed teams from bureaucratic to concertive control. He documents how concertive control evolved from the value consensus of the company's team workers, but how such value consensus subsequently led to a system of normative rules that were formalized and increasingly rationalized. Cardinal's (2001) study of a pharmaceutical firm analyzed the impact of input, behavior, and output control on incremental and radical innovation. In a 10-year longitudinal study, Cardinal et al. (2004) analyzed the emergence of organizational control in a moving company. The main focus of the study is on factors that drive changes in control mechanisms. Its main finding is that imbalance among formal and informal controls is the key driver of shifts in control configurations. Cardinal et al. (2010) focus on the emergence of control configurations, that is, systems made up of several control mechanisms that include formal and informal input, behavior, and output control. They investigated the emergence of control configurations in a moving company, considering both the individual control forms and the control configurations in place in different phases of the firm's development. Their paper confronts different theoretical explanations for the transitions that were observed in the case.

The dearth of studies of the emergence and development of control configurations is notable because one well-established fact about organizations is that in their history, organizations change organizational control mechanisms (and configurations of control mechanisms). Ouchi (1977: 99), for instance, observes that 'as organizations grow larger, the number of levels of hierarchy increases, thus compounding problems of control loss. In response to this loss of control, they will turn from behavior control to output control, which is less susceptible to this kind of loss'. Focusing especially on coordination, Mintzberg (1979) has argued that organizations typically coordinate informally after they are founded, by mutual adaptation, then pass to direct supervision (where a superior directs the work of subordinates). When this coordination mechanism becomes strained because of growth, organizations shift to standardization of inputs (skills), work (behavior for accomplishing tasks), and outputs. At one point in time, relying on standardization might not be adequate to deal with changing demands from the environment and with uncertainty and complexity, so that organizations come to rely on mutual adaptation again (ibid.). The organizational control modes that organizations employ thus typically change over their lifetime, involving the emergence of control modes that were not previously implemented in the organization. Moreover, in the case of clan control, it is even more difficult as providing the prerequisites for clan-based control and generating clan control is not trivial because clan control is challenging (Ouchi, 1979). I therefore address the question 'How can the actions of top management contribute to the emergence of clan control?'.

3   CASE SELECTION AND METHOD

For a research question that focuses on process, longitudinal research is called for (Pettigrew, 1990). Because the research question is a 'how' question that requires insights into complex social processes, qualitative data are particularly suited (Eisenhardt and Graebner, 2007). A case study is appropriate in order to develop rich insights into a phenomenon in its context (Eisenhardt, 1989; Yin, 1994). The method I apply is, therefore, a longitudinal, historical case study. I employed theoretical sampling, selecting a case that was 'very special in the sense of allowing one to gain certain insights that other organizations would not be able to provide' (Siggelkow, 2007: 20), and that provided 'opportunities to explore a significant phenomenon under rare or extreme circumstances' (Eisenhardt and Graebner, 2007: 27).

The case I selected is Carl Zeiss, a manufacturer of optical instruments such as microscopes. The Zeiss firm, founded in 1846 and at least since Ernst Abbe's breakthrough discoveries in the 1860s a decidedly science-based firm, is one of the first firms to have a strong emphasis on science-based product development. Zeiss thus represents an R&D-intense firm, where there are particularly demanding challenges of control. Moreover, this makes the Zeiss case extreme, where the phenomenon in question stands out particularly clearly, and which provides the occasion for learning a good deal about it (Eisenhardt, 1989; Siggelkow, 2007).

The main data source I draw on is secondary literature on the Zeiss firm, Carl Zeiss, and Ernst Abbe. Much of the secondary literature on the history of the Zeiss firm is authored by eye-witnesses, such as its past top managers. Abbe himself also left a large set of published articles (running to five volumes of collected works), including papers on social and management issues. While I have also studied the firm's archives, in this chapter I draw on the rich secondary literature.

4   THE CARL ZEISS FIRM

Carl Zeiss was a manufacturer of optical instruments. Today, Zeiss offers products such as microscopes, measurement instruments, medical technology, optical sensor systems, and semiconductor manufacturing equipment. It is fully owned by the Carl Zeiss Foundation, which also owns Schott, the glass maker. It was founded in 1846 by Carl Zeiss in Jena, Germany. Zeiss made instruments, among others for the scientists at Jena University. He specialized in microscopes and quickly acquired fame for his high-quality microscopes. From 1863 on, Zeiss collaborated with a young physics professor at Jena University, Ernst Abbe. Abbe's task was to find a scientific basis for designing microscopes (at the time, craftsmanship, experience and trial and error guided microscope design). By 1871, Abbe had indeed managed to develop an analytical theory of the microscope that served as the foundation for calculating its characteristics (Markowski, 1997). This theoretical basis allowed compensation to be made for varying glass quality by modifying the geometry of the lenses (Buenstorf and Murmann, 2005). The way to mass-manufacture microscopes was cleared, and Zeiss established a reputation in high-quality microscopes that would endure.

By the end of the 1870s, Abbe had advanced the theory, design, and manufacturing process of the microscope so much that the quality of glass became the new bottleneck in further improving microscope technology (Hendrich, 1993). In 1879, Zeiss and Abbe started collaborating with Otto Schott, a chemist who experimented with glassmaking (Stolz and Wittig, 1993). After several years of experimentation, Schott found the combination of chemicals that produced glass with the characteristics desired for optical instruments, characteristics that were not previously available. This allowed Zeiss to produce microscopes of so far unknown quality. Subsequently, the Zeiss firm grew rapidly (Mütze, 2004; for more on the firm's history, see several company histories, some written by some of the leading figures of the Zeiss firm, such as Auerbach, 1918, 1925; Schomerus, 1940, 1952; Hellmuth and Mühlfriedel, 1996; Mütze, 2004).

When Zeiss died in 1888, leadership of the firm was left to Abbe (who also owned half of the Zeiss firm by then). In 1891, Abbe set up the Carl Zeiss Foundation and transferred ownership to the Foundation. In setting up the Foundation, Abbe provided very detailed guidelines for the firm's management in the statutes of the Foundation, consisting of 122 paragraphs (see Buenstorf and Murmann 2005 for an analysis of the statutes).

5   FINDINGS

One of the early biographers of Zeiss distinguished three phases in the early development of the Zeiss firm: (i) the initial phase, 1846 to 1872, which was capped by the realization of Abbe's theories, (ii) the transition period, 1872 to 1889, characterized by the development of different product lines of microscope technology, and by the development of the firm into a large manufacturing enterprise, and (iii) the period of maturity, from 1889 to before the First World War (Auerbach, 1925). Our focus is on the second period, where clan control emerged, as I shall show in the following. What did Abbe, who by that time had largely taken over from Zeiss as the main top manager, do to support the emergence of clan control?

Organizational Control in the Initial Phase (1846–1872): Output Control

As a background foil against which to consider Abbe's action, I first describe organizational control before Abbe became actively involved in the firm's management. From the beginning, Carl Zeiss had considered high precision and high quality in his products essential (Abbe, 1887 [1940]; von Rohr, 1930a). Undoubtedly, that made controlling output very important. Zeiss was known for being extraordinarily demanding. Some sources, such as the local newspaper, spoke of Zeiss's 'iron-clad strictness' (von Rohr, 1930a, App. IV: 9). Abbe mentioned that 'from the beginning, Zeiss did everything to make a highly exact technique customary in his small workshop, and always put the uncertain manual dexterity under the control of strict control mechanisms' (Wittig, 1989: 98). Zeiss not only had the will and the personal characteristics to exercise control, he also had the opportunity to do so because he spent much time in the workshop, in the beginning with a small, then with a gradually growing number of employees. This enabled him to control because he could observe both behavior and output. There is textual evidence that Zeiss engaged in output control. For instance, we know that he carried out rounds on the shop floor, where he personally inspected products in order to uphold high-quality standards (Schomerus, 1952: 69). Moreover, from the very beginning, each product that left Zeiss production had a serial number that made it possible to trace each instrument back to those who had produced it, so that errors in production or customer complaints could be thoroughly investigated (von Rohr, 1930a: 175). Furthermore, Zeiss took pride in the fact that each product was of top quality, 'thanks to the precise, and multiple, controls of each individual instrument' (ibid.: 175). An anecdote purported that on the occasion of such an inspection, Zeiss saw some microscope stands that a craftsman had just finished. He tested the mechanism, moved the controls, extended the tube, but did not say a word. Finally, he asked the craftsman to bring the stands to the anvil in the workshop. There, he took a heavy hammer and destroyed one stand after the other, six altogether. 'So, now we are finished with each other!' The craftsman packed up and left the Zeiss firm. For those who remained, however, the message that there was no 'cutting corners' stuck powerfully in their memory for a long time (Schomerus, 1952: 69). Zeiss therefore personally monitored output, employing output control.[1] Under Zeiss, the organizational control system at the firm thus depended very much on his presence, and was what could be called 'simple control' (Edwards, 1981), mainly relying on output control.

The Emergence of Clan-Based Control under Ernst Abbe

In order to trace how clan-based control emerged under Abbe after 1872, I shall use the four hallmarks of clan-based control as identified in the literature review.

Commitment and agreement on values

A distinctive feature of clan control is social agreement on a broad range of values and beliefs (Ouchi, 1979: 838). Because the clan lacks the explicit price mechanism of the market and the explicit rules of the bureaucracy, it relies for its control upon a deep level of common agreement between members on what constitutes proper behavior, and it requires a high level of commitment on the part of each individual to those socially prescribed behaviors (ibid.: 838). Two principles stand out in terms of guiding behavior at Zeiss: high precision and science-based product development.

Precision   Zeiss himself was famous for his rigor. From the very beginning, his abiding principle was to produce instruments of high precision and high quality (von Rohr, 1930a). The first person that Zeiss hired was a mechanic, August Löber. It turned out that Löber was a gifted mechanic, with a particular strength in high precision. Abbe further remarked how important it was that the first person Zeiss hired 'had such a highly developed sense for precision and exactness, and such complete dedication to these principles' (Abbe, 1896a: 71).

In phase two, staff numbers grew substantially. In 1872, there were fewer than 40 employees; in 1889, there were over 350 (Auerbach, 1914: 192). How did Abbe ensure that Zeiss staff continued to pursue high precision, while staff numbers increased? In this subsection, I shall argue that he did so by making high precision a value that was shared among Zeiss staff, thus fostering the emergence of clan control for assuring high precision.

One move appears to be especially crucial in making precision a value shared throughout the firm: Abbe started to invoke and emphasize an earlier German manufacturer of telescopes, Joseph Fraunhofer. Fraunhofer had defined the state of the art in making lenses, and it took half a generation after his death before anyone managed to produce lenses with the same quality as he did. Abbe invoked the three principles that had been the foundation of Fraunhofer's success: increasing precision, increasing the depth of theoretical understanding, and improving materials

(Mütze, 2004: 38). For instance, Abbe gave a speech on the anniversary of Fraunhofer's death, and also repeatedly invoked Fraunhofer and his principles in speeches on occasions such as the 50th anniversary of the Zeiss firm in 1896, and in what we would today call strategy documents (Abbe, 1887 [1940]).

Moreover, since he had joined the Zeiss firm in 1866, Abbe had enabled Zeiss employees to *be* more precise by making two major contributions. His overwhelming contribution was to have developed an analytical theory of the microscope, furnishing the basis for making precise calculations (Markowski, 1997). This allowed compensation to be made for varying glass quality by modifying the geometry of the lenses (Buenstorf and Murmann, 2005). Because lens design could be calculated, rather than arrived at by trial and error, precision could be enhanced substantially. Furthermore, high precision could be produced reliably. As Abbe wrote, by 1872, 'mass manufacturing of microscopes could be organized without depreciating quality in the least' (Abbe, 1887 [1940]: 63–4). Abbe's second contribution was to design instruments and tools for measurement and testing, based on the application of his theories (Auerbach, 1925). Thereby, he gave Zeiss employees the tools to produce high-quality instruments and check for high precision. Finally, he also studied the work process in the workshop (Mütze, 2004) and started to increase the division of labor and the specialization of workers (Buenstorf and Murmann, 2005), thus further supporting and enabling high precision.

Science-based product development   At the beginning, Zeiss had the idea of developing products on the basis of underlying scientific knowledge. He had faith in the 'power of science' and wanted to draw more on the help it could provide (Abbe, 1887 [1940]: 62). The problem was that such a scientific basis did not yet exist. Not easily deterred, Zeiss embarked on finding such a basis. A first attempt with a physics professor from Jena University from 1850 to 1854 turned out to be 'a complete failure' (ibid.: 62). In 1863, however, Zeiss persuaded Abbe to give it a try. Surprisingly, Abbe did in fact manage to discover the scientific basis for developing microscopes, ushering in phase two of the development of the Zeiss firm. With his scientific discoveries and by providing Zeiss employees with the tools and organization to deploy them in microscope technology, Abbe was instrumental in shifting to science-based product development. How did he manage to make such development a principle that came to be *shared* by the Zeiss employees, though?

The most important means was that Abbe established a *tradition* for science-based product development. (I shall develop this in the following subsection.) But Abbe did more. In 1889, he set up the Carl Zeiss Foundation, and handed over his 50 percent share in the Zeiss firm to the Foundation (he also persuaded Zeiss's heirs to do the same, so the Foundation owned 100 percent of the Zeiss firm). The Foundation is governed by statutes, which Abbe wrote himself. The statutes are still legally binding for the firm's management. As Buenstorf and Murmann (2005) described, the statutes contain comprehensive principles along which the Zeiss firm is to be managed, which are surprisingly modern. In any case, Abbe specifically wrote into the statutes of the Foundation a commitment to support science.

First, Abbe made furthering scientific progress an objective of the Zeiss firm, rather than just making a profit. §42 of the statutes specifies:

> [The objective] is not just making a profit, but also general progress of the technical arts present in the firms, the interests of scientific research, and increased satisfaction of the demands of technology and of everyday life that rely on those arts. That means it is within the scope of the Foundation's firms' tasks, and within the natural task of their top managers, to also pursue such objectives with full force whose pursuit does not promise any immediate advantage, but seems suited to further general interests of the precision-mechanics industry or particular matters of its technology, in particular, wants of science and of practical life within the Foundation's firms.

§101 further specifies that the Zeiss firms are to engage in 'improving the performance of this *industry* regarding tasks it faces from scientific research and practical demands; further developing its scientific foundations, improving its technical tools and increasing the cooperation of science and technology' (emphasis added). Moreover, the statutes specify particular ways in which the Zeiss firm is to engage in improving the performance of scientific research, that is, by

> undertaking or supporting scientific studies and experiments or other endeavors that regard tasks of the industry as a whole, and that are suited to further the interests of the industry – independently of whether they are linked to the activity of the Foundation's firms and can be carried out in their institutions and with their staff, fully or partly, or whether they are triggered by outsiders and have to be carried out by them; by triggering or supporting literary works of any kind that relate to matters of interest to the profession; by encouraging gifted people to undertake higher education at the Foundation's expense, to serve the industry that the Foundation's firms are in (§102)

and by supporting studies in the natural sciences and mathematics, in research and academic teaching (§1.3.B).

Again, as with the principle of high precision, Abbe also used the statutes to provide the prerequisites that enabled Zeiss employees to use science as a base for product development. In the statutes, Abbe inserted provisions to ensure that funds for pursuing science as described in the paragraphs cited above would always be provided. He determined that a part of the profits of the Zeiss firm was to be used to fund research at Jena University. To this end, he established the 'University Fund', to be funded by a share of the Zeiss firm's profits. The relevant provision in the statutes reads: 'The University Fund . . . is to provide means to Jena University for increased attention to subjects of mathematics and natural sciences, as well as to other subjects close to the foundation's interests' (Supplementary statutes, §1). Moreover, the statutes specify how those means are to be used:

> To support, directly or indirectly and without any consideration of faculty boundaries, scientific research or the efficacy of teaching in the disciplines of mathematics and the natural sciences, as well as in other subject matters that are more closely related to the interests of the Carl Zeiss Foundation, such as economics, commercial and trade law, hygiene, technological disciplines etc. (Supplementary statutes, §7)

It is noteworthy that while the statutes provide strong guidance, they do not prescribe a particular behavior. They do not describe how to accomplish particular tasks. Rather, recognizing that it will be impossible to prescribe behavior for the future, Abbe formulated the statutes' provisions in such a way as to convey the 'guiding philosophy' (Buenstorf and Murmann, 2005: 555), namely, what it means to act in accordance with the key values when it comes to decisions in key management areas. §35, for instance, explains what a focus on science means for diversification. The paragraph bars the Zeiss firm from unrelated diversification. The paragraphs cited above can serve as further examples of what it means to afford science a high value. From the perspective of writing rules that can diminish goal incongruence, it is significant that Abbe also wrote a commentary on the statutes' provisions, 'to identify the intentions underlying his prescriptions' and 'to record the intentions underlying the statutes for future generations of foundation leaders' (ibid.: 544). This is very different from prescribing how particular tasks are to be accomplished. For instance, as Abbe writes, that document provides 'some pointers for interpreting the statutes, should that become necessary in the future' (Abbe, 1896b: 330). As Buenstorf and Murmann (2005: 571) argue, 'by articulating the intentions underlying [the statutes' provisions], he added meaning to the individual provisions and thus facilitated their subsequent interpretation'. Abbe therefore wrote the statutes in a way that gave employees guidelines of how to act in accordance with the central values when they had to take decisions, and also provided them with hints at how to interpret the guidelines he had codified.

The statutes were shared and became accepted and 'lived' by Zeiss employees, influencing their behavior. For example, after some of the Zeiss staff were brought to what became West Germany in 1945, from a legal point of view, the new firm was not an enterprise that belonged to the Carl Zeiss Foundation and its statutes thus had no legal power. Nevertheless, 'top management and the works council still felt obliged to follow the provisions of the statutes and whenever the economic situation permitted at all, acted in the spirit of the founder' (Hermann, 1989: 60–61). In the German Democratic Republic, 'with its early and ongoing involvement in laser technology the firm followed the principles laid out by Ernst Abbe in the Zeiss Foundation statutes, and thus sustained its traditional corporate vision even in the socialist environment', where the statutes were no longer in force (Buenstorf and Murmann, 2005: 567–8). It therefore appears that the statutes served an important role in generating commitment to values in the Zeiss firm.

Traditions
According to Ouchi, traditions are a feature of clan control because they provide important informational requirements. This is because traditions are perhaps the simplest form of information about what behavior is desirable. They are crude, because they are usually stated

> in a general way which must be interpreted in a particular situation. On the other hand, the set of traditions in a formal organization may produce a unified, although implicit philosophy or point of view, functionally equivalent to a theory about how that organization should work. A member who grasps such an essential theory can deduce from it an appropriate rule to govern any possible decision, thus producing a very elegant and complete form of control. (Ouchi, 1980: 139)

Traditions are, therefore, a means for communicating what principles and values employees should commit to.

Modern biographers of Zeiss argue that he laid the foundations of traditions, for instance for precision, and Abbe continued those traditions (Hellmuth and Mühlfriedel, 1996: 306). I shall go further and argue that Abbe not only continued this and other traditions, but that he actually turned much that had 'just' happened under Zeiss into a tradition. Von Rohr, one of the leading microscope experts in Zeiss at the beginning of the twentieth century, remarked that while Michael Faraday had also noted the threefold direction of Fraunhofer's effort, it was Abbe who crystallized it into 'this marvellous picture of Fraunhofer's objectives' (von Rohr, 1930b:

82). In speeches, Abbe started to invoke his crisp and inspiring image of the three principles that had been the foundation of Fraunhofer's success: increasing precision, increasing the depth of theoretical understanding, and improving materials (ibid.: 19). Von Rohr writes that 'Abbe *attributed* the implementation of Fraunhofer's way of working to Carl Zeiss' (ibid.: 19; emphasis added). Invoking Fraunhofer's principles, he set Zeiss's, and then his own, achievements in a long-term perspective which linked back to Fraunhofer. He built up a perspective that stretched from Fraunhofer, hero of the previous generation, via Zeiss to himself, and by implication, projected it onto present and future Zeiss employees. Consider the following quotations: 'Fraunhofer's form of working has now found its strictest and most perfect realization in the case of the microscope' (Abbe, 1887 [1940]: 63). Moreover, '60 years after Fraunhofer's death, some of those fertile dispositions . . . have come to be unfolded here in Jena' (ibid.: 47).

The following excerpt from his speech on the occasion of the 50th anniversary of the Zeiss firm further shows how he retrospectively framed what Zeiss had been doing:

> This is the idea that Carl Zeiss has introduced to microscope optics, and has brought to realization despite all problems and barriers: the idea of a strictly *rational* [that is, science-based] construction of the optical functions of the microscope. That is the seed from which all internal progress and all external successes have grown that his activity has led to. That is what we mean by calling it Carl Zeiss' merit to have consciously worked towards bringing about a new cooperation of science and technical art in his specific field of activity. (Abbe, 1896a: 65; original emphasis)

Abbe used occasions such as an anniversary, where the Zeiss employees remembered their origins and their deceased founder, to forge a tradition: a tradition that said success was achieved by the pursuit of a few principles. Abbe extended the shadow of the past to his listeners, upon whom these principles were impressed.

Fraunhofer's principles also became a point of reference for others in the firm. Moritz von Rohr, for instance, felt inspired to write a treatise on 'Joseph Fraunhofer: His Life, Achievements, and Impact' (von Rohr, 1929).

Other aspects of the firm, too, came to be seen as part of this larger tradition. A modern biographer of Zeiss noted that in his later years, Abbe used to call August Löber, the first person hired by Zeiss, 'the founder of the Zeiss school of subtle mechanics, because he developed Zeiss production from the state of trial and error to a technology' (Mütze, 2004: 33). Friedrich Schomerus, a board member from 1945 to 1949, also adopted this way of thinking and extended it to others:

Carl Zeiss himself was the first specifically Zeissian precision mechanic and August Löber the first specifically Zeissian precision optician. Out of their school emerged the first generation of specifically Zeissian foremen, precision mechanics and precision opticians . . . The continuous tradition of technical skills from the older to the younger ones has developed a relatively large number of employees to unusually high ability. (Schomerus, 1952: 323)

Abbe, in turn, 'was the first Zeissian scientist and researcher. Out of his school emerged the long series of specifically Zeissian scientists that drew from the source of the insights of the master and added their own' (ibid.: 323). Schomerus further explained how such a tradition also led to the fact that principles and values were passed on from one generation to the next. In the design offices and the administration, too, 'ideas and principles of the first generation took further shape, were refined by the next generation and perfected by the third one' (ibid.: 323). To provide another example, the spirit of maintaining the technical equipment at the highest possible level was kept alive and was passed on from Zeiss to Abbe, and from Abbe to later managers such as Straubel, Bauersfeld, Kotthaus and the foremen (ibid.: 323). All these instances show how people saw themselves in the shadow of a long tradition. Abbe had managed to instill a sense of tradition, and Zeiss employees became accustomed to seeing themselves as part of this tradition.

Socialization processes
The central control lever in clan control is a relatively complete socialization process which effectively eliminates goal incongruence between individuals (Ouchi, 1979: 833; 1980). Socialization mechanisms and long socialization processes are requirements for socialization. In phase one, under Zeiss, socialization mechanisms were provided in the form of the master–apprentice system, as was common at the time. Abbe continued and reinforced the socialization mechanisms in place, but also extended them beyond the realm they typically applied to, that is, the crafts. Although some of the top managers he hired were not of course part of the master–apprentice system as the mechanics craftsman under Zeiss were, Abbe also provided similar socialization mechanisms when he taught staff himself. This included very rich, intense, and frequent communication. For example, Max Fischer was the first board member to specialize in administration. When he was hired, Abbe spent two hours a day with him over a period of two years, when he discussed Fischer's concerns and made sure that Fischer learned to make decisions just like Abbe would have done (von Rohr, 1930a). Siegfried Czapski, his eventual successor, moreover became a close friend of the family, and also spent much time with Abbe outside work. Importantly, Abbe's way of socializing with

new employees was subsequently imitated by those very employees, who applied it to the next generation.

Abbe also put much emphasis on selecting important staff. One example is the choice of Czapski: Abbe had been looking for a person who could become his successor as CEO. One of Abbe's biographers writes that '[w]hat Abbe needed was not merely a scientific assistant; it was the malleable soul of a youngster who was so similar to him in nature that to become the receptacle into which the soul of his idol could be poured would mean to fulfil his destiny' (Auerbach, 1918: 266). This serves as an indication that Abbe was aware of fit of character and malleability as selection criterion for hiring new top staff, which would make sense if socialization mechanisms were in place.

Finally, modern biographers of Zeiss come to the following conclusion

> [T]he attitude towards the workers, employees and leading staff of the Zeiss firm was highly unusual for the times. It aimed at developing a highly knowledgeable and highly qualified staff, and at binding it to Jena and its production of precision mechanics. Ernst Abbe realized that principle through the social circumstances of Zeiss staff . . . and through shaping the social and cultural circumstances of the city of Jena. (Hellmuth and Mühlfriedel, 1996: 455)

For instance, the Zeiss firm later founded an optician's school in Jena, which provided skilled opticians that would use Zeiss products. Under Abbe, the Zeiss firm also adopted workers' benefits that were more generous than the industry standard, and in fact, were ahead of their time (Buenstorf and Murmann, 2005). Abbe founded such benefits as a firm-wide health insurance, pension fund, and preventive medical examinations, but also set up and funded the municipal library, the Zeiss swimming pool, and a multipurpose hall (Auerbach, 1925: 254–5). Such measures contributed to the pride of being a 'Zeissian' that runs through many accounts (for one example, see Auerbach, 1925), and to a sense of identification with the Zeiss firm that reinforced socialization because of the motivation provided by a sense of 'belonging'. Such measures boost intrinsic motivation (Deci, 1975). In contrast to extrinsic motivation, for instance provided through monetary rewards, intrinsic motivation does not require measurement in order to allocate rewards.

Stable membership
A necessary, if not sufficient condition for socialization is the length of time that socialization mechanisms can apply (Ouchi, 1979). Stable membership in an organization is therefore conducive to socialization. Already under Carl Zeiss, membership in the Zeiss firm was very stable. We know from the accounts of some of the employees that many spent their whole

career in the Zeiss firm (Schomerus, 1952). Although that was not unusual at the time, it also applied to the firm under Zeiss. Under Abbe, member-ship stability was enhanced. Abbe took very specific measures to provide for stable, long-term membership in the Zeiss firm. Once more, Abbe used the statutes for this purpose. For instance, he inserted provisions into the statutes that linked long membership in the firm to social benefits, thus making long and stable membership attractive. For instance, social ben-efits were provided according to age and length of time spent in the Zeiss firm (Hellmuth and Mühlfriedel, 1996: 245).[2]

Clan Control in Place in the Period of Maturity (after 1889)

As a result of Abbe's actions, clan control was in place at Zeiss by the beginning of the period of maturity (after 1889), at least as far as the top staff were concerned. This can be read off at the dimensions of clan control as identified earlier. For instance, there was strong *commitment* and agreement on two principles, precision and science-based product development. This is particularly traceable in leading staff. Abbe said of his successor, Siegfried Czapski, that Czapski 'was fully convinced that he would . . . consider it the task of his life to incessantly contribute to ensure and develop the Zeiss firm in the sense of the objectives I have pursued' (Hermann, 1989: 114). Max Fischer, board member from 1895 to 1926, 'agreed with the fundamental provisions of the statutes concern-ing business and social and political ideas so much, that they fit to his way of thinking and his ideas without any problem' (Schomerus, 1952: 109). Otto Schott, who built up the Schott glassworks together with Abbe and Zeiss, was also considered similar to Zeiss and Abbe in his drive to launch himself into an entirely novel and highly uncertain endeavor, and not to stop until it was accomplished (Auerbach, 1925: 18). Finally, to appreciate the strong agreement between people such as Zeiss, Abbe, Schott, Czapski and Fischer, it is interesting to note a case of disagreement. Roderich Zeiss, Carl Zeiss's son, had joined the firm's board when his father retired. As one of the biographers notes,

> Abbe always had a lot of ideas, inventions and plans, and as a farsighted entre-preneur he saw great opportunities for developing the firm and wanted to use them. Roderich Zeiss, to the contrary, was risk averse and preferred a good and safe income from a firm with 300 employees. Thus, he was not very accommo-dating of Abbe's plans. (Schomerus, 1940: 118)

After some years, Abbe made it clear that he wanted Roderich Zeiss to leave the firm, which Zeiss eventually agreed to. Abbe had also crystallized strong *traditions* that would last long beyond his lifetime. The secondary literature on Zeiss abounds with descriptions – covering all the decades from Abbe's time to the present – where Zeiss employees take pride in their precision and in applying science in developing new products (see Auerbach, 1925; Schomerus, 1952). Powerful *socialization processes* also remained in place. Like other firms, Zeiss made full use of the German master-apprentice tradition, and continued to recruit top staff (such as Kotthaus or Küppenbender) from among the scientific assistants of university professors. Zeiss also dedicated particular attention to socialization. Finally, *membership* in the Zeiss firm has remained stable since Abbe's time. Many employees still spent most of their working life at Zeiss (Schomerus, 1952).

6   DISCUSSION AND CONCLUSION

What did top management do to support the emergence of clan control? And how did the actions of top management contribute to its emergence? The gist of the answer is that Ernst Abbe focused the attention of Zeiss staff on two principles, high precision and relying on science for product development, and created strong agreement on these two values, and commitment to them. While Carl Zeiss had laid the foundations of traditions, for instance for precision products, Abbe not only continued those, but actually *made* something that had 'just' happened under Zeiss into a tradition. He forged a tradition around these two values by invoking Fraunhofer, and by putting Zeiss, himself, and the employees in a grander perspective. Such a framing projected the 'shadow of the past' onto current and future employees, and with it, some moral force deriving from the admiration for the founder and from his success, which undergirded his principles and values. Abbe also enabled Zeiss employees to successfully employ the two principles in their daily work. He then used the Foundation's statutes to commit the firm's management and employees to his principles, in particular, to pursuing science-based product development. He did so by using the statutes to break down what it means to apply the two values in business decisions, and to convey his intentions and thinking behind how to do that.

This set of mechanisms turned out to be very powerful and to have long-lasting effects. For example, it actually helped the emergence of clan control. This is non-trivial because clan control is the most demanding form of organizational control, posing the most difficult organizational challenge (Ouchi, 1979: 838). The transition from personal, informal output monitoring to clan control is non-trivial, for instance because it is tempting to shift to behavior control for purposes of coordination

(Mintzberg, 1979). In fact, there are often many rules in R&D environments, even down to standard operating procedures for how to develop new products (Cooper and Kleinschmidt, 1995). Getting people to 'buy into' and adopt certain values and act in accordance with those values is not simple. Putting in place mechanisms for socialization is a very exacting task, and its success is anything but certain. Yet, it succeeded in the Zeiss firm. Moreover, the effect was very long-lasting as clan control seems to have survived not just for a long time, but also extreme discontinuities such as the two World Wars. For example, after the Second World War, the Zeiss firm had to be largely rebuilt, having been essentially destroyed in the war (both physically as well as in form of losing its written records, and many of its staff). When the firm was rebuilt in Jena, and in what would become West Germany, secondary literature indicates that clan control structures seem to have re-emerged from the rubble (Schomerus, 1952).

With regard to why the measures taken by Abbe led to the emergence of clan control, and to make it lasting, several points appear noteworthy. Without doubt, the statutes of the Foundation played an important role. They offered the opportunity to codify what it means to apply the guiding values and principles in a range of concrete situations, thus providing a means of communicating the values and principles. Creating a tradition (for high precision and science-based product development) provides a second powerful means for communicating what principles and values employees should commit to, but a very different one from the statutes. Traditions are crude because they are stated in a general way that needs interpretation. That makes them both easy to communicate, and has the effect that 'a member who grasps such an essential theory can deduce from it an appropriate rule to govern any possible decision, thus producing a very elegant and complete form of control' (Ouchi, 1980: 139). Abbe further boosted this role of the traditions he crystallized by providing the statutes, and in particular the document in which he explains his intentions with the statutes' provisions. Abbe therefore communicated his idea of how the Zeiss firm should work in two ways that were very different, and which seem to have the potential to mutually reinforce each other.

Identifying principles and providing a powerful means of communicating these principles is the first important requirement of clan control. The second requirement is mechanisms for creating commitment, in this case, strong socialization mechanisms. Abbe extended and reinforced the socialization mechanisms in place, for instance, by extending the intense interaction typical for the master–apprentice system to future top scientists and managers that he hired, with whom he would spend much time in intense, face-to-face interaction. Importantly, his way of socializing new employees was subsequently imitated by those very employees, who applied it to the next generation. The intrinsic motivation derived from a sense of pride and identification with the firm, as well as the generous social benefits that bound employees to the firm more closely, also seem to have boosted the willingness to incorporate socialization into the firm's values.

The emergence of clan control poses the question how different control forms coexist. Cardinal et al. (2004) show that they coexist in organizations and can be arranged in different combinations to achieve multifaceted goals, and Cardinal et al. (2010) explore some combinations in which they appear, and the drivers of these combinations. Cardinal et al. (2004) also identify the need to balance formal and informal control mechanisms as a driver as the need to adapt the 'mixture' of control mechanisms in the control figurations present at one point of time. These findings, as well as the findings from this chapter, raise questions for the future research agenda in innovation management. We know that product development also relies on standard operation procedures and rules, which prescribe particular behavior such as the use of stage-gate models in developing new products (Cooper and Kleinschmidt, 1995). Given that clan control has emerged, what is the 'appropriate' proportion of clan control among other control mechanisms in the bundle of control mechanisms? Are there ways of answering that question other than waiting for negative performance feedback that indicates problems with the organizational control mechanisms in place (which require, for instance, rebalancing the set of mechanisms)?

NOTES

* I gratefully acknowledge support for this research from the Agence Nationale de Recherche (ANR), Grant JC05_440239, and the Danish Social Sciences Research Council. For helpful comments, my thanks go to Stephan Billinger, Bo Eriksen, Jade Maneja, Ulrik Nash and Svend Thomsen. I am particularly grateful to Dr Wolfgang Wimmer of the Zeiss archives for supporting my work on Zeiss. All errors and omissions are mine.
1. Zeiss's daily rounds also provided an opportunity for observing how employees accomplished their task, that is, for behavior control, something that was part of the master–apprentice system.
2. A separate section on Ouchi's fifth characteristic of clans, rituals and ceremonies is omitted here because I do not have much textual evidence to offer from the data I collected. To provide one indication, however, that rituals might also have been present, consider how the invocation of Fraunhofer by Abbe was repeated by Zeiss employees later on (for example, von Rohr, 1930; Mütze, 2004), thus coming close to a ritual that would be a means for upholding and strengthening the tradition described above.

REFERENCES

Abbe, E. (1887 [1940]), 'Denkschrift vom 4. Dezember 1887', in F. Schomerus (ed.), *Werden und Wesen der Carl Zeiss-Stiftung*, Jena, Germany: Gustav Fischer, pp. 35–78.

Abbe, E. (1896a), 'Gedächstnisrede zur Feier des 50 jährigen Bestehens der Optischen Werkstätte. 12. Dezember 1896', Abbe (ed., 1906), *Sozialpolitische Schriften*, 3rd edn, Jena, Germany: Gustav Fischer, pp. 60–101.

Abbe, E. (1896b), 'Motive und Erläuterungen zum Entwurf eines Statuts der Carl-Zeiss-Stiftung', Abbe (ed., 1906), *Sozialpolitische Schriften*, 3rd edn, Jena, Germany: Gustav Fischer, pp. 329–87.

Aldrich, H.E. (1999), *Organizations Evolving*, Thousand Oaks, CA: Sage.

Anthony, R.N. (1952), *Management Controls in Industrial Research Organizations*, Cambridge, MA: Harvard University Press.

Anthony, R.N. (1965), *Planning and Control Systems: A Framework for Analysis*, Boston, MA: Division of Research, Harvard Business School.

Auerbach, F. (1914), *Das Zeisswerk*, 4th edn, Jena, Germany: Gustav Fischer.

Auerbach, F. (1918), *Ernst Abbe: Eine Lebensbeschreibung*, Leipzig, Germany: Akademische Verlagsgesellschaft.

Auerbach, F. (1925), *Das Zeisswerk und die Carl-Zeiss-Stiftung in Jena: Ihre wissenschaftliche, technische und soziale Entwicklung und Bedeutung*, 5th edn, Jena, Germany: Gustav Fischer.

Barker, J.R. (1993), 'Tightening the iron cage: concertive control in self-managing teams', *Administrative Science Quarterly*, **38**, 408–37.

Berry, A.J., A.F. Coad, E.P. Harris, D.T. Otley and C. Stringer (2009), 'Emerging themes in management control: a review of recent literature', *British Accounting Review*, **41**, 2–20.

Buenstorf, G. and J.P. Murmann (2005), 'Ernst Abbe's scientific management: theoretical insights from a nineteenth-century dynamic capabilities approach', *Industrial and Corporate Change*, **14** (4), 543–78.

Cardinal, L.B. (2001), 'Technological innovation in the pharmaceutical industry: the use of organizational control in managing research and development', *Organization Science*, **12** (1), 19–36.

Cardinal, L.B., S.B. Sitkin and C.P. Long (2004), 'Balancing and rebalancing in the creation and evolution of organizational control', *Organization Science*, **15** (4), 411–31.

Cardinal, L.B., S.B. Sitkin, C.P. Long and C. Miller (2010), 'The genesis of control configurations during organizational founding', paper presented at the 2010 Academy of Management meeting, Montreal, QC.

Chen, D., S.H. Park and W. Newburry (2009), 'Parent contribution and organizational control in international joint ventures', *Strategic Management Journal*, **30**, 1133–56.

Cooper, R.G. and E.J. Kleinschmidt (1995), 'Benchmarking the firm's critical success factors in new product development', *Journal of Product Innovation Management*, **12** (5), 374–91.

Cyert, R.M. and J.G. March (1963 [1992]), *A Behavioral Theory of the Firm*, 2nd edn, Oxford: Blackwell.

Daft, R.L. and N.B. Macintosh (1984), 'The nature and use of formal control systems for management control and strategy implementation', *Journal of Management*, **10** (1), 43–66.

Deci, E.L. (1975), *Intrinsic Motivation*, New York: Plenum Press.

Edwards, R.C. (1981), 'The social relations of production at the point of production', in M. Zey-Ferrell and M. Aiken (eds), *Complex Organizations: Critical Perspectives*, Glenview, IL: Scott, Foresman, pp. 156–82.

Eisenhardt, K. (1989), 'Building theories from case study research', *Academy of Management Review*, **14** (4), 532–50.

Eisenhardt, K. and M.E. Graebner (2007), 'Theory building from cases: opportunities and challenges', *Academy of Management Journal*, **50** (1), 25–32.

Flamholtz, E.G., T.K. Das and A.S. Tsui (1985), 'Toward an integrative framework of organizational control', *Accounting Organizations and Society*, **10** (1), 35–50.

Gambino, A. and M. Gartenberg (1979), *Industrial R & D Management*, New York: National Association of Accountants.

Hellmuth, E. and W. Mühlfriedel (1996), *Zeiss 1846–1905: Vom Atelier für Mechanik zum führenden Unternehmen des optischen Gerätebaus*, Weimar, Germany: Böhlau Verlag.

Hendrich, J. (1993), 'Otto Schott', in R. Stolz and J. Wittig (eds), *Carl Zeiss und Ernst Abbe: Leben, Wirken und Bedeutung, Wissenschaftshistorische Abhandlung*, Jena, Germany: Universitätsverlag Jena, pp. 263–8.

Hermann, A. (1989), *Nur der Name war geblieben: Die abenteuerliche Geschichte der Firma Carl Zeiss*, Stuttgart, Germany: Deutsche Verlags-Anstalt.

Kirsch, L.J. (1996), 'The management of complex tasks in organizations: controlling the systems development process', *Organization Science*, **7** (2), 1–21.

Kirsch, L.J., D.-G. Ko and M.H. Haney (2010), 'Investigating the antecedents of team-based clan control: adding social capital as a predictor', *Organization Science*, **21** (2), 469–89.

Markowski, F. (1997), 'Präzisionsarbeit, Massenproduktion und Gruppensystem: Arbeit und Technik bei Carl Zeiss bis zur Weltwirtschaftskrise', in F. Markowski (ed.), *Der letzte Schliff: 150 Jahre Arbeit und Alltag bei Carl Zeiss*, Berlin: Aufbau-Verlag, pp. 54–75.

Mintzberg, H. (1979), *The Structuring of Organizations*, Englewood Cliffs, NJ: Prentice-Hall.

Mütze, K. (2004), *Die Macht der Optik. Industriegeschichte Jenas 1846–1996. Band 1: Vom Atelier für Mechanik zum Rüstungskonzern. 1846–1946*, Weimar and Jena, Germany: Hain Verlag.

Otley, D. (2003), 'Management control and performance management: whence and whither?', *British Accounting Review*, **35**, 309–26.

Otley, D., J. Broadbent and A. Berry (1995), 'Research in management control: an overview of its development', *British Journal of Management*, **6**, Special Issue, S31–S44.

Ouchi, W.G. (1977), 'The relationship between organizational structure and organizational control', *Administrative Science Quarterly*, **22** (1), 95–113.

Ouchi, W.G. (1978), 'The transmission of control through organizational hierarchy', *Academy of Management Journal*, **21** (2), 173–92.

Ouchi, W.G. (1979), 'A conceptual framework for the design of organizational control mechanisms', *Management Science*, **25** (9), 833–48.

Ouchi, W.G. (1980), 'Markets, bureaucracies, and clans', *Administrative Science Quarterly*, **25** (1), 129–41.

Ouchi, W.G. and M.A. Maguire (1975), 'Organizational control: two functions', *Administrative Science Quarterly*, **20**, 559–69.

Pettigrew, A.M. (1990), 'Longitudinal field research on change: theory and practice', *Organization Science*, **1** (3), 267–92.
Rockness, H.O. and M.D. Shields (1984), 'Organizational control systems in research and development', *Accounting, Organizations and Society*, **9** (2), 165–77.
Schomerus, F. (1940), *Werden und Wesen der Carl Zeiss-Stiftung*, Jena, Germany: Gustav Fischer.
Schomerus, F. (1952), *Geschichte des Jenaer Zeisswerkes*, 1846–1946, Stuttgart, Germany: Piscator Verlag.
Siggelkow, N. (2007), 'Persuasion with case studies', *Academy of Management Journal*, **50** (1), 20–4.
Stolz, R. and J. Wittig (eds) (1993), *Carl Zeiss und Ernst Abbe: Leben, Wirken und Bedeutung, Wissenschaftshistorische Abhandlung*, Jena, Germany: Universitätsverlag Jena.
Tannenbaum, A.S. (1968), *Control in Organizations*, New York: McGraw-Hill.
Thompson, J.D. (1967), *Organizations in Action: Social Science Bases of Administrative Theory*, New York: McGraw-Hill.
Turner, K.L. and M.V. Makhija (2006), 'The role of organizational controls in managing knowledge', *Academy of Management Review*, **31** (1), 197–217.
Urwick, L.F. (1928), 'Principles of direction and control', in J. Lee (ed.), *Dictionary of Industrial Administration*, vol. 1, London: Pitman, pp. 161–79.
von Rohr, M. (1929), *Joseph Fraunhofers Leben, Leistungen und Wirksamkeit*, Leipzig, Germany: Akademische Verlagsgesellschaft.
von Rohr, M. (1930a), 'Zur Geschichte der Zeissischen Werkstätte bis zum Tode Ernst Abbes', *Forschungen zur Geschichte der Optik* (Beilagenhefte zur Zeitschrift für Instrumentenkunde), **1** (3), January, pp. 91–201.
von Rohr, M. (1930b), 'Zur Geschichte der Zeissischen Werkstätte bis zum Tode Ernst Abbes', *Forschungen zur Geschichte der Optik*, Sonderabdruck [special reprint] aus den Forschungen Zur Geschichte der Optik (Beilagenhefte zur Zeitschrift für Instrumentenkunde), pp. 1–110.
Waterhouse, J. and P. Tiessen (1978), 'A contingency framework for management accounting system research', *Accounting, Organizations and Society*, **3** (1), 65–76.
Weber, M. (1978), *Economy and Society*, edited by G. Roth and C. Wittich, Berkeley and Los Angeles, CA: University of California Press.
Wittig, J. (1989), *Ernst Abbe – Sein Nachwirken an der Jenaer Universität Zu Seinem 150. Geburtstag am 23 Januar 1990*, Jena, Germany: Jenaer Reden and Schriften, Friedrich-Schiller-Universität.
Yin, R.K. (1994), *Case Study Research: Design and Methods*, Thousand Oaks, CA: Sage.

8. Creativity, human resources and organizational learning

Thierry Burger-Helmchen and Patrick Llerena

1 INTRODUCTION

Resource-based theories of the firm draw attention to a firm's ability to explore and exploit new knowledge as the source of value creation and sustainable development (Conner and Prahalad, 1996). How to achieve a good balance between exploration and exploitation activities in a firm is a puzzling question for the manager. For the applied economist, it is difficult to develop effective criteria of decision in a dynamic context for dispatching the resources between the two activities (O'Reilly and Tushman, 2004). The problem becomes even more cumbersome in creative industries where production and creation are intimately related. In those industries, creation often occurs during the production phase. Therefore the notion of value creation and the sources of value creation become an even more important topic. Our contribution will be to add a new perspective to the debate: the distinction between division of knowledge and division of labor.

Knowledge is the essence of the resource-based perspective and it is also the source of innovation. In a strategic perspective, knowledge can be viewed on the one hand as a stock (Dierickx and Cool, 1989) or base (Asheim, 2007) when we refer to accumulated routines, skills and expertise in relation to a specific domain. On the other hand, knowledge is transformed into a flow when we refer to transfer, integration and development of new knowledge. Knowledge bases are essential for the exploitation activities of the firm and knowledge flows are indispensable in exploratory activities, creativity is then at the genesis of these flows (Kang et al., 2007; Teece, 2007). The literature highlights the necessity to adapt the governance modes dynamically to ensure an optimal fit between the resource allocated to exploration and exploitation in order to create value and to capture the created value (Youndt et al., 2004; Subramaniam and Youndt, 2005; Reed et al., 2006).

We propose a representation of how the knowledge bases are sources of value creation during the exploitation/productive activities by re-enforcing the division of labor. Then we integrate the idea that the division of knowledge can be a source of creativity and value creation during the exploration activities. As a linchpin model we take the special case of creative activities where exploration and exploitation coexist and coevolve, and where a single type of individual stands at the crossroads of the division of labor and of knowledge. From that model basis, and following Antonelli (2006), we induce some implications on governance and on how a firm can limit opportunism and grasp the value created.

To reach our goal we use a methodology that fits intermediate theory development, an interaction between existing theory and case study findings (Edmondson and McManus, 2007). Here we reinvestigate mature bodies of literature (work on the ambidextrous firm and division of labor) through the lenses of the division of knowledge and communities in creative entrepreneurial firms. The empirical findings we call upon to illustrate and justify the theory development stem from studies on biotech, cell phones, video games and university spinoffs (Llerena and Matt, 2005; Maurer and Ebers, 2006; Burger-Helmchen, 2008; Burger-Helmchen et al., 2009, 2010).

In order to reach this deeper understanding of how learning, knowledge bases and creativity are interrelated and can be managed through adequate division of labor and division of knowledge to create and capture value, we proceed as follows. First, we reinvestigate the notion of value creation and value capture. This is done by seeking the difference between the value created by an individual, a work group or a firm as a whole. It is also the place to recall the notions of knowledge bases. Then, in Section 3 we clarify the relations between knowledge flows and bases, organizational learning and value creation and link them to the puzzles of division of knowledge and division of labor. This allows us to rephrase the notion of division of labor and division of knowledge depending on the position inside the firm or outside of the asset considered. In Section 4 we propose a linchpin model where the creative knowledge worker is the pivotal element, and in Section 5 we give some management insights concerning this specific linchpin model. A final section concludes.

2   CREATING AND CAPTURING VALUE: LABOR, KNOWLEDGE BASES AND KNOWLEDGE FLOWS

Value creation is a central concept in management science and economics at both the micro level (individual, group) and the macro level (the firm or nexus of firms). Nevertheless, there is little consensus on what value creation and creativity really are, where they come from, how they can be achieved and how to capture the outcomes of the creativity. This may reflect the multidisciplinary nature and/or the multilevel aspects of value creation. Researchers in human resource management (HRM) and organizational theory rather consider value creation from the point of view of employees and teams. Finally, economists often take a broader approach encompassing several firms, a network of firms and institutions or even a whole industry or country. These few examples show the differences that may exist between these approaches. Each of them focuses on a different level of analysis for the creation of value but also for the beneficiary of the value. From a labor and knowledge perspective this raises the question of whether the division of labor is possible between the different levels of analysis (from the bottom up, an individual can divide the labor in a team or a firm, or from the top down a firm can divide the labor between the different individuals) or is the division of labor only possible on a same level of analysis if the goal is to create value by this division? The same question is relevant for the division of knowledge. Must there be a quantitatively or qualitatively greater base in one level to be able to divide that stock and dispatch it to other levels?

Value is often created at one level of aggregation and captured at another. For example an employee can develop a new way to perform a specific task, diminishing his/her effort and thereby reducing the firm's costs; it is likely that the firm will be the main beneficiary of this creation. Or, if a firm develops a new product by combining modular parts, it is likely that a network of firms (those producing the modular parts) will benefit from the creation and catch a large part of the value.

As mentioned, there are many possible vantage points in the literature on value creation depending on the theoretical stream followed. In the following we focus our efforts on three points that we link to the division of labor and knowledge in the subsequent sections. First, we discuss a definition of value creation that can take into account the interactions between various levels of analysis and different knowledge bases. Second, we illustrate how the value creation process may vary depending on the path taken by the creative activity and the intervening knowledge bases. Third, we discuss the process of value capture and show how it can change depending on the creation path. Figure 8.1 summarizes these points by representing the value creativity path and capturing processes that are possible between the different levels of analysis.

Value Creation and Knowledge Bases

Value is a concept deeply rooted in the economic literature; therefore it is not surprising that management science studies of value creation

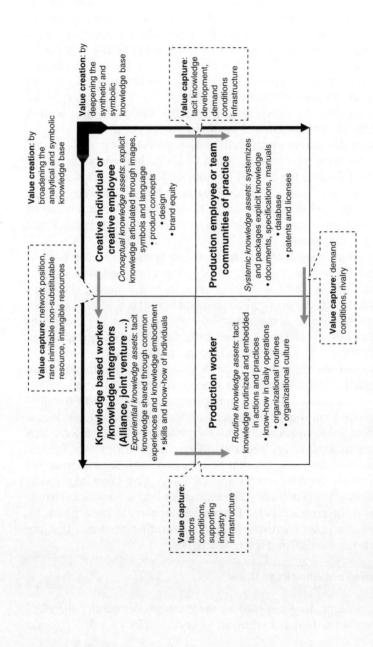

Sources: Based on Nonaka and Konno (1998), Asheim (2007), Lepak et al. (2007).

Figure 8.1 Categories of knowledge assets, value creation and value capture

follow a standard established in economics by dividing the value into (i) use value and (ii) exchange value (Bowman and Ambrosini, 2000). Use value refers to the uniqueness, quality and nature of a new job, a task, a good or service received by users in relation to their needs (price, quality, functionalities, artistic components, aesthetics, and so on). Use value is essentially subjective, relative and specific to each individual. 'Specific and subjective' because the use each may make of a product or a service can be appreciated very differently and 'relative' because the value in this case can be appreciated by referring to other products or services, the value of which are already appreciated. Exchange value is defined as the monetary equivalent that the final user gives to the supplier in exchange for the use value of the service or product. In this case, exchange value depends not on a specific individual but on the views of all individuals who may have an interest in the exchange (Hirshleifer et al., 2005: 416).

Both definitions imply that the creation of value is a subjective and relative amount obtained by an economic agent (who is the target of value creation). This agent may be an individual, a group, a firm or a nexus of firms, and this creation is marked by the willingness to exchange a specific amount of money against that value. Also the creation of value is clearly a multilevel activity going from individuals to firms: (i) the amount of money exchanged should be higher than the cost of the producer (as measured by the total costs over a given period); and (ii) the amount that the applicant is prepared to provide for the exchange depends on the expected performance difference between the new value and existing substitutes, or existing in the near future.

If those are the two basic economic features of value, management scholars developed the definition of creativity behind the value. Creativity is generally defined as the production of novel, useful ideas or solutions to a problem. It refers to both the process of idea generation or problem solving and the actual idea or solution (Amabile, 1988; Amabile and Mukti, 2008). To be able to assess the novelty of a task, product or service users must have specialized knowledge related to the subject in question and to the alternatives available. Then users will adapt the product to their own specific context. This context is dependent on the social and cultural universe in which the user employs the object. Amabile (1988) mentions the nature of value creation as a subjective and context-specific activity but also specific to the level of analysis. Users evaluate differently the novelty, value and ownership rights based on their knowledge and their representations (Boisot and MacMillan, 2004). This also implies that the supplier has a possible explanation why the product is new and in what context it can be used.

Figure 8.1 represents a matrix that we completed stepwise during this work following several aspects. In this figure we show all participants and the different knowledge assets occurring in the creative exploration and exploitation processes. The basic drawing considers whether the employees are inside and outside the firm (the horizontal axis: on the left mainly outside the firm, on the right mainly inside the firm) and the type of knowledge used (the vertical axis: the upper row corresponds to specific intellectual assets, the lower row to more trivial assets). In the matrix we indicate the types of employees concerned in each box and the types of knowledge they are mainly handling (Nonaka and Konno, 1998). As noted by Asheim (2007, p. 224): 'there is a large variety of knowledge sources and inputs to be used by organizations and firms, and there is more interdependence and division of labor among actors (individuals, companies and other organizations) . . . Innovation processes of these firms differ substantially between various industries and sectors whose activities require specific knowledge bases'.

We distinguish between three types of knowledge base: analytical, synthetic and symbolic. These bases correspond to different mixes of tacit and codified knowledge, skills and qualifications and lead to different forms of creativity and innovations:

- *Analytical knowledge base*   This base corresponds to the know-why for the development of new knowledge in a framework depending on scientific knowledge. This type of knowledge is best obtained by collaboration within and between research units.
- *Synthetic knowledge base*   This is merely know-how, applying or combining existing knowledge, and it is strongly tacit. The development of this base can be achieved through interaction with customers and suppliers.
- *Symbolic knowledge base*   This corresponds to know-who, and develops strong aesthetic qualities. It is fostered by learning by doing inside specific project teams and is highly context specific.

We mention that there are different knowledge bases, but we do not say that one of these bases is pre-eminent in one of the boxes of Figure 8.1. As we shall see, to create value and be creative is not so much a question of the initial size of each base, but rather a question of how each base develops. In the following we shall see how these different bases interact to create value for the firm and link this creation of value with the notions of division of labor and division of work.

Creativity Paths: The Value Creation Processes

How is value created? It is possible to represent the value creation process in many ways, depending on the level of analysis used, which is why we chose two approaches, both of which are contingent on the level of analysis chosen or a particular source of value creation. When the individual is the level of analysis, the process on which we focus is the creative activity carried out by a certain individual by taking into account the attributes of the individual (ability, motivation, intelligence, and so on) and her/his interactions with the environment. When the organization is the source of value creation, then attributes such as the creation and management of knowledge flows become prominent.

These two approaches are linked in the following manner with Figure 8.1. If we consider the individual as the source of creativity, then we focus on the upper-right box of the matrix that we labeled 'creative individual'. If we take the firm as a source of creativity then we consider the entire right column corresponding to the firm (we then speak of 'creative employee' instead of 'creative individual'). The exchanges between the boxes in the right column are the interactions inside the firm, and the exchanges with the left column are the interactions with individuals or organizations outside the firm.

The individual as the source of creativity
People create value by developing new products and services or any contributions with a certain value perceived by a user by taking into account his/her future needs and the monetary amount he/she is ready to commit in comparison to alternatives or a combination of alternatives. The creation has therefore to produce a higher utility at the same cost, or the same value at lower cost. For Felin and Hesterly (2007) and Teece (2007), the micro level of the individual should be the starting level of analysis. For these authors, knowledge creation is the source of value creation, creativity is the transformation of the stock of knowledge into a process, a dynamic, creative value. As noted by Dierickx and Cool (1989), if knowledge can be both a stock and a flow, creativity is always a flow (Amabile, 1996).

In Figure 8.1, the creative individual is characterized as a conceptual knowledge asset (Nonaka and Konno, 1998), explaining his/her knowledge and creation through images, symbols, language, and so on. These types of individuals are at the origin of the product concept, the design, and so on which corresponds to a source of possible value, but the main value is created by interacting with others. The creative individual puts down the roots of use value; the concept must be given a reality which will enhance use value and develop the exchange value. For this, creative individuals interact with knowledge-base and production workers following two different, often complementary value-creating paths.

The first creativity path corresponds to the interaction with knowledge-base workers. Those workers mainly rely on know-how, explicit technical and scientific knowledge obtained by the embodiment of explicit knowledge by experience. When creative individuals interact with this type of worker what is obtained is the technical/scientific building of the product or service, which corresponds to the enhancement of use value. From a knowledge-base point of view, the interaction between the two types of individuals leads to the broadening of the analytical and symbolic knowledge base, by, for example, a creative process that gives a working prototype.

The second creativity path corresponds to the interaction with production workers or a production team. These are characterized as a systemic knowledge asset, producing documents, specifications, manuals, and so on, and can be assimilated, when effective, into a community of practice. The interaction between creative individuals and production work teams leads to an industrially exploitable product or service. The interaction probably creates a higher exchange value by diminishing the production costs. This concerns the synthetic and symbolic knowledge base. We can speak of a deepening of the bases rather than a broadening because what is created is a better and more detailed use of the existing stock.

The firm as the source of creativity

When we consider the firm as a whole or a network of firms linked by creative activity, value creation is often a development of a sustainable competitive advantage that allows the firm to produce a unique valuable product or service. For many writers, the act of invention and innovation at the enterprise level has an intentional content much stronger than the individual level (Van de Ven et al., 1999). This upper level of intent expressed encompasses many resources allocated to the creation process (financial, technical, organizational, time allocation, and so on) that are not present in the same way at the individual level. Creativity and value creation are apparently facilitated if the firm facing uncertainty has organizational slack and is managed as an entrepreneurial organization relying on a large social network constituted by communities, partners and users (Brown and Eisenhardt, 1998). The rich literature on the dynamic capabilities is largely focused on the internal factors of firms and the renewal of the firm's operative functions through the creation of knowledge, the entrepreneurial process and also the reconfiguration of the firm's networks (Zollo and Winter, 2002; Smith et al., 2005). However, as noted by Lepak et al. (2007), this literature focuses heavily on the internal functions of the firm and not enough on the external partners and on the beneficiaries of these efforts. Lepak et al. also identify organizational practices, such as the strategic management of human resources including knowledge and labor division and governance methods as an alternative source of value creation. Thus, the performance of knowledge-intensive firms, employees with high intellectual capital and their combinations with other assets and resources within and outside the firm can be a significant source of value creation.

From a firm's point of view, more worrying is the fact that it must decide how to organize the exchanges between the employees inside the firm with those outside the firm. It seems that the exchange with knowledge-base workers both inside and outside the firm is mainly a division of knowledge problem and that the interaction with production teams in order to obtain better performance is mainly a division of labor problem.

The division of knowledge and division of labor are two levels of management of an innovative firm. As explained by Becker et al. (2007), for Adam Smith the division of labor leads to the division of knowledge. The development of skills is more a consequence than a cause of the division of labor, in particular through learning-by-doing mechanisms. The division of labor entails a process of learning by doing that contributes to increasing skills and expertise and thus to enhancing the accumulation of specialized knowledge. The opposite position, that of the division of knowledge, implies that knowledge distribution drives the division of labor.

Therefore from a division of labor point of view a progressive specialization of work induces progressive specialized knowledge through learning by doing. This occurs under the following conditions: the pre-existing division of labor, to be coordinated, to produce given (or even changing) artefacts. As a consequence, the firm's organization follows a functional division of labor. Routines are then the 'memory' of organizations, truces to handle divergence of interests and conflicts, and the focus is on the 'activities' and their coordination (Nelson and Winter, 1982). The implications of the hypothesis 'the division of labor precedes the division of knowledge' on the theory of the firm is that transactions drive competences and define the boundaries of the firm. The explanation of networking, partnering, alliances, and acquisitions of a given firm mostly rely on strategic considerations related to the processing of information, to the level of transaction costs. In such a context it becomes extremely difficult to explain the functioning of the creative firm.

From a division of knowledge point of view, the differences in skills and 'mental labor' precede the division of labor and are also subject to learning and specialization. This suggests that one can unbundle the labor skills and pay only for the exact quantity the firm needs to produce. Many conditions must be fulfilled for such a mechanism to work. The main conditions are that there is an individual with all the necessary competences who knows how much of each type of labor must be acquired and that the required variety of labor also exists. As a consequence, the division of knowledge does not necessarily match the division of labor; the organization/coordination of dispersed knowledge does not necessarily overlap with the organization/coordination of activities.

For these reasons, the creation of exchange value is more likely to be dependent on the division of labor, but this division is only possible when knowledge division has been achieved in the first place. Therefore the creation of value is only efficient if the firm masters the two types of creativity path. Before we discuss in more detail how a firm can do this, we investigate the capture of value mechanisms.

The Diffusion and Capture of Value

As we have mentioned above, creation of value does not always go hand in hand with the appropriation of the created value. Obviously the firm must distribute the value created among employees, suppliers, shareholders and business partners. Often this distribution is fixed by contract. However, all beneficiaries of the created value are known in advance by the firm. There are other unknown beneficiaries who can capture value at the expense of the firm. This happens when use value is high but exchange value is low, or when the division of knowledge is not efficient enough to obtain a good division of labor. The difference in value can be grounded by different mechanisms affecting the relations between groups of individuals. For example, when a new product is introduced, and if it is perceived as valuable, it must increase both use value and exchange value. If it is new, the supply is limited (often only the innovator produces it) and the demand is relatively strong for a single supplier. The competitive process will attract new suppliers and reduce the gap between supply and demand, reducing prices, and therefore decreasing exchange value. This mechanism means that the firm that has spent most resources in the value creation process must share it with competitors. Of course there are ways to protect it (licensing, patenting) against this type of leakage in value, but it remains constrained due to the type of product or service (rival/not rival, excludable/non-excludable) and to the possibility for competitors to offer substitute products.

Competition is not limited to business-to-consumer relations but spreads to all levels influencing the amount of value captured by newly created businesses, for example in factors of production markets such as the labor market. In such a market if a particular type of worker is in an activity niche and requests a salary increase, this increase is limited to the value retained by the firm over the increasing costs. From the demand point of view the reverse analysis can also be done: competition between firms can lower the price, which corresponds to a growth in the value retained by the consumers. However, this competition may be limited by several mechanisms such as specific knowledge or legal, physical and technical barriers. These mechanisms prevent or limit the replication of the process of value creation or appropriation of value created. If such barriers exist, the creator of the value has more power to retain the benefits.

Catching value at the individual level

At the individual level many attributes can be the source of the appropriation of value, such as the position of the individual in a network (Baum and Rowley, 2008), the nature of relationships with others within and outside the production process and also the specialization of knowledge. This set is hardly imitable and therefore in the short term it will be difficult for competitors to deprive an individual of the value he/she has created.

Catching value at the firm level

The best-known appropriation characteristics are made on the basis of a resource node characterized by the adjectives valuable, rare, inimitable and non-substitutable (VRIN). When these conditions are satisfied, the firm can benefit from these resources for some time (Barney, 2001). Also, as we have mentioned, it is only when the firm has achieved sufficient experience in the division of knowledge that it can buy the needed resources at the smallest cost. Then, to catch the created value, the firm must have the relevant match between the division of knowledge and the division of labor.

Like the process of value creation, this match can be explored following different academic perspectives. The development of the theory of the firm and strategic management in recent years bridges the views based on the resources and on knowledge. Quite naturally the first works focused on the resources and knowledge within a single firm. These resources are related to the VRIN characteristics of competitive advantage (Kogut and Zander, 1992). Then, in a second phase, attention is paid to the combination of resources and knowledge held separately by several firms and the combination reinforces the strategic nature. In this approach, the management of the division of labor and division of knowledge has become a centerpiece of the strategy and value creation (Burger-Helmchen and Llerena, 2008).

What we are interested in is the management of flows and stocks of knowledge within a collaborative relationship between individuals inside or outside the firm which implies a certain division of labor. Existing knowledge (know-how, routines) is, according to Dierickx and Cool (1989), part of the firm inventory and can be analyzed as a stock. By contrast, the knowledge being acquired by creation, learning or transfer corresponds to a flow. The knowledge stock provides firms with the foundation of their core competences, flows of knowledge enable them to modify the existing stock. Therefore knowledge flows are part of dynamic capabilities (Kogut and Zander, 1992). This distinction is important because in the absence of flows the stock of skills of the firm is fixed and in the long run leads to the firm's decline. This implies that the management of knowledge stocks is an important activity in order to match well the division of labor with the tasks to be performed. The management of knowledge flows is equally important, adding a forecasting difficulty.

A large proportion of work in strategic management focuses on management of knowledge stocks as the source of value creation. Lepak and Snell (2002) follow this approach which allows them to represent the portfolio of knowledge of the firm and its specific management. However, the management of existing stocks of knowledge, if these stocks are distributed among several firms, immediately encompasses the management of labor flows between different groups of workers inside the same firm or employed between several firms.

The process of knowledge sharing within and between firms, and thereby the broadening and deepening of the knowledge bases, is often managed following social interaction codes rather than using IT-based processes or another formal exchange structure. It is therefore important to identify the relationships that facilitate the flow of knowledge and to organize the learning process. The objective of the following section is to clarify the value creation, this time by taking the point of view of the learning processes. For this we distinguish between two types of organizational learning (exploration and exploitation) which must both be present to efficiently create value. Then we examine the importance of the three characteristics (network structure, trust and cognition) of each of the mechanisms of learning and subsequently determine the appropriate division of knowledge and division of labor for the firm. This allows us to identify two extreme prototypes of relationships: one based mainly on the division of knowledge and the other based mainly on the division of labor. Within each prototype, the three characteristics that we have mentioned are combined to achieve the learning activity in relation to the exploitation or exploration.

3   CREATIVITY, VALUE, ORGANIZATIONAL LEARNING AND SOCIAL CONTEXT

The success of a firm depends on its ability to regularly create value for consumers. The source of this value creation lies in two alternative forms of learning: learning by exploration and learning by exploitation (March, 1991). Both types of learning are based on an organization with very different structures of knowledge flows which is expressed by the costs/benefits obtained, flexibility, specialization or division of these flows. Learning through exploration is the search for knowledge that does not exist within the firm to create value. This knowledge may exist in other firms or can be radically new. The learning operation corresponds to the development of knowledge and leads to an enhancement of the value or extension of perceived value by consumers. Learning through exploitation corresponds basically to the same definition, with two main differences: expected outcomes are less radical and the costs of the learning are smaller because the learning activity is simultaneously performed with the exploitation (production activity) of the firm. In many cases, companies create value by using most of their stock of knowledge (via a better division of labor). This behavior corresponding to the learning operation is often described as less risky and less diverse, but also more incremental and more routinized (Schulz, 2001).

If we were to define the alternative learning activities by the difference between benefits and costs, then the learning through exploitation generates more short-term benefits and the associated costs are much more predictable and so it should enhance the exchange value. Incorporating the benefits of improved productivity, incremental innovation and this learning are a weak form of dynamic capabilities which can improve continuously the skills and knowledge in a stable environment by improving the integration of knowledge and division of labor.

However, as mentioned, if the firm engages only in this type of learning, it may see the overall performance deteriorating in the long term (Levinthal and March, 1993). If the firm relied entirely on this type of learning, it would deplete its stock of knowledge and fail to renew it. To avoid this, the firm can try to create value by developing radically different ideas, innovative ideas – that is, the firm must be creative. For the firm this means engaging in learning through exploration with the objective of generating flows of new knowledge, and thus radically changing the product or process. Therefore this type of learning gives the firm a strong form of dynamic capacity.

From the point of view of value creation, this type of learning is characterized by higher benefits, higher costs and deeper uncertainty, and it generates new use value. Potentially this type of learning can influence each item of the business or have no influence at all. The daily survival of a firm cannot be based solely on this type of learning because it is too random. Many empirical studies therefore conclude that the sustainable development of a firm depends on the balance between these two learning mechanisms (Kang et al., 2007). Many models exist for understanding the balance between exploration and exploitation, including the nature of production, a balanced portfolio of options, the distribution of risk, environmental change and the division of labor and knowledge (Burger-Helmchen et al., 2009).

The general distinctions that we have mentioned show the importance of each form of learning in the creation of value, but we have not discussed the management of these forms of learning. Much of this involves management of the learning system which includes social interactions, in particular through the creation of communities. Management of learning and value creation implies the management of these communities and of contexts favorable to their creation and development (for example, the 'Ba', the place that favors the creation of knowledge, developed by Nonaka and Konno, 1998). To be effective, management must take into account the network structure, trust and the cognitive dimensions (Kang et al., 2007). In the remainder of this section we draw a parallel between these dimensions and forms of learning, in particular we are interested in the impact of variations on the flow of knowledge (a division of knowledge) and the divisions of labor.

The Network Structure Dimension

Several authors have suggested that organizational learning is primarily determined by the structure of relations in a network – the interactions between actors – within a firm and between firms. The network structure is crucial because it gives an individual the opportunity to evaluate and appropriate the knowledge of others within the network. The best-known measures are found in Granovetter (1973) and Uzzi (1997) on the strength of ties and proximity to see the links between two members of the same network and the network density (the average intensity among all members of the network). The strength of the links depends on the frequency of relations between two individuals of the same network, while the density determines who can interact with whom.

Learning by exploitation, network density and division of labor
The density of the network and the strength of the ties positively influence learning by exploitation. The stronger the links, the more efficient the exchange of knowledge will be with a high level of sophistication and precision. The more frequently people interact, the more easily they recognize the value and importance of the knowledge of others and then try to learn from them.

Learning by exploration, sparse network and division of knowledge
Too dense links in a network can block exploration by locking individuals into a specific type of knowledge, and thus lower their creativity (Gargiulo

and Benassi, 2000). This possibility was recognized by Granovetter (1973) for whom sparse links leave the network sufficiently flexible to identify entrepreneurial opportunities and use new knowledge. A similar result can be obtained by opening the network to other firms or even users as suggested in the fast-growing literature on open innovation (Chesbrough, 2003; Von Hippel, 2006; Penin et al., 2011).

The Trust Dimension

If the network structure dimension raises the issue of quantity of interactions, the affective dimension corresponds to the quality of the interaction to be experienced based on the motivations of the individuals, their expectations and behavior standards. These elements will influence the nature and quality of knowledge exchanged within the network. An expectation of reciprocity is necessary so that the network members are willing to learn and share their knowledge with others. Also, it can create value only if the members trust each other (Nooteboom, 2003).

This dimension can be studied by using two main forms of trust. Institutional trust is an impersonal form of trust which is given to people in relation to their employer firm or who belong to an institution or a group, but does not depend on their personal merits. Dyadic trust, the second form, refers to the trust between two individuals resulting from their past interactions.

Learning by exploitation, institutional trust and division of labor
The literature suggests that the development of a bundle of knowledge has very little to do with the confidence that we give to the members of an institution but a lot to do with the confidence we have in institutions. Thus members of different institutions can exchange information without having to know each other in advance insofar as they trust the person on the basis of the institution to which he or she belongs. Shared standards allow the creation of value between members of different institutions who share these values, and conversely there is no value creation possible between individuals from institutions which do not share these standards. Institutional trust helps to develop knowledge in a very precise domain but does, or does not sufficiently, allow for the development of knowledge outside this area.

Learning by exploration, dyadic trust and division of knowledge
Dyadic trust can develop knowledge in a rich way by facilitating learning through exploration. By its nature this type of trust allows for more flexibility and is obtained more rapidly than institutional trust.

The Cognitive Dimension

The cognitive dimension is related to the nature of the exchange and addresses the issue of what is exchanged. It focuses on the importance of common representations and the same system of value, the mental models, and the same code book, all of which allow learning in the organization (Bureth et al., 2000). Many authors acknowledge that it is not possible to recognize an idiosyncratic knowledge exchange in the absence of a framework and common references. This common repository corresponds to the firm's absorptive capacity, depending on the individual and the organization.

Henderson and Clark (1990) and Nooteboom (2009) divide knowledge into two categories: knowledge related to a specific component and architectural or integration knowledge. These two sets of knowledge should be identified when companies seek to develop the value of a good or service. Knowledge related to components, as its name indicates, refers to the components, parts of modules, rather than to the whole product or service, while architectural knowledge related to the interconnection of components covers the overall product or service. The same classification applies to the body of knowledge held by an individual and the knowledge exchanged within a network. It is worth noting that each of the firms in the network is related to a particular type of learning.

Learning by exploitation, architectural knowledge and division of labor
A better understanding of everyone's job and its importance in relation to the value and costs of the whole process improves the efficiency of each individual. Also, obtaining a certain level of knowledge related to architecture allows everyone to be more motivated and perform better in their own learning by exploitation (Kang et al., 2007). Therefore since each individual learns more from the exploitation activity, the knowledge related to architecture should be improved.

Learning by exploration, knowledge related to components and division of knowledge
During the exploration of new areas, the need to have the same knowledge related to architecture becomes less prevalent, as it focuses on a component whose integration can be addressed only after its own definition. However, it is necessary that individuals share the same knowledge related to the components if they wish to collaborate and explore the same area.

Antithetical Prototype, Organizational Learning and Division of Knowledge and Labor

Each of the three dimensions just mentioned is conceptually distinct and complementary to the others for the creation of relationships and the high creation of value. If these three dimensions are distinct conceptually they are linked in practice, as shown in a number of studies. Thus Nahapiet and Ghoshal (1998) and Yli-Renko et al. (2001) show that there is a causal relation where network structure influences trust, that trust influences cognition, cognition influences the network structure and so on. Therefore it is unproductive to separate these three effects; rather they should be put together in bundles whereby they provide synergies to each other. Kang et al. (2007) in a context similar to ours but with an HRM perspective identify two configurations of these three attributes that are consistent with learning by exploration or exploitation. Both configurations are based more on the theoretical work we have mentioned than on empirical work. These two relationships are summed up in Table 8.1.

The first row of the table represents the type that characterizes a division of labor-intensive prototype with a dense social network, strong institutional trust and shared architecture knowledge. The knowledge base involved is synthetic and symbolic because of the practical nature of the learning going on. It is based on a high degree of division of labor, but the learning process can challenge the division of knowledge (and ultimately lead to a better division of labor). This is the ideal type for learning by exploitation, a deepening of the knowledge held and a better distribution of activities corresponding to a more efficient division of labor.

In the second row, the division of the knowledge-intensive relation prototype is characterized by a sparse and flexible network, dyadic relationships between individuals sharing a common stock of knowledge about the components. This is the ideal type for learning by exploration, a broadening of the knowledge held and a better distribution of the creative fostering activities and allowing a future division of knowledge that is more efficient.

4 THE LINCHPIN ACTOR IN THE DIVISION OF LABOR AND THE DIVISION OF KNOWLEDGE

In order for a firm to be able to create value for its short- and long-term needs, these two prototypes must coexist in a certain proportion without any damaging prey/foe competition over the resources. But there is no predisposition for this to happen naturally. This is the fundamental argument of

Table 8.1 Learning forms and creativity development factors

	Network structure	Trust	Cognitive	Value	Knowledge base involved	Intensive in	Challenges
Learning by exploitation	Dense network, strong ties	Institutional trust	Common architectural knowledge	Mainly exchange value	Synthetic and symbolic knowledge base	Division of labor	Division of knowledge
Learning by exploration	Sparse network, weak ties	Dyadic trust	Common component knowledge	Mainly use value	Analytic and symbolic knowledge base	Division of knowledge	Division of labor

Kogut and Zander on the management of organizational learning. For them, the management of the employees and the relationships between employees within a firm but also between different firms is the basic endeavor of the knowledge management activity. To be executed correctly this management must implement a division of labor and a division of knowledge. To meet this objective, we propose to concentrate our effort on a linchpin actor in the firm concerned with both types of division: the creative employee.

The Creative Employee: Between Division of Knowledge and Division of Labor

We base our approach on a matrix inspired by the works of Lepak and Snell (1999, 2002) and the Ba types of Nonaka and Konno (1998). These authors take into account two dimensions of the value of human capital and the scarcity of these knowledge assets. This distinction allows them to highlight a preferred mode of employment (internal, external) and the form to be given to this employment (a relational or transactional basis). The character of scarcity expressed is formulated from the point of view of the firm to which the employees are primarily attached.

The value is the value added created by this activity. In this matrix, two other zones appear, one for the allocation of resources, internal or external to the firm. Clearly if the value is high the firm should ensure control by internalizing these resources. On the other hand if the value is low, the firm benefits from having them from an external partner whose form is to be specified. This observation is also valid for the case where knowledge is scarce. Indeed, if it is rare but of a low value, the firm will not have frequent use but the scarcity may be tainted by excessive costs that the firm should not have to bear over a long period. Therefore this knowledge could be externalized.

The other area corresponds to the form of management of the relationship between the firm and the individuals, whether they are within or outside the firm. But when the activity is less knowledge intensive or involves trivial knowledge, it is easier for the firm to describe what it expects and to control the execution of the tasks and the results. Such a relationship can be contracted with many details. When the relationship, on the other hand, requires rare knowledge and is therefore difficult to control, the approach is necessarily more than a contractual relationship and cannot be based on a precise description of the implementation.

Figure 8.2 shows that the critical knowledge held by employees is actually a part of existing knowledge, and it suggests that internal knowledge is primarily a stock of resources obtained by learning and inclusion of knowledge originating from outside the firm.

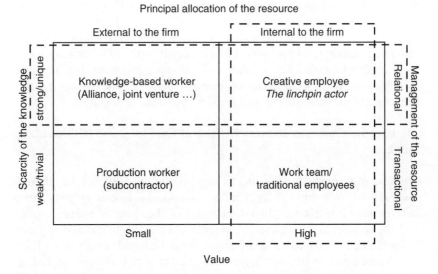

Sources: Based on Kang et al. (2007) and Burger-Helmchen and Llerena (2008).

Figure 8.2   Value creation linchpin from a management perspective

Knowledge and Labor-intensive Tasks: Premium to Creativity

Is there a parallel between the three characteristics (cognitive, network structure and trust) and how the stocks and flows of knowledge can be managed to achieve better creativity? In theory, it would not be surprising to find such a relation because it would imply that the management of the opportunities, opportunism, motivation and the interaction between individuals within the same firm or belonging to different firms are of utmost importance. But this necessitates a point-by-point discussion following the nature of the two prototypes we showed previously:

- *Creative employees and cognitive connections* First, based on the intellectual capital characteristics of the partners, different forms of knowledge can be developed by and between the different employees (this corresponds to knowledge asset types in the Nonaka and Konno representation). If the partners have knowledge that can be adapted and customized to the knowledge of the firm, as is the case for service providers such as consultants or experts, then they work in a defined timeframe with some employees during a short period of time. This type of contract leads to knowledge development related to components between partners outside the firm and employees in the firm (Brown and Duguid, 2001).

- *Creative employees and network structure* The management of employment relationships is dependent on the network structure and influences the management of the interactions between employees and partners as well as the opportunities that can be created and captured. Expectations and results vary greatly between the internal and external partners in relation to this criterion. External partners have a sparser network with the employees of the firm, especially those with strong intellectual capital and weaker ties. Therefore this type of approach is more common for interactions between different firms insofar as it concerns employees with high intellectual capital.

- *Creative employees and the development of trust* The third dimension that allows us to distinguish between individuals in those prototypes based on employment relationship is the amount of trust as well as the reciprocal obligations between employers and employees and between the employees. Lepak and Snell (1999) note that external partners and internal employees with high intellectual capital often have co-specialized knowledge, knowledge that can only be a source of value when combined. There is a synergy between the two. Such an alliance cannot be permanently maintained unless there is reciprocity between the individuals and mutual trust. Only in this case do companies develop mutual investments and mutual benefits. In this type of exchange it is essentially institutional trust that is created through the development and recognition of shared standards.

We can summarize the previous discussions in Figure 8.3. We see that creative employees with strong intellectual capital attract division of knowledge and division of labor activities. Creative employees are the linchpin between these two types of division. The relationships between knowledge-intensive workers and others are generally denser in the firm than the relations with external partners. Does this mean that any other relationship would not be strategic, that is, does not use the stocks of knowledge efficiently to create immediate value and generate flows of knowledge that allow the creation of future value? Several examples of firms that follow different strategies exist (Youndt et al., 2004). They show that firms can choose original strategies. Such strategies are not implemented naturally but indicate an intense effort of different firms that manage the stocks and flows of knowledge. They are essentially the exceptions that prove the rule. When relations between employees with high intellectual capital and external partners are governed mainly on the basis

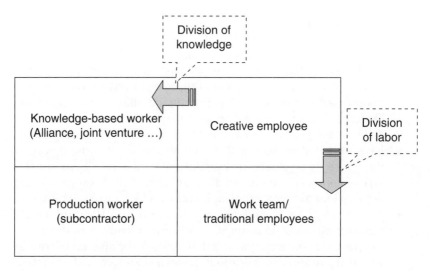

Figure 8.3   Division of labor and division of knowledge balance

of divisions of labor rules, then links between knowledge workers and the other employees reap the benefits of learning related to exploration rather than those coming from exploitation.

5   CREATIVE MANAGEMENT OF THE DIVISION OF LABOR AND THE DIVISION OF KNOWLEDGE

In the following we present two management techniques to develop creativity and produce value in accordance with learning mechanisms and the flows and stocks of knowledge that we described above. These two schemes are summarized in Table 8.2. The recommendations we make apply primarily to creative employees with high intellectual capital and their productions in ways that simplify their interactions with other employees (within and outside the firm).

Many studies have shown that management techniques can and must be reduced to the management of opportunities, motivation and accounting of each of the three elements that influence performance (Katz, 2003): (i) building labor structures that specify the content, scope, independence and interdependence which determine the opportunities for each employee and under what condition they interact with others in the accomplishment of tasks; (ii) the structure of incentives, including salary, performance evaluation and the safety of the employees, which provides a way to motivate

Table 8.2   Management modes of division of labor and knowledge

	Network structure	Trust	Cognitive
Division of labor	Flexible structure organization	Monetary and nonmonetary incentive based on individual results	Development of knowledge related to the specialty
Division of knowledge	Interdependent work structures	Monetary and nonmonetary incentive based on group results	Development of knowledge related to different specialties

employees to seek and acquire new knowledge; and (iii) the development of new skills (by training) which allows employees to understand and combine new knowledge.

Management of the Division of Labor Relations

The management of the division of labor is simplest when (i) the structures of work are independent, (ii) remuneration is introduced at the team level and (iii) it allows the development of specific expertise or extends the knowledge insights that link them.

Management of creative employees and interdependent work structures

When work is interdependent then strong links can be developed and maintained with interdependence between employees with high intellectual capital, other employees and external partners. Specifically, teamwork that requires interdependent and reciprocal interaction may help improve the interaction between these different types of employees and lead to mutual adjustments and coordination. This fosters the improvement of architectural knowledge (Brown and Duguid, 2001).

Management of creative employees and group spirit

Institutional trust between employees with high intellectual capital and internal and external partners can be improved through initiatives creating groups and communities that reinforce goals and shared values. The creation of this type of community and reinforcement of values can also be helped by systems of performance management which focus on the collective results (Lepak et al., 2007). A system of collective remuneration can also strengthen the relationship. This system can be particularly effective if the remuneration depends on the collective performance obtained through exchange with employees outside the firm. Indeed, it encourages people to participate in communities and to develop common frameworks.

Management of creative employees and the development of intraspecialty expertise

Knowledge connected to the architecture can be built through exchanges between different functions within the firm as well as intrafirm exchange when firms are affected by the same process. Joint training can also be a way to construct knowledge related to the architecture between employees with high intellectual capital and other employees of the firm or outside of the firm. Socialization programs are practices that help employees and partners understand and internalize the values, goals, history and culture of the firm and share tacit knowledge.

Management of the Division of Knowledge Relations

Unlike the division of labor, the basis of the business relationship behind the division of knowledge is the identification and exploitation of new ideas through interactions within and between enterprises. Also the management tasked with facilitating this type of relationship should strive to create infrastructures that allow flexibility to work in creative networks but also the mechanisms that enhance the flexibility of this network and its development.

Management of creative employees and flexible work structures

Flexible structures authorize temporary exchanges between employees with high intellectual capital and other members within or outside the firm. This holds for both short- and long-term exchanges. This flexibility goes hand in hand with high autonomy granted to this type of shared knowledge. Autonomy and flexibility should allow for greater access to the exploration for enhanced creativity.

Management of creative employees and individual results

The behavior necessary to obtain and use knowledge is difficult to identify and standardize a priori. Exchanges of knowledge for business development should not be expected if the individuals do not obtain a fair profit in return. This is why we have a system that rewards all the partners on the basis of their relationship and builds dyadic confidence. Leonard-Barton (1995) shows that the most-creative and best-paid employees are those who practice 'creative abrasion' of employees to link ideas, sometimes even conflicting ideas in order to create value.

Management of creative employees and the development of interspecialty expertise

To obtain more advanced knowledge related to components an individual must develop knowledge in different specialties. Also, employees with strong intellectual capital to develop such a type of knowledge must be able to better understand and improve their own work but also to better understand the integration of different elements. To achieve this, firms may include in the employment management specific career paths in which each individual is employed in a different position successively, and therefore can broaden his/her expertise based on many different contexts and develop knowledge in relation to several specialties. This also requires that employees recognize the value of the knowledge of others.

6   CONCLUSION

In this chapter we addressed the strategy of firms for managing their assets by developing the division of knowledge and labor aspects. For this, we emphasized the differences between stock and flow of knowledge in relation to the division of labor and knowledge. We investigated the relationship between employees within and between firms for value creation, and the deepening or broadening of the knowledge this implies. Then we linked learning by exploration and exploitation to the different forms of knowledge and labor division. This allowed us to specify some standard management rules which enable a firm to create value in the most efficient way.

This approach is based on a linchpin actor, at the center of all the exchange in this description: the creative employee. Future work could continue to explore the management rules by investigating the best knowledge/labor mix to capture the value and not only to create it. Also a further step could be to identify the peculiarities of some creative industries following our linchpin model.

REFERENCES

Amabile, T.M. (1988), 'A model of creativity and innovation in organizations', *Research in Organizational Behavior*, **10**, 123–69.

Amabile, T.M. (1996), *Creativity in Context* (update to *The Social Psychology of Creativity*), Boulder, CO: Westview Press.

Amabile, T.M. and K. Mukti (2008), 'Creativity and the role of the leader', *Harvard Business Review*, **86**, 100–109.

Antonelli, C. (2006), 'The business governance of localized knowledge: an information economics approach for the economics of knowledge', *Industry and Innovation*, **13**, 227–61.

Asheim, B. (2007), 'Differentiated knowledge bases and varieties of regional innovation systems', *Innovation: The European Journal of Social Sciences*, **20**, 223–41.

Barney, J. (2001), 'Resource-based theories of competitive advantage: a ten-year retrospective on the resource-based view', *Journal of Management*, **27**, 643–50.

Baum, J. and T. Rowley (2008), *Network Strategy, Advances in Strategic Management 25*, Bingley: Emerald Insight, JAI Press.

Becker, M., P. Cohendet and P. Llerena (2007), 'Division of labor and division of knowledge: why the nature of the causality really matters for the evolutionary theory of the firm?', in U. Cantner and F. Malerba (eds), *Innovation, Industrial Dynamics and Structural Transformation: Schumpeterian Legacies*, New York: Springer Verlag, pp. 49–66.

Boisot, M. and I.C. MacMillan (2004), 'Crossing epistemological boundaries: managerial and entrepreneurial approaches to knowledge management', *Long Range Planning*, **37**, 505–24.

Bowman, C. and V. Ambrosini (2000), 'Value creation versus value capture: towards a coherent definition of value in strategy', *British Journal of Management*, **11**, 1–15.

Brown, J.S. and P. Duguid (2001), 'Knowledge and organization: a social-practice perspective', *Organization Science*, **12**, 198–213.

Brown, S. and K.M. Eisenhardt (1998), *Competing on the Edge: Strategy as Structured Chaos*, Boston, MA: Harvard Business School Press.

Bureth, A., B. Ancori and P. Cohendet (2000), 'The economics of knowledge: the debate about codification and tacit knowledge', *Industrial and Corporate Change*, **9**, 255–87.

Burger-Helmchen, T. (2008), 'Plural-entrepreneurial activity for a single start-up: a case study', *Journal of High-Technology Management*, **19**, 94–102.

Burger-Helmchen, T., P. Cohendet and P. Llerena (2009), 'Division of labour and division of knowledge: a case study of innovation in the video game industry', in J.L. Gaffard, L. Nesta and U. Cantner (eds), *Schumpeterian Perspectives on Innovation, Competition and Growth*, New York: Springer, pp. 313–36.

Burger-Helmchen, T. and P. Llerena (2008), 'A case study of a creative start-up: governance, communities and knowledge management', *Journal of Innovation Economics*, **2**, 127–48.

Chesbrough, H. (2003), *Open Innovation: The New Imperative for Creating and Profiting from Technology*, Boston, MA: Harvard Business School Press.

Cohendet, P. and P. Llerena (2003), 'Routines and incentives: the role of communities in the firm', *Industrial and Corporate Change*, **12**, 271–97.

Cohendet, P., P. Llerena and L. Simon (2010), 'The innovative firm: nexus of communities and creativity', *Revue d'Économie Industrielle*, **129–30**, 139–70.

Conner, K.R. and C.K. Prahalad (1996), 'A resource-based theory of the firm: knowledge versus opportunism', *Organization Science*, **7**, 477–501.

Dierickx, I. and K. Cool (1989), 'Asset stock accumulation and sustainability of competitive advantage', *Management Science*, **35**, 1504–13.

Edmondson, A. and S.E. McManus (2007), 'Methodological fit in management field research', *Academy of Management Review*, **32**, 1155–79.

Felin, T. and W.S. Hesterly (2007), 'The knowledge-based view, heterogeneity, and new value creation: philosophical considerations on the locus of knowledge', *Academy of Management Review*, **32**, 195–218.

Gargiulo, M. and M. Benassi (2000), 'Trapped in your own net? Network cohesion, structural holes, and the adaptation of social capital', *Organization Science*, **11**, 183–96.

Granovetter, M.S. (1973), 'The strength of weak ties', *American Journal of Sociology*, **78**, 1360–80.

Henderson, R.M. and K.B. Clark (1990), 'Architectural innovation: the reconfiguration of existing product technologies and the failure of established firms', *Administrative Science Quarterly*, **35**, 9–30.

Hirshleifer, J., A. Glazer and D. Hirshleifer (2005), *Price Theory and Applications, Decisions, Markets and Information*, 7th edn, Cambridge: Cambridge University Press.

Kang, S.C., S. Morris and S.A. Snell (2007), 'Relational archetypes, organizational learning, and value creation: extending the human resource architecture', *Academy of Management Review*, **32**, 236–56.

Katz, R. (2003), *The Human Side of Managing Technological Innovation*, Oxford: Oxford University Press.

Kogut, B. and U. Zander (1992), 'Knowledge of the firm, combinative capabilities, and the replication of technology', *Organization Science*, **3**, 383–97.

Leonard-Barton, D. (1995), *Wellsprings of Knowledge*, Boston, MA: Harvard Business School Press.

Lepak, D.P., K.G. Smith and S. Taylor (2007), 'Value creation and value capture: a multilevel perspective', *Academy of Management Review*, **32**, 180–94.

Lepak, D.P. and S.A. Snell (1999), 'The human resource architecture: toward a theory of human capital allocation and development', *Academy of Management Review*, **24**, 31–48.

Lepak, D.P. and S.A. Snell (2002), 'Examining the human resource architecture: the relationship among human capital, employment, and human resource configurations', *Journal of Management*, **28**, 517–43.

Levinthal, B. and J.G. March (1993), 'The myopia of learning', *Strategic Management Journal*, **14**, 95–112.

Llerena, P. and M. Matt (2005), *Innovation Policy in a Knowledge-based Economy: Theory and Practice*, New York: Springer.

March, J.G. (1991), 'Exploration and exploitation in organizational learning', *Organization Science*, **2**, 71–87.

Maurer, I. and M. Ebers (2006), 'Dynamics of social capital and their performance implications: lessons from biotechnology start-ups', *Administrative Science Quarterly*, **51**, 262–92.

Nahapiet, J. and S. Ghoshal (1998), 'Social capital, intellectual capital, and the organizational advantage', *Academy of Management Review*, **23**, 242–66.

Nelson, R.R. and S. Winter (1982), *An Evolutionary Theory of Economic Change*, Cambridge, MA: Belknap Press of Harvard University Press.

Nonaka, I. and N. Konno (1998), 'The concept of "Ba": building a foundation for knowledge creation', *California Management Review*, **40**, 40–54.

Nonaka, I., R. Toyama and N. Konno (2000), 'SECI, Ba and leadership: a unified model of dynamic knowledge creation. Preview', *Long Range Planning*, **33**, 5–34.

Nooteboom, B. (2003), *Trust: Forms, Foundations, Functions, Failures and Figures*, Cheltenham, UK and Northampton, MA, USA: Edward Elgar.

Nooteboom, B. (2009), *A Cognitive Theory of the Firm: Learning, Governance and Dynamic Capabilities*, Cheltenham, UK and Northampton, MA, USA: Edward Elgar.

O'Reilly, C. and C. Tushman (2004), 'The ambidextrous organization', *Harvard Business Review*, **62**, 74–82.

Penin, J., C. Hussler and T. Burger-Helmchen (2011), 'New shapes and new stakes: a portrait of open innovation as a promising phenomenon', *Journal of Innovation Economics*, **7**(1), 11–29.

Reed, K.K., M. Lubatkin and N. Srinivasan (2006), 'Proposing and testing an intellectual capital-based view of the firm', *Journal of Management Studies*, **43**, 867–93.

Schulz, M. (2001), 'The uncertain relevance of newness: organizational learning and knowledge flows', *Academy of Management Journal*, **44**, 661–81.

Smith, K., C. Collins and K. Clark (2005), 'Existing knowledge, knowledge creation capability, and the rate of new product introduction in high-technology firms', *Academy of Management Journal*, **48**, 346–57.

Subramaniam, M. and M.A. Youndt (2005), 'The influence of intellectual capital on the types of innovative capabilities', *Academy of Management Journal*, **48**, 450–63.

Teece, D.J. (2007), 'Explicating dynamic capabilities: the nature and microfoundations of (sustainable) enterprise performance', *Strategic Management Journal*, **28**, 1319–50.

Uzzi, B. (1997), 'Social structure and competition in interfirm networks: the paradox of embeddedness', *Administrative Science Quarterly*, **42**, 35–67.

Van de Ven, A., D. Polley, R. Garud and S. Venkataraman (1999), *The Innovation Journey*, New York: Oxford University Press.

Von Hippel, E. (2006), *Democratizing Innovation*, Cambridge, MA: MIT Press.

Yli-Renko, H., E. Autio and H.J. Sapienza (2001), 'Social capital knowledge acquisition and knowledge exploitation in young technology-based firms', *Strategic Management Journal*, **22**, 587–613.

Youndt, M.A., M. Subramaniam and S.A. Snell (2004), 'Intellectual capital profiles: an examination of investments and returns', *Journal of Management Studies*, **41**, 335–61.

Zollo, M. and S.G. Winter (2002), 'Deliberate learning and the evolution of dynamic capabilities', *Organization Science*, **13**, 339–51.

PART III

Evolving firms as drivers of economic development

9. Economic development as a branching process

Koen Frenken and Ron A. Boschma

1 INTRODUCTION

The central question in economics has been, at least historically, the question of economic development (or 'the wealth of nations'). Classical economists typically viewed this as a historical process of structural change, in particular as a process of modernization through industrialization. Later, the question of economic development was approached in a narrower sense by equating economic development with economic growth, namely, with upward movements in macroeconomic variables such as productivity, GDP, or export volume. Of course, it has always been known that the *quantitative* process of economic growth is accompanied by a *qualitative* process of economic development in the form of structural change in the industry composition of a country. However, the large majority of macroeconomists tended to assume that specific qualitative dynamics are of no interest to an understanding of economic growth.

In more recent macroeconomic literature, the interest in structural change reappeared. For example, Harberger (1998) argued that the remarkable interindustry variation in productivity growth, and the changes therein over time, calls for theories that take the industry level seriously. He argued that the effect of broad externalities, for example, due to the growth of knowledge or human capital as central in new growth theory, is negligible compared to industry-specific productivity growth. Metaphorically, Harberger compared economic growth to the way mushrooms grow, where growth in particular industries can take place 'overnight', as opposed to growth likened to the way yeast grows, as implied by the new growth theorists.

Others have looked at the relationship between industry variety and economic growth, and found that, for most countries, economic growth is historically accompanied by an increase in variety (Funke and Ruhwedel, 2002; Imbs and Wacziarg, 2003). Subsequent research has suggested that variety increases through a process of diversification in related industries (Hidalgo et al., 2007; Saviotti and Frenken, 2008; Hidalgo and Hausman, 2009). This process, akin to a branching process, can be understood as the result of entrepreneurs re-employing their capabilities built up in one industry, by entering a related industry.

The new vision of growth as a process of economic development driven by diversification in a related industry, naturally links to an explicit geographical view of economic development. As the branching process of related diversification is driven by entrepreneurs switching from one industry to another, related, one, we typically observe that this branching process is localized in space. Entrepreneurs moving into related industries tend to remain located in the city or region in which they were already active. Thus, there is 'regional path dependence' (Martin and Sunley, 2006; Boschma and Wenting, 2007; Buenstorf and Klepper, 2009): since the first generation of entrepreneurs come from related industries, regions that host industries related to the new industry are more likely to create this new industry. However, regional success in an industry is not automatically reproduced in the next one, as the success of a firm is only partly determined by pre-entry experience. As new industries also rely on newly created knowledge, the 'windows of locational opportunity' are open, at least to some extent, for any region (Storper and Walker, 1989; Boschma, 1997). Yet, regions hosting related industries clearly enjoy an advantage, because related industries provide a large pool of potential experienced firms and experienced entrepreneurs.

Below, we present a very general framework of economic development as a branching process. We understand the process of economic development explicitly as a spatial process, where development is fundamentally uneven across cities, regions and countries. We proceed by proposing a minimalist theory of firm and urban growth inspired by Gibrat's principle of proportional growth. This framework can be regarded as a 'null-model', in the sense that empirical deviations from the null-model require an explanation that goes beyond the logic of randomness. Following a previous contribution (Frenken and Boschma, 2007), we shall take product division as the unit of analysis. A growth event concerns setting up a new product division within an existing firm or a new firm, and within an existing city or a new city. First, it considers firm growth dynamics and urban growth dynamics as stemming from a single process. Second, it introduces a parental lineage structure between product divisions, which allows one to introduce explicit branching dynamics regarding the inheritance of relevant knowledge and experience. These hypotheses are further elaborated in the remainder of the chapter.

2   NULL-MODEL

Let us conceive of firms and cities as aggregates of product divisions. Each product division belongs to a particular firm and is located in a particular city. The size of a firm at time t is simply expressed in the number of product divisions it contains at time t. Similarly, the size of a city at time t is simply expressed in the number of product divisions that are located in that city at time t. These definitions imply that a single firm may locate its divisions all in one city or over multiple cities, and, vice versa, a city may host divisions of a single firm or of multiple firms. In short, firms and cities are orthogonal aggregates of product divisions. One can thus derive from a single set of product divisions the firm size distribution by aggregating product divisions into firms and the city size distribution by aggregating product divisions into cities.

In our framework (Frenken and Boschma, 2007), firm and urban growth occur simultaneously through the establishment of new product divisions. In terms of Simon's (1955) seminal model, the lumps that drive growth can be considered as product innovations that are exploited by entrepreneurs by establishing a new product division. By reformulating Simon's stochastic model as a growth process fueled by new product divisions, and by assigning each new product division simultaneously to a firm and a city, the firm- and the city-size distributions can be derived from one single growth process.

We further assume that new product divisions are founded by former employees, who become entrepreneurs. One may think of such an employee as someone who comes up with a new product idea, which leads to the founding of a new product division. One can then introduce two organizational *parameters* (*p and p**) and two *locational parameters* (*q and q**). With probability p the employee will commercialize the innovation in-house, leading to a new product division within the parent firm. With probability p^* the employee will commercialize the product innovation in another firm by changing jobs. The remaining probability $(1 - p - p^*)$ is the probability that the employee creates a spinoff firm. And, with probability q the innovation will be commercialized in the city of origin. With probability q^* the innovation will be commercialized in another city where the probability that a particular city attracts the product innovation is proportional to its size. And with the remaining probability $(1 - q - q^*)$ the innovation will be commercialized in a new city.

This reformulation of Simon's model incorporates nine possible events resulting from a product innovation (see Table 9.1). As such, the framework provides a rich repertoire for formal modeling approaches with only four parameters (p, p^*, q and q^*). Since firms and cities are the aggregates

Table 9.1   Possible events resulting from a product innovation

Probability	Possible event
$(p)(q)$	Internal firm growth in city of origin
$(p)(q^*)$	Internal firm growth in another city
$(p)(1 - q - q^*)$	Internal firm growth in a new city
$(p^*)(q)$	Firm growth through labor mobility in city of origin
$(p^*)(q^*)$	Firm growth through labor mobility in another city
$(p^*)(1 - q - q^*)$	Firm growth through labor mobility in a new city
$(1 - p - p^*)(q)$	Spinoff in city of origin
$(1 - p - p^*)(q^*)$	Spinoff in another city
$(1 - p - p^*)(1 - q - q^*)$	Spinoff in a new city

Source: Frenken and Boschma (2007).

of product divisions, the model will produce the Zipf law for both the firm- and the city-size distributions in a single model as long as $(1 - p - p^*)$ and $(1 - q - q^*)$ are close to zero, following Simon (1955). What needs to be added here, as an assumption, is that in the case of interfirm or intercity mobility, the probability that an employee chooses a firm or city is proportional to its size (otherwise growth ceases to be proportional to size).

3   GENEALOGY

Mobility patterns of former employees who found their own product division create genealogical trees between product divisions. Such a link is created once an employee who previously worked for one product division, founds his/her own division. Having the arc point from the pre-existing division (parent) to the newly created division (child), the resulting genealogical tree is an a-cyclical, directed graph in which all the nodes have an in-degree equal to one and an out-degree of zero or higher.

In studies of industrial dynamics, genealogy has been used to explain the differential performance of firms (Klepper, 2002). The main idea behind such a genealogical analysis is to explain the performance of a firm from the pre-entry experience of the founder. If the founder has previously been working for a firm active in the same or similar economic activity as the newly founded firm, the survival probability of the newly founded firm is higher than if the founder has previously been working for a firm active in an activity that is different from that of the newly founded firm. In short, the more related the activity of the parent firm and its 'spinoff', the higher the survival probability of the spinoff firm, *ceteris paribus*. Meanwhile, empirical evidence for the hypothesis has been found for many industries including the US, the UK and German car industries (Klepper, 2002; Cantner et al., 2006; Boschma and Wenting, 2007), the US and German laser industries (Klepper and Sleeper, 2005; Buenstorf, 2007), the global fashion design industry (Wenting, 2008), the US tire industry (Buenstorf and Klepper, 2009) and the Dutch publishing industry (Heebels and Boschma, 2011).

This principle of inheritance can also be introduced in our model where product divisions, rather than firms, are the unit of analysis. We assumed that each new product division comes into existence as a result of a product innovation. This means that the activity of the newly founded division is by definition different from the activity of the parent division. However, the activities can be more or less related, for example, in terms of the technology employed in the product or the production process, or in terms of the specific organizational routines, business models, marketing strategies, logistics, and so on. In the remainder of this chapter, we shall speak of 'technological relatedness' for the sake of brevity.

The introduction of technological relatedness in our framework can be elaborated in two different ways, which nevertheless both result in the same evolutionary pattern of economic development. One way to incorporate technological relatedness is to assume that entrepreneurs can invent any product with equal probability, which means that the degree of relatedness of the activity of the entrepreneur and the activity of the parent division is a random variable. In that case, those who happen to have invented a product that is technologically related to the product of the parent division will have the highest probability of survival, while those who happened to have invented a product that is technologically unrelated to the product of the parent division, will quickly exit the market. Hence, there will be a correlation between the geodesic distance in the genealogy graph connecting product divisions and the degree of technological relatedness between their products. Alternatively, one can assume that entrepreneurs have a tendency to develop new products that are related to the product of the parent division in order to be able to re-use the knowledge and experience that they have gained as an employee in their newly founded division. Again, there will be a correlation between the geodesic distance in the genealogy graph connecting product divisions and the degree of technological relatedness between their products. Obviously, the two lines of argument are not mutually exclusive.

The second question that follows is whether the degree of technological relatedness between the product innovation of the entrepreneur and that of the parent division affects the organizational and locational

parameters as introduced before. Concerning the organizational parameters, one can assume that a firm is more willing to accept the creation
of a new division by one of its employees, the more the new activities
involved are technologically related. A higher technological relatedness
will generally result in higher economies of scope, which explains why
firms tend to diversify in related products. If the employee's new product
is only weakly technologically related to a firm's existing products, the
employee may approach other firms that are already active in technologically related activities, as such firms can benefit from economies of
scope if they found a new product division. In that case, we have again
an example of a firm that diversifies in a related product. In the rare
instance that an entrepreneur develops a product that is unrelated to the
activities of any other firms, the entrepreneur is forced to 'go it alone'
and to found a spinoff firm. Since such a newly founded firm cannot
profit from the pre-entry experience of the founder, or from economies of scope associated with the production of multiple products, the
chances of observing such firms are rather small. This may explain why
– even if technologically unrelated activities are more likely to be organized in a spinoff firm than in an existing firm – most of the spinoff firms
that one observes empirically are still active in technologically related
activities.

Concerning the locational parameters, one can follow the analogous
reasoning as for the organizational parameters. An entrepreneur will
tend to stay in the city where (s)he was previously employed, the more
the new activity is technologically related to other activities present in the
city. By doing so, the entrepreneur will profit from agglomeration advantages associated with the co-location of technologically related products
(Frenken et al., 2007). Where the employee's new product is only weakly
technologically related to a city's activities, the employee may migrate to
another city where technologically related activities are present. Again, the
entrepreneur will profit from agglomeration advantages associated with
the co-location of technologically related products. In the rare instance
that an entrepreneur develops a product that is unrelated to any economic
activity, the entrepreneur may found a new city.

The pattern of economic development that follows from our discussion is one where (i) entrepreneurs tend to move into technologically
related activities and (ii) such technologically related activities tend to be
organized as a new product division within the parent firm so as to profit
from economies of scope and within the parent city so as to profit from
economies of agglomeration. This implies that the genealogical evolution
of products is highly localized within firms and within cities, giving rise to
related diversification trajectories at firm and city levels.

4   ECONOMIC DEVELOPMENT AS A WALK THROUGH PRODUCT SPACE

As entrepreneurs tend to move to technologically related products when setting up a new product division, be it in the same or a different firm and in the same or a different city, the structure of the 'product space' affects the entrepreneurial opportunities for every potential entrepreneur. Following Hidalgo et al. (2007), one can think of the product space as a weighted graph specifying the degree of technological relatedness – or shorter 'technological proximity' – between each two products.

It is most likely the case that such a graph is complex in the sense that it contains dense areas with strong links among products (say, electronics) and sparsely connected areas with weak links (say, natural resources). Indeed, both Hildago and colleagues (Hildago et al., 2007; Hildago and Hausmann, 2009) and Neffke and colleagues (Neffke and Svensson-Henning, 2008, 2009; Neffke et al., 2011), find that the graphs display 'cores' with many interrelated industries and peripheries with relatively isolated industries.

Depending on the position of a product in product space, entrepreneurial opportunities differ. If a product is strongly linked to many other products (to be developed or to be imitated), there are many entrepreneurial opportunities to be exploited. Conversely, if a product is weakly linked to a few products, there are only a few entrepreneurial opportunities to be exploited. Indeed, at the country level, Hildago et al. (2007) showed that countries tend to move to new export industries that are close to their previous export specializations as mapped in product space. This means that countries that happen to be located in the high-density part of the industry graph grow faster than countries whose industries are located in the low-density parts, as the former have many more opportunities to upgrade their export products than the latter. Similarly, at the regional level, Neffke et al. (2011) showed that in Sweden, industries that were technologically related to pre-existing industries in the region were more likely to enter, and industries that were unrelated to industries in the region were more likely to exit.

5   EXTENSIONS

We have argued that the organizational and locational parameters are likely to be different for different types of innovation. The more the innovation is technologically closely related to the products of the parent firm, the higher the probability of the entrepreneur exploiting the innovation in-house. Similarly, an entrepreneur will tend to stay in the city where (s) he was previously employed, the more the new activity is technologically related to other activities present in the city. Thus, the type of innovation *vis-à-vis* the existing activities in a firm or a city determine the degree of path dependence in firm and urban growth.

This model can be extended by taking into account other contexts that affect the organizational and locational decision of the entrepreneur. First, country-specific institutions affecting the locational and organizational parameters can be incorporated. For example, regarding the organizational parameters, countries differ markedly in the extent to which new products are commercialized within spinoffs. And countries differ in non-compete clauses in labor contracts. Regarding the locational parameters, the extent to which institutions are standardized across the country may greatly affect intercity mobility (apart from transportation costs). More generally, one can ask how national institutions differ and how these affect the organizational and locational behavior of entrepreneurs. Studying these institutional varieties in depth may shed new light on the differential development path of countries.[1]

Another extension of our framework is to make organizational and locational parameters specific to industries. From empirical work, we know that industries differ systematically in their technological regimes (Pavitt, 1984; Malerba and Orsenigo, 1993, 1996, 1997). For example, if appropriability conditions are such that inventions can easily be patented by firms, spinoffs may be less likely. And, obviously, if technological opportunities are more abundant, spinoffs are more likely to occur, as is typically the case at the start of a new industry (Klepper, 2002).

A second extension of the model is to change the organizational and locational parameters in the framework into decision variables of firms. In particular, one expects organizational and locational decisions to be dependent on the nature of the innovation. As innovations can be considered as being more or less radical, the radicalness of innovation will impact on the organizational form and locational behavior of firms. Regarding the organizational forms, the probability that an innovation leads to internal firm growth is likely to decrease with radicalness. To exploit organizational routines built up in the past, firms tend to prefer incremental over radical innovations (Tushman and Anderson, 1986). Radical innovations, therefore, are more likely to lead to labor mobility or the creation of a spinoff firm than incremental innovations. Regarding locational decisions, the radicalness of the innovation is expected to play a role as well. The more radical an innovation, the less likely it will benefit from existing routines, be it within the firm or within the city. For that reason, radical innovations are more likely to be commercialized in a location different from that in which they are conceived, compared to less radical innovations. In other words, the openness of the windows of locational opportunity increases with the radicalness of the innovation in question (Storper and Walker, 1989; Boschma, 1997).

6   QUESTIONS FOR FURTHER RESEARCH

The first obvious question that follows from viewing economic development as a process of related diversification is how to measure relatedness. Attempts to map technological relatedness range from using SIC codes (Jacquemin and Berry, 1979; Frenken et al., 2007), to input–output tables (Fan and Lang, 2000), to co-specializations in traded sectors (Porter, 2003) and exports (Hidalgo et al., 2007), to co-occurrences of products in plants (Neffke and Svensson-Henning, 2008), to interindustry labor mobility flows (Neffke and Svensson-Henning, 2009). Although the use of SIC codes is very convenient as the hierarchical classification structures indicate different degrees of relatedness, and entropy measures different degrees of related variety (Jacquemin and Berry, 1979; Frenken et al., 2007), the question remains whether SIC codes capture technological relatedness. Indeed, the classification structure has not been designed to reflect such technological relationships at all. In the context of the framework proposed here, which reasons from mobility of individuals across industries, the approach by Neffke and Svensson-Henning (2009) seems most appropriate as relatedness is derived from labor mobility flows between two industries.

A second question that follows from our framework is what is actually being inherited among product divisions, be it within the firm, between firms, or between parent firm and spinoff firm. From the research on spinoff performance (Klepper, 2002), it is apparent from the high correlation in performance between parent and spinoff that 'something' is being transmitted from parent firm to spinoff. However, whether the spinoff inherits knowledge, or organizational capabilities, or network relations, or reputation remains unclear. And, one can also ask under what conditions transmission is more or less noisy, leading to higher or lower correlation in performance. Both what has been transmitted and how noisy the transmission process has been, are likely to depend on industry characteristics (nature of knowledge, appropriability conditions, capital intensity, and so on), the motivation to start a spinoff (whether a disagreement is underlying the spinoff), and the geographical distance between parent and spinoff (if a spinoff is located far away, it may be less able to copy the parent's success).

Finally, one can ask whether the branching logic as described applies equally to manufacturing, services and creative industries. In this context, note that the local branching and spinoff process underlying the studies on manufacturing industries (such as cars, tires, lasers, and so on) was found to be operating in services and creative industries as well. As studies show on publishing services (Heebels and Boschma, 2011), and on fashion design as a creative industry (Wenting, 2008), the patterns of industrial dynamics (for example, spinoffs outperforming other entrants) and spatial distribution (one or a few dominant clusters gradually emerging) are in line with earlier studies on manufacturing. An interesting difference, however, is the location of branching and spinoffs: finance, publishing and fashion tend to cluster in large 'world cities' (for example, London, Paris, New York, Los Angeles and Tokyo), while manufacturing clusters typically emerge in smaller towns (for example, Detroit, Coventry, Akron and San Francisco). This particular pattern remains to be incorporated into the framework sketched above.

NOTE

1. The literature on 'varieties of capitalism' may be particularly useful (Hall and Soskice, 2001).

REFERENCES

Boschma, R.A. (1997), 'New industries and windows of locational opportunity: a long-term analysis of Belgium', *Erdkunde*, **51**(1): 1–19.
Boschma, R.A. and R. Wenting (2007), 'The spatial evolution of the British automobile industry: does location matter?', *Industrial and Corporate Change*, **16**(2): 213–38.
Buenstorf, G. (2007), 'Evolution on the shoulders of giants: entrepreneurship and firm survival in the German laser industry', *Review of Industrial Organization*, **30**(3): 179–202.
Buenstorf, G. and S. Klepper (2009), 'Heritage and agglomeration: the Akron tyre cluster revisited', *Economic Journal*, **119**: 705–33.
Cantner, U., K. Dreßler and J.J. Krüger (2006), 'Firm survival in the German automobile industry', *Empirica*, **33**(1): 49–60.
Fan, J.P.H. and L.H.P. Lang (2000), 'The measurement of relatedness: an application to corporate diversification', *Journal of Business*, **73**(4): 629–60.
Frenken, K. and R.A. Boschma (2007), 'A theoretical framework for evolutionary

economic geography: industrial dynamics and urban growth as a branching process', *Journal of Economic Geography*, **7**(5): 635–49.

Frenken, K., F.G. Van Oort and T. Verburg (2007), 'Related variety, unrelated variety and regional economic growth', *Regional Studies*, **41**(5), 685–97.

Funke, M. and R. Ruhwedel (2002), 'Export variety and export performance: empirical evidence for the OECD countries', *Weltwirtschaftliches Archiv*, **138**: 97–114.

Hall, P.A. and D. Soskice (eds) (2001), *Varieties of Capitalism: The Institutional Foundations of Comparative Advantage*, Oxford: Oxford University Press.

Harberger, A.C. (1998), 'A vision of the growth process', *American Economic Review*, **88**(1): 1–32.

Heebels, B. and R. Boschma (2011), 'Performing in Dutch book publishing 1880–2008: the importance of entrepreneurial experience and the Amsterdam cluster', *Journal of Economic Geography*, **11**: 1007–29.

Hidalgo, C.A. and R. Hausmann (2009), 'The building blocks of economic complexity', *Proceedings of the National Academy of Sciences*, **106**: 10570–75.

Hidalgo, C.A., B. Klinger, A.-L. Barabasi and R. Hausmann (2007), 'The product space conditions the development of nations', *Science*, **317**: 482–7.

Imbs, J. and R. Wacziarg (2003), 'Stages of diversification', *American Economic Review*, **93**(1): 63–86.

Jacquemin, A.P. and C.H. Berry (1979), 'Entropy measure of diversification and corporate growth', *Journal of Industrial Economics*, **27**(4): 359–69.

Klepper, S. (2002), 'The capabilities of new firms and the evolution of the U.S. automobile industry', *Industrial and Corporate Change*, **11**(4): 645–66.

Klepper, S. and S. Sleeper (2005), 'Entry by spin offs', *Management Science*, **8**: 1291–306.

Malerba, F. and L. Orsenigo (1993), 'Technological regimes and firm behavior', *Industrial and Corporate Change*, **2**: 45–74.

Malerba, F. and L. Orsenigo (1996), 'Schumpeterian patterns of innovation are technology-specific', *Research Policy*, **25**, 451–78.

Malerba, F. and L. Orsenigo (1997), 'Technological regimes and sectoral patterns of innovative activities', *Industrial and Corporate Change*, **6**: 83–118.

Martin, R. and P. Sunley (2006), 'Path dependence and regional economic evolution', *Journal of Economic Geography*, **6**(4): 395–437.

Neffke, F. and M. Svensson-Henning (2008), 'Revealed relatedness: mapping industry space', Papers in Evolutionary Economic Geography (PEEG) 0819, Utrecht University.

Neffke, F. and M. Svensson-Henning (2009), 'Skill-relatedness and firm diversification', Papers on Economics and Evolution 2009-06, Max Planck Institute of Economics, Jena.

Neffke, F., M. Svensson-Henning and R. Boschma (2011), 'How do regions diversify over time? Industry relatedness and the development of new growth paths in regions', *Economic Geography*, **87**(3): 237–65.

Pavitt, K. (1984), 'Sectoral patterns of technical change: towards a taxonomy and a theory', *Research Policy*, **13**: 343–73.

Porter, M.E. (2003), 'The economic performance of regions', *Regional Studies*, **37**(6–7): 549–78.

Saviotti, P.P. and K. Frenken (2008), 'Export variety and the economic performance of countries', *Journal of Evolutionary Economics*, **18**(2): 201–18.

Simon, H.A. (1955), 'On a class of skew distribution functions', *Biometrika*, **42**(3–4): 425–40.

Storper, M. and R. Walker (1989), *The Capitalist Imperative: Territory, Technology and Industrial Growth*, New York: Basil Blackwell.

Tushman, M.L. and P. Anderson (1986), 'Technological discontinuties and organizational environments', *Administrative Science Quarterly*, **31**: 439–65.

Wenting, R. (2008), 'Spinoff dynamics and the spatial formation of the fashion design industry, 1858–2005', *Journal of Economic Geography*, **8**: 593–614.

10. Spin-off growth and job creation: evidence on Denmark

Pernille Gjerløv-Juel and Michael S. Dahl*

1 INTRODUCTION

It is well established that entrepreneurial spin-offs are distinct performers in several industries. Firms founded by former employees from incumbent firms in the same industry tend to outperform other new entrants and sometimes even incumbent firms as well (see Klepper, 2001a, 2009 for reviews of this literature). This fact has sparked considerable interest among politicians and civil servants, since future industrial and entrepreneurial policy might gain by looking more closely at this. Most of the existing studies focus on the life cycle of single industries and on survival as a key performance indicator. Spin-offs have been found to be key entrants at specific stages of the life cycle, but are spin-offs universally the best entrants? To answer this question, we need to add studies of firms from a variety of industries, across different stages of the life cycle and with other performance measures as well. Dahl and Reichstein (2007a) and Dahl et al. (2009) have established that spin-offs are relatively more successful entrants across industries in terms of survival. The question is more open when it comes to other performance measures.

This chapter adds to this discussion by studying in greater detail the performance differences between spin-offs and other entrants in terms of employment growth and job creation. We use a comprehensive dataset covering all entrants in the Danish economy from 1995 to 2004. We find that spin-offs are not only surviving longer, as the existing literature suggests, but they are also relatively more important for job creation in the economy.

One of the reasons for the increasing attention to entrepreneurship is the expectation that new and younger firms are the driving force behind economic growth and job creation. Policy makers promote them to provide future employment and prosperity, and their industrial policy is often focused on increasing the number of start-ups. If spin-offs are a particularly successful type of entrant in terms of job creation and generation of prosperity, it might be a particularly interesting type of entry to promote in industrial policy.

The chapter is structured as follows. In Section 2, we discuss the relative performance of spin-offs presenting selected literature from organizational ecology and human and social capital theory. Based on this discussion, we develop our hypotheses on spin-off employment growth. In Section 3, we describe the dataset and selection of firms. We introduce notation and measures of growth rates, job creation and job destruction. In Section 4, we test our hypotheses and present the results, and also illustrate the impact of spin-off entrepreneurship on overall employment. Finally, in Section 5 we summarize major results and discuss implications of our findings.

2   EMPLOYMENT GROWTH OF *DE NOVO* ENTRANTS

A great number of studies have illustrated how spin-offs are more likely to survive compared to other *de novo* entrants. This has been demonstrated for a number of different industries from Silicon Valley law firms to the Detroit automobile industry (Klepper, 2001b, 2007; Phillips, 2002; Agarwal et al., 2004; Klepper and Sleeper, 2005). Assuming identical rates of employee turnover, increased likelihood of survival implies a proportional increase in job security for spin-off employees. Furthermore, it indicates more homogeneous growth rates for firms that survive longer. These characteristics also describe the job creation among relatively older firms (Davis et al., 1997). In this chapter, we argue that stability and homogeneity are also features of the job creation of spin-offs. However, there is not the same trade-off between growth and stability that these studies observe with older firms.

We build our hypotheses departing from the liability of newness argument presented by Stinchcombe (1965). He explains the liability of newness based on three central factors. First, there must be internal distribution of roles among the employees. The roles need to be not only distributed but also defined. A vague distribution of roles might give rise to problems and inefficiencies as division of tasks and responsibility might be unclear. Distribution of roles is partly based on history and experiences. It takes time and might require some trial and error which can be costly.

Second, new firms have not yet established a social structure for communication. Thus, the communication in new firms might resemble communication among strangers. It takes time to establish social relations and relationships of trust among the employees and the employees and management when there is no basis of communication; this also complicates knowledge sharing. In sum, communication might be more complicated in younger firms compared to older firms.

Finally, lack of reliance is not only a potential internal problem regarding employees, it also includes customers, investors and suppliers. As was the case internally in the organization, it also takes time to establish stable relations to these external parties. In opposition to older firms, new and young firms do not yet have a reputation for reliability. Older firms potentially have a number of regular customers who are familiar with the products and services of the firms and, perhaps, not willing to substitute what they are already conversant with, in order to win minor cost savings which, possibly, could be achieved by changing to a new but unknown supplier. Likewise, the investors are interested in the firms' ability to produce, service customers and run a cost-effective business, but new firms have not yet had the opportunity to prove their worth (Hager et al., 2004).

Along similar lines, Brüderl and Schüssler (1990) develop the theory of liability of smallness by introducing the term 'liability of adolescence', suggesting that the hazard of exit is not necessarily at its highest at the time of start-up. Instead, the likelihood of exit increases in the first period, peaks in the middle, and then gradually decreases with firm age. The argument for this U-shaped hazard rate, as opposed to the monotonously decreasing risk suggested by the liability of newness, is that new firms often have an initial capital to draw on and the firm does not exit until it has exhausted its initial resources. The more initial resources, the longer the firm is capable of surviving (ibid.).

Several studies have demonstrated a positive correlation between startup size and new-firm survival (see, for example, Freeman et al., 1983; Brüderl et al., 1992; Dahl and Reichstein, 2007a). Economies of scale, systematic research and development and access to capital and qualified labor are explanations of the liability of smallness (Audretsch and Mahmood, 1995; Agarwal et al., 2002; Dahl and Reichstein, 2007a). However, while the likelihood of survival on the one hand is increasing with firm size, the above arguments further point to an inverse relationship between employment growth and firm size. As the number of employees increases, growth rates tend to subside. This indicates a trade-off between growth and survival (Dunne et al., 1989).

The above arguments suggest that differences in survival rates might be explained by the liability of smallness. If so, the higher survival of spin-offs can be explained by them being larger at entry. Industry experience tends to improve productivity. Greater technological knowledge of the spin-off entrepreneurs might allow spin-offs to produce at lower unit costs, giving them a competitive advantage over other entrants. For that reason, spin-offs are expected to enter more markets, leading to an increased startup size (Roberts et al., 2011). Moreover, Audretsch and Mahmood (1995) point out the potential reverse causality that startup size is an indicator of the founders' expectations. Supporting this, Roberts et al. suggest that spin-off entrepreneurs found initially larger businesses than others, as they are aware of the (competitive) advantages arising from superior qualifications. Apart from technological knowledge regarding production processes, prior industry experience also includes knowledge concerning relevant organizational structures and routines, customers, suppliers, markets, products, and so on, giving spin-off entrepreneurs a superior endowment of knowledge and helping them to identify unexplored business opportunities, thereby giving them a head start over their peers (see, for example, Burton et al., 2001; Helfat and Lieberman, 2002; Shane, 2003; Chatterji, 2009). Brüderl et al. (1992) show that industry-specific experience has a positive effect on start-up size. They argue that greater human capital increases founders' productivity by managing and organizing the production process more efficiently and attracting more customers and investors. This reflects on production efficiency and results in higher profits. Therefore, despite possibly greater initial size, the risk spin-off entrepreneurs take is relatively smaller due to greater competency at the time of entry.

Hypothesis 1: Spin-offs have more employees at the time of entry

Yet another explanation to the spin-offs' relatively higher likelihood of survival relies on the theory of liability of newness. As presented above, the liability of newness is triggered by a lack of organizational routines which are not yet fully incorporated in younger firms. New firms are founded on the routines implemented by the founders. These routines are often based on founders' prior experience as they will lean on routines already familiar to them. One might expect founders to differentiate their organization from their prior employer depending on the estimated quality of the organizational structures of the latter. Immediately, this is rarely the case (Baron and Hannan, 2002). But, Baron and Hannan argue further that the founders are actually better off sticking to a model familiar to them independently of how good it might be objectively (see also Hannan and Carroll, 1992). Prior experience is important as organizational culture and structures already start to take shape in the early years, making the priorities and choices made during this initial period crucial, as they might have long-lasting and permanent effects on the organization's routines and through that the firm's performance (Stinchcombe, 1965; Schein, 1983). In other words, the performance of new firms is determined by the founders' experiences prior to the start-up (Klepper, 2001b; Helfat and Lieberman, 2002).

Klepper (2001b) explains the superior performance of spin-offs over other entrants based on the notion of routines from Nelson and Winter (1982). As spin-offs are established in industries where the founder has prior experience, their routines are more likely to fit the challenges characteristic of that particular industry. The spin-off entrepreneur has more experience of how to run a business in that industry and how to make that business profitable (Agarwal et al., 2004).

Returning to the core of liability of newness, Stinchcombe (1965) emphasizes the three central factors described above. First, the division of tasks and responsibility in new and young firms is unclear as internal roles among the employees are not yet distributed; a distribution that is partly based on history and experience. Additionally, new firms lack a social structure of communication. Potentially, spin-off entrepreneurs already have a network within the industry helping them in the early recruitment phase. They might recruit former colleagues as well as others who are already part of their network. It is possible that this could limit the liability of newness as a number of employees as well as managers already share a history of experiences and organizational culture. Thus, relationships and a basis of trust might already be established among members of the organization and this could ease communication and knowledge sharing, limit the degree of misunderstandings and, taken together, result in increased efficiency compared to other start-ups.

Relationships of trust are not only a relevant internal matter. The above arguments point to lack of reputation and relationships to external partners as other significant factors. Following the argument of Dahl and Reichstein (2007a), a spin-off might inherit something other than technological knowledge and organizational routines from its prior employer. In the case that the prior employer (the parent firm) has a good reputation, this blueprint might be transferred from the parent firm to the spin-off, giving the spin-off entrepreneur a great advantage (for example, help the entrepreneur to raise finance and attract the most talented employees). In other words, external parties (for example, investors) cannot observe the new firm's potential directly and therefore need to rely on *signals* of legitimacy, credibility and profitability – even if the effect on performance is only symbolic. The founders' career history and network are examples of indicators that might affect outsiders' perception of the new firm (Brüderl et al., 1992; Stuart et al., 1999; Higgins and Gulati, 2003). Following similar lines of argument, Chatterji (2009) shows that new firms, within the US medical device industry, secure funding more quickly than other entrants do, when spawned by incumbent firms in the industry. Finally, studies on the role of parent firms suggest that spin-offs from better parent firms survive longer, and better parent firms have higher spawning rates (see, for example, Phillips, 2002; Agarwal et al., 2004; Gompers et al., 2005; Dahl and Reichstein, 2007b; Klepper, 2007).

Taken together, the above arguments explain how stronger skills/competences embedded in the spin-offs help them cope with the barriers that lie in the liability of newness. In addition to increased survival, this also makes the spin-offs a more homogeneous group. As previously discussed, the great heterogeneity observed among new and younger firms is partly explained by differences in the skills acquired by the founders prior to the time of entry. Different initial endowments of knowledge make the entrepreneurs differ in ability to identify and explore opportunities. As the less-skilled, -gifted or -experienced entrepreneurs exit during the selection process, the remaining (older) firms make up a more homogeneous group of viable firms. But spin-offs already constitute a group of higher-skilled entrepreneurs at the time of entry. For that reason, we expect spin-offs to reflect the homogeneity and stability in job creation otherwise characteristic of relatively older firms:

Hypothesis 2:   Spin-offs constitute a more homogeneous group with more stable growth patterns than other young firms

If spin-offs have a higher likelihood of survival, are a more homogeneous group and show greater stability in overall job creation compared to other entrants, it might seem a natural conclusion that they, like older firms, should experience a trade-off, as discussed above, between growth and survival. In other words, they might contribute less to the overall (net) job creation in comparison to other young firms despite improved survival. Moreover, a common default assumption in economics is the positive correlation between risk and return. When entering, spin-off entrepreneurs might lower their risk by imitating the business model, products, organizational structures and so on of their parents. In a related model, Jovanovic (2004) shows how firms, switching from new product development to safer returns, gain initial higher earnings at the expense of long-run profits. Spin-offs might have a higher likelihood of survival because they take less risk, indicating a similar trade-off between risk and return. Other entrants, in contrast, might be more explorative and innovative which, in turn, will lower survival but increase overall growth (for example, job creation). In contrast to this, we argue that spin-off net job creation exceeds that of other young firms.

First, the above arguments on greater spin-off performance mention suitable (and quickly established) organizational routines, structures and culture. While older firms might find themselves locked into existing routines, spin-offs are better able to change their organization and routines, if it is required by the market, thereby making them more flexible (Klepper, 2001b). This higher flexibility enables them to challenge incumbent firms, whereas other young (and equally flexible) firms lack experience and routines to compete with both incumbents and spin-offs. Second, as described above, the spin-off entrepreneur's prior industry experience includes knowledge regarding the market and competitors helping him/her identify *unexplored* business opportunities (see, for example, Burton et al., 2001). In contrast to the above discussion, this speaks against the perception of spin-offs as less innovative and less willing to explore new markets. Supporting this, Chatterji (2009) finds that non-technological rather than technological knowledge is important for spin-off performance. Finally, Roberts et al. (2011) show that spin-offs do not experience higher (or lower) growth rates than other young firms. On the other hand, we argue that if spin-offs experience the same (gross) job creation as others, but are less likely to exit or have negative growth, their net job creation should be greater.

Hypothesis 3: Spin-offs have higher net job creation than other young firms

This suggests that the relative net contribution to job creation by spin-offs exceeds that of other new firms. If supported empirically, this stresses not only the importance of spin-offs to continuous job creation, but also the economic and political potential of promoting spin-off entry rates.

3   METHOD

Data

We exploit two databases: the Danish Entrepreneurship Database and the Danish Integrated Database for Labor Market Research (referred to by its Danish acronym, IDA). Both databases are maintained by Statistics Denmark. IDA is a linked employer–employee database containing all incorporated companies in Denmark and their employees from 1980 to 2006, which allow us to follow the year-on-year employment flow of Danish firms. The Danish Entrepreneurship Database identifies the primary founder of all new limited liability and privately owned firms in Denmark from 1994 to 2004.[1]

Following Dahl et al. (2009) our sample consists of all (active) start-ups in Denmark from 1995 to 2006. We include only startups from the private sector. Additionally, due to regulation and reduced competition we exclude start-ups from the primary and energy sectors. As we are investigating job creation, our interest is confined to those start-ups that are (or become) actual active businesses. We define this as start-ups with a minimum employment of one full-time equivalent in addition to the founder. Using this definition (minimum one full-time equivalent), we determine firm age from the first observed activity. Similarly, we consider the firm closed after two successive years without activity. Thus, we allow for a single year without activity (less than one full-time equivalent).[2] If the firm is later observed in the dataset we consider it to be re-entered and we reset the age variable. We use information on activity to determine the start-up year even though the year of official registration is in the database. The reason for this is that in many cases, no (or very limited) activity is observed in the start-up until several years later. We argue that the level of experience within these firms – and thus expected growth and likelihood of exit – does not mirror that of established firms. In other words, using business registration as a measure of start-up year would impose uncertainty regarding job creation within different age groups.

We identify a total of 142,278 start-ups from 1994 to 2004. From this population, approximately only one in three has any employees (in addition to the founder) at any point and even fewer ever employ as many as one full-time equivalent. This reduces our population to 37,080 start-ups from 1994 to 2004. All the start-ups in our sample are registered in the Danish Entrepreneurship Database. Using the IDA database we run a series of additional controls to verify that these start-ups are new businesses in compliance with the above definition. This reduces the population further by approximately 7,500 start-ups. Finally we exclude founders younger than 18 or older than 65 years of age (this has only very little effect on the population size). The final population consists of 29,583 start-ups, including 6,645 spin-offs. Spin-offs are businesses founded by previous employees from incumbent firms in the same industry (same four-digit SIC code).

We cannot track individual positions but only make yearly observations of the employment level in each firm. The implication of this is that we are not able to capture whether a firm, within the same year, both creates and cuts one or more position (for example, expands its research department and outsource cleaning). Instead we observe the year-to-year net employment changes for each firm.[3] Thus, the disadvantage of this timeframe is that the actual job flow within our population is underestimated. If two employees are laid off in August and two employees are hired in October, then it is not revealed in the statistics. The advantage, on the other hand, is that an annual statement does not include every temporary and provisional change. We assume that annual counts will provide a more accurate picture of the more permanent job flow (Davis et al., 1997).

Job Creation

In order to confirm (or reject) Hypotheses 2 and 3, we need a detailed investigation of employment growth by spin-offs and other entrants. Following Davis and Haltiwanger (1992), we compute employment growth for a particular firm, j, as:

$$g_{j,t} = \frac{E_{j,t} - E_{j,t-1}}{X_{j,t}} \tag{10.1}$$

$$X_{j,t} = \frac{E_{j,t} + E_{j,t-1}}{2}. \tag{10.2}$$

The growth rate, $g_{j,t}$, is the difference between the number of employees in firm j at time t, $E_{j,t}$, and the number of employees the previous year, $E_{j,t-1}$, in proportion to the *average* number of employees within the two-year period, $X_{j,t}$. The advantage of using the average employment level, $X_{j,t}$, over the initial employment level, $E_{j,t-1}$, is that it allows for job creation and job destruction by entry and exit, respectively, and it is symmetric around zero for job creation and job destruction. Using $E_{j,t-1}$ instead would overestimate the growth rate for job creation ($g_{j,t} > 0$) and underestimate the growth rate in the case of job destruction (leading to a numerically smaller $g_{j,t}$) (ibid.). Equation (10.1) also takes into account the intuitive correlation between size and growth. We expect more small than large businesses to double employment within a year. A business with only one employee, which recruits additionally two employees, would have a growth rate of 200 percent using $E_{j,t-1}$ and just 100 percent using $X_{j,t}$ (equation (10.1)), whereas a business with an initial employment level of 50 employees and an equivalent increase in staff by two employees by comparison would have a growth rate of 4 and 3.92 percent, respectively.

To investigate Hypothesis 3 and evaluate the potential differences in economic contribution in terms of employment further, we are interested in the overall net job creation from the two categories of start-ups (net job creation is explained in equation (10.6)). The net job creation is divided into the two components, gross job creation (*JC*) and gross job destruction (*JD*). The gross job creation in subpopulation s at time t is the sum of employment increases in all firms which either start up or expand in the period between $t - 1$ and t:

$$JC_{Gross_{s,t}} = \sum_{g_{j,t}>0, j \in s} \frac{X_{j,t}}{X_{s,t}} \cdot g_{j,t} \qquad (10.3)$$

$$X_{s,t} = \sum_{j \in s} X_{j,t}. \qquad (10.4)$$

The employment growth for each firm, $g_{j,t}$, is weighted by the firm's size (the average number of employees, $X_{j,t}$) relatively to the size of the entire subpopulation, $X_{s,t}$, which is the overall employment within firms characterized by s, which represents different age ranges. Finally, the weighted growth rates are added up. Likewise, the gross job destruction at time t is the sum of all jobs that are lost among all firms, which either reduce their staff or exit over the period from $t - 1$ to t:

$$JD_{GROSS_{s,t}} = \sum_{g_{j,t}<0, j \in s} \frac{X_{j,t}}{X_{s,t}} \cdot |g_{j,t}|. \qquad (10.5)$$

Firms with an unchanged employment enter neither job creation nor job destruction. We point out that the job creation, $JC_{GROSS_{s,t}}$, also includes start-ups, in which case employment will increase from zero to a positive number, generating a net growth rate, $g_{j,t}$, of 200 percent. Similarly, job destruction, $JD_{GROSS_{s,t}}$, includes firms which exit, in which case employment declines from positive to zero generating a net growth rate of –200 percent. The overall employment net change is computed as the difference between employment at year t and $t - 1$:

$$JC_{NET_{s,t}} = JC_{GROSS,t} - JD_{GROSS,t}. \qquad (10.6)$$

Thus, the net growth rate is total employment growth[4] in percentages of the average employment level within firms characterized by s (for example, total employment growth of spin-offs aged one to three).

The overall reallocation accounts for the number of jobs which are created and destroyed, respectively:

$$Reallocation_{s,t} = JC_{GROSS,t} + JD_{GROSS,t}. \qquad (10.7)$$

Job reallocation at time t is the sum of the total job creation and job destruction which has taken place within the period $t - 1$ to t. Job creation captures the opportunities of employment within different locations, industries, age groups and so on, depending on the classification, s. An increase in job creation improves the chances of finding employment, all things being equal. Likewise, an increase in job destruction increases uncertainty among those already employed. These opposite trends are summarized in the job reallocation. Thus, job creation and job destruction are indicators of the heterogeneity of employment growth within different age groups or within spin-offs and other entrants, and we shall interpret a higher job reallocation as an indicator of greater heterogeneity within the group of firms in question. Additionally, we include the standard deviation of individual firm growth rates ($g_{j,t}$, equation (10.1)) as an indicator of heterogeneity in firm growth patterns.

4 RESULTS

Size Differences at Start-up

Table 10.1 presents the average number of full-time equivalents employed at spin-offs and other entrants each year from age zero to nine. Comparing the average start-up size, we find that the average spin-off employs 1.84 full-time equivalents at the time of entry, whereas other new firms, on average, only employ 1.64. This provides support to Hypothesis 1, that spin-offs are larger than other startups at the time of entry. This is also true for the two subsequent years. However, one problem arises, as firms can never be reduced to fewer than zero employees, whereas there is no upper limit. This should result in a right-skewed distribution where the mean employment level might give an inaccurate impression of the employment level in Danish startups.[5] For this reason, we further investigate the

Table 10.1   Average firm size for spin-offs and other entrants, classified by age

Age	Average size (95% confidence interval)			
	Others		Spin-offs	
0	1.64	(1.62–1.67)	1.83	(1.78–1.89)
1	2.59	(2.53–2.66)	2.88	(2.78–2.98)
2	3.18	(3.09–3.28)	3.47	(3.30–3.63)
3	3.70	(3.56–3.85)	3.90	(3.64–4.12)
4	4.15	(3.94–4.36)	4.21	(3.88–4.53)
5	4.66	(4.41–4.91)	4.59	(4.15–5.03)
6	5.29	(4.91–5.67)	5.13	(4.56–5.69)
7	5.53	(5.08–5.98)	5.82	(4.96–6.68)
8	5.70	(5.09–6.31)	6.31	(4.97–7.65)
9	6.52	(5.54–7.50)	6.52	(5.36–7.67)

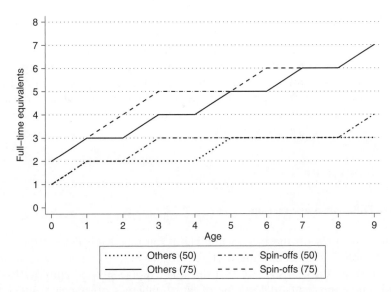

Figure 10.1   Median and 75th percentile of number of full-time equivalents of spin-offs and other entrants, classified by age

median and 75th percentile of employees at different ages for spin-offs and other start-ups, respectively. These are illustrated in Figure 10.1. We no longer find size differences between the typical spin-off and other entrants at start-up and the following year. Comparing Table 10.1 and Figure 10.1 we reconfirm that outliers increase the mean value, as the median at all ages is well below the mean. Investigating the median for different points in time we find that the typical spin-off is larger than the typical start-up in the third, fourth and ninth years. For the remaining years, the 50th percentiles are equal in the two groups. Looking at the 75th percentile we observe even more differences, as the 75th percentile for spin-offs exceeds that of other young firms in the second, third, fourth and sixth years. These results indicate that within some age ranges, the typical spin-off is larger than the typical start-up. This supports the argument that spin-offs might experience a higher likelihood of survival as they are less exposed to the liability of smallness.

Job Creation and Stability in Growth

Investigating Hypotheses 2 and 3, Table 10.3 shows the job creation and job destruction at younger firms from zero to nine years of age, categorized as spin-offs and others. As job creation for firms of the age range

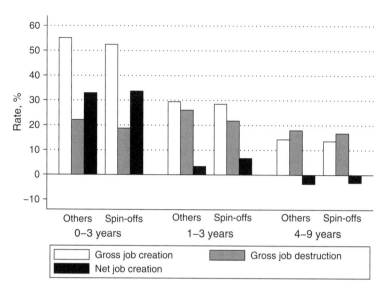

Figure 10.2   Job creation and job destruction of spin-offs and other entrants, classified by age

zero to three also includes jobs created by entry (as opposed to growth in established firms) we also include the age range one to three. Furthermore, the main results are summarized in Figure 10.2.

The subject of Hypothesis 2 is homogeneity and stability in growth. For all age ranges, we find that job creation as well as job destruction is higher for non-spin-offs, which results in similarly higher rates of reallocation for these firms, corresponding to a higher variation in job creation compared to spin-offs. Substantiated with a relatively lower standard deviation for spin-off growth rate we can confirm the notion of overall smaller variation in spin-off growth rates. This smaller variation is further illustrated by Figure 10.3, which shows a boxplot of employment growth for spin-offs and other entrants from age one to nine. Job creation by entry is excluded, as it is always a growth rate of 200 percent with zero standard deviation. Figure 10.3 shows that the observations of spin-off employment growth are more clustered around the mean (in both cases zero), indicating a smaller degree of dispersion in the distribution compared to other young firms.[6]

In Table 10.2, we group the firms according to their growth. We find that a relatively larger share of spin-offs have positive growth rates each year. This result applies to most age groups, supporting the argument that spin-offs are able to convert initial better endowments of human and social

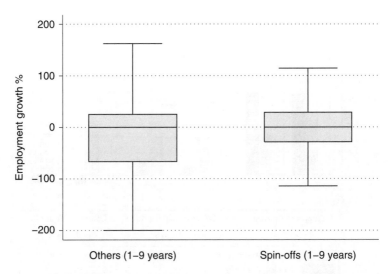

Figure 10.3   Boxplox of employment growth, classified as spin-offs and others

Table 10.2   Share of firms with positive, negative and zero growth, respectively, of spin-offs and other entrants, classified by age

Age	Growth rate < 0		Growth rate = 0		Growth rate > 0	
	Spin-offs (%)	Others (%)	Spin-offs (%)	Others (%)	Spin-offs (%)	Others (%)
0	0	0	0	0	100	100
1	25.93	32.81**	36.38	35.90	37.69	31.30**
2	29.50	33.25**	38.30	37.86	32.20	28.89**
3	29.09	32.23**	39.18	39.76	31.74	28.02**
4	29.36	32.17**	39.03	39.94	31.60	27.89**
5	31.28	31.92	41.36	41.69	27.36	26.40
6	27.28	31.84**	42.22	40.44	30.50	27.72*
7	31.40	30.90	41.79	42.54	26.81	26.56
8	30.31	29.12	41.12	44.21	28.57	26.67
9	26.43	26.17	42.68	46.05	30.89	27.78
10	25.79	28.54	42.63	44.32	31.58	27.15†
11	34.78	32.16	30.43	40.70	34.78	27.14*

Note: Significance levels: † 10%, * 5%, ** 1% indicates differences between spin-offs and other entrants using a chi-square test (not calculated for 'Growth rate = 0').

Table 10.3   Job creation and job destruction of spin-offs and other entrants, classified by age

	0–3 years:		1–3 years:		4–9 years:	
	Others	Spin-offs	Others	Spin-offs	Others	Spin-offs
JC (%)	55.11	52.46	29.42	28.49	14.17	13.48
JD (%)	22.12	18.72	26.04	21.77	17.53	16.56
Net growth rate (%)	32.99	33.73	3.38	6.72	−3.36	−3.07
Standard deviation	139.42	130.20	106.19	98.11	83.70	78.06
Reallocation rate	77.23	71.19	55.47	50.26	31.70	30.04

capital into larger and more rapidly growing businesses. Moreover, it is indicated that a relatively smaller share of spin-offs have negative growth rates during the first years. After the sixth year, however, we find no systematic pattern.

In Table 10.3, gross job creation and gross job destruction give us the net job creation, which was the focal point of Hypothesis 3. The net job creation for firms of age range zero to three is 33.73 percent and 32.99 percent for spin-offs and non-spin-offs, respectively. This results in only a small difference in net job creation of 0.74 percentage points. The difference in net job creation is more pronounced for firms of age range one to three and with a net rate of 6.72 percent, spin-offs' net job creation is almost twice the magnitude of that in other young firms. For firms older than four years, the difference in net job creation decreases once again. Net growth is negative for both spin-offs and others but it is less negative for spin-offs. For the three age groups investigated, we can confirm Hypothesis 3 that spin-offs have higher net job creation than other new firms. An obvious explanation of this result is a proportional higher gross job creation in spin-offs. Table 10.3, however, tells a different story. Within each age group, gross job creation is actually relatively smaller for spin-offs but at the same time, they also show a relatively smaller job destruction, which more than offsets this. Thus, despite a lower rate of gross job creation, spin-offs actually achieve a higher net job creation. Higher likelihood of survival for spin-offs drives this higher net growth (Figure 10.4), indicating that employment growth does not necessarily have to happen at the expense of job security.

The importance of survival to net job creation becomes more obvious when we investigate the job flow excluding job creation by entry. For both spin-offs and others the main job creation happens in firms within age group zero to three. This was expected as this category includes job creation by entry, which always equals a growth rate of 200 percent. The

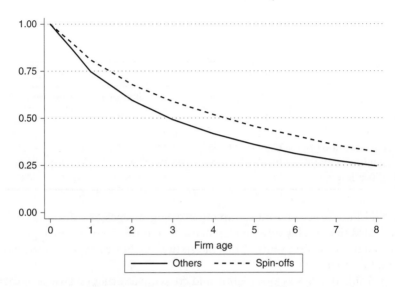

Figure 10.4   Kaplan–Meier survival rates for spin-offs and other entrants

importance of entry to employment growth is evident from the large difference in job creation between the two categories of younger firms (0–3 years
and 1–3 years). Because of their relatively low hazard rate and thereby
fewer exits, growth by entry accounts for a smaller share of employment
growth for spin-offs compared to other entrants. For that reason, the spin-
offs experience a relative smaller decrease in net job creation when moving
from age range zero to three and up. Similarly, exit has a significant effect
on job destruction in both categories. We find that the average number of
employees in spin-offs in the year of exit exceeds that of other young firms.
This makes exit more crucial to the destruction rate. However, because of
their smaller hazard of exit, job destruction by exit actually accounts for a
smaller share of spin-off job destruction.

Overall, Table 10.3 and the additional results give strong evidence to
support Hypothesis 3. This superiority in (net) job creation emphasizes
the spin-offs' great economic significance. But, exactly *how* important are
spin-offs to employment in Denmark? Moreover, what might the policy
implications of these results be? We shall explore these questions in the
next subsections.

Relative Importance of Spin-offs to Employment Growth in Denmark

High survival rates, increased stability and high net growth are indicators
that spin-offs are important to employment growth. In order to verify

this, we need to consider the spin-offs' effect on *total* employment in the economy. However, using the population of this chapter makes such an analysis very difficult and at best imprecise. Our population includes only Danish start-ups satisfying certain criteria. As previously discussed, we take a rather conservative approach when selecting our population in order to ensure that all firms are in fact real entrants and only true spin-offs are included. This is likely to underestimate the actual job creation, as we leave out some potential entrants. Therefore, proving the importance of new firms to job creation will not be the aim of this chapter. Instead, we shall continue to focus on spin-offs' performance relative to other entrants, when investigating their significance to employment. However, references to the literature on job creation by new and young firms are considered. As described above, the crucial role played by job creation in new and young firms to overall employment, is well established (Davis et al., 1997; Westergård-Nielsen and Ibsen, 2005; Dahl et al., 2009; Haltiwanger, 2009). We shall rely on these studies when we evaluate the importance of spin-offs to employment based on their relative performance. Investigating employment and job creation in Denmark, Westergård-Nielsen and Ibsen (2005) find that new establishments account for approximately one-third of job creation (excluding the public sector). This is supported by Dahl et al. (2009) who show that new and young firms (0–3 years) account for 61 percent of the gross job creation.[7] Moreover, 69.1 percent of the jobs created by new and young firms arise from entry, corresponding to 43 percent of total job creation. As stated above, we add to this literature, investigating the spin-offs' significance to employment compared to other entrants. We illustrate the impact of spin-offs' increased stability and high net growth on overall job creation by new and young firms.

For each category – gross job creation, gross job destruction and net job creation – we divide the total number of jobs created (or destroyed) into spin-offs and other entrants, respectively. Then the spin-offs' share of job creation is compared to their share of firms and share of employment. As previously discussed, we include two categories of young firms: 0–3 and 1–3 years, the latter being exclusive of entry. Results are shown in Table 10.4.

In their first years, spin-offs account for approximately 23 percent of the population but, as a result of their higher survival rates, this share increases with the age of the spin-offs. Similarly, the spin-offs' share of employment rises from 25.92 to 27.98 percent. As clarified in the following subsection, this is the result of both superior survival and net job creation. As expected, based on Table 10.3, the spin-offs' share of job destruction is less than their share of firms and share of employment (for example, spin-offs account for 26.41 percent of the employment, but only 22.79 percent

Table 10.4   Share of job creation and job destruction of spin-offs and other entrants, classified by age

	0–3 years:		1–3 years:		4–9 years:	
	Others	Spin-offs	Others	Spin-offs	Others	Spin-offs
Share of firms (%)	76.83	23.17	76.47	23.53	72.63	27.17
Share of employ- ment (%)	74.08	25.92	73.59	26.41	72.02	27.98
Share of JC (%)	75.08	24.92	74.52	25.48	73.10	26.90
Share of JD (%)	77.21	22.79	77.21	22.79	73.47	26.53
Share of net JC (%)	73.71	26.29	58.74	41.26	74.94*	25.06*

Note: *Share of negative value.

of the job destruction within firms of age group one to three). This applies to all age groups. On the other hand, spin-offs create fewer jobs (gross) than one would expect based on their employment share. Nevertheless, they still outperform others regarding net job creation.[8]

The object of Table 10.4 is to examine the magnitude of the spin-offs' job creation and their impact on total employment compared to other new and young firms. When investigating the spin-offs' significance to employment, our interest concentrates on *net* job creation. As already stated above, spin-offs have higher rates of net job creation and they are slightly larger at start-up. The effect is that spin-offs account for 26.3 percent of net job creation for age range zero to three, while only accounting for 23.2 percent of the population. Moreover, spin-offs are responsible for an impressive 41.3 percent of the net job creation within age range one to three, while only making up a quarter of the population. Recalling the magnitude of job creation in new and young firms, this strongly underlines the significance of spin-offs to overall employment and job creation.

Do Spin-offs Matter in the Long Run?

So far, we have investigated performance differences for different age groups separately. Generally, the tendency seems to be a superior performance by spin-offs in terms of job creation. However, what is the overall effect of increased survival, higher net job creation and greater average firm size in the long run? Overall, do spin-offs rather than non-spin-offs result in a marked improvement in employment or is the difference barely perceptible in the long run? We explore this question in the following, as our focus shifts from growth rates to absolute employment.

Table 10.5   Yearly average of total employment for spin-offs and other entrants, classified by age (year of startup: 1995–1998)

Age	Others			Spin-offs		
	Firms	Jobs	Share of total jobs (%)	Firms	Jobs	Share of total jobs (%)
0	4,970	8,446	75.59	1,397	2,728	24.41
1	3,662	9,207	73.27	1,146	3,359	26.73
2	2,886	8,967	71.41	988	3,590	28.59
3	2,409	8,636	70.69	859	3,580	29.31
4	2,028	8,324	71.04	746	3,393	28.96
5	1,731	7,823	71.19	651	3,166	28.81
6	1,484	7,302	69.80	580	3,159	30.20
7	1,305	6,875	68.72	518	3,129	31.28
8	1,167	6,651	69.31	467	2,945	30.69

Investigating long-term effects on job creation, the scale of data bounds us. Our population includes start-ups from 1995 to 2006. This implies that we can observe some entrants for 11 years and others for just one. This makes comparisons difficult and investigation of long-term effects is only possible for part of the population. As a solution to the latter, we include only start-ups for the period from 1995 to 1998 in the following analysis. Thus, we are able to track the total net job flow from four generations of entrants (1995–98) during their first eight years. The total net job flow is the total year-to-year development in employment by one generation. We measure it as the number of jobs created by entry, adding and subtracting the yearly job creation and job destruction, respectively, the latter including both negative growth and job destruction by exit. Table 10.5 shows the total net job flow provided by the four generations of entrants.

In total, 4,970 non-spin-offs and 1,397 spin-offs start up between 1995 and 1998. At the time of entry they employ 8,446 and 2,728 full-time equivalents, respectively.[9] In other words, in their first year, spin-offs account for 24.41 percent of a generation's employment. In the second year (corresponding to age one), the number of total employees rises for both spin-offs and other entrants, whereas the number of firms is reduced. The total number of employees depends on the effect from two opposing factors. The first factor (the negative effect) is the continuous reduction in the number of firms and the second factor (the positive effect) is a yearly increase in the average firm size (the number of employees). For both spin-offs and others, total employment peaks in the third year, after which

Table 10.6   Total employment per 100 start-ups (year of start-up: 1995–1998)

Year since start-up	Average (1995–1998)	Others only	Spin-offs only
0	175	170	195
1	197	185	240
2	197	180	257
3	192	174	256
4	184	167	243
5	173	157	227
6	164	147	226
7	157	138	224
8	151	134	211

total employment gradually declines as the negative effect of firm exit becomes stronger. After eight years, only 1,167 of the other start-ups still exist, whereas 467 of the spin-offs remain. The important conclusion of this analysis, however, is not the higher survival rate for spin-offs, which is already an established fact, but the spin-offs' relatively large share of a generation's employment. During the first nine years the spin-offs' share of total employment has increased from 24.41 percent in the year of start-up to 30.69 percent of the employment eight years later. Recall that both survival and average firm size have previously been illustrated for the entire population in Figure 10.4 and Table 10.1 We find a similar survival rate and average firm size for the 1995–1998 cohort. This suggests that the increase in share of employment is the result of not only a higher survival rate, but also a relatively larger firm size on average.

Finally, to make a clear illustration of what these differences in job creation mean to new firms' long-term contribution to employment, we estimate the total employment effect after eight years. Based on the data presented in Table 10.5, we find the expected returns on employment for spin-offs compared to other entrants. In other words, we obtain an estimate of spin-offs' relative contribution to absolute employment, all things considered. Results are presented in Table 10.6. In order to make a comparison of the two groups and expose the performance difference, we report the absolute job creation per 100 firms.

For each 100 non-spin-offs that enter the economy, there is an immediate contribution to employment of 170 full-time equivalents, corresponding to an average firm size of 1.7 employees. After eight years, however, this number diminishes to only 134 employees. In contrast, 100 spin-offs employ 195 employees in the year of start-up and eight years later this number increases to 211 as the positive effect from increases in firm size offsets the negative effect from exit. We find this to be the case only for spin-offs. Of course, it is not realistic (or desirable) that spin-offs would ever account for 100 percent of the start-up rate in Denmark. Furthermore, we must emphasize that the difference in return on employment applies only to this ratio of spin-offs and non-spin-offs, even though we have no reason to suspect that the results would change dramatically by an increase in the share of spin-offs. This being said, it is food for thought that while today's[10] ratio of spin-offs to other entrants gives an expected return on employment after eight years of 151 employees for each 100 new firms established, it is likely that there is a potentially much higher return if we were to increase the spin-offs to non-spin-offs ratio. Table 10.6 indicates that an increase in spin-offs' share of start-ups by 10 percentage points from approximately 22 percent today to 32 percent, would result in an increase in the return to employment of 0.077 employee per start-up or, in terms of Table 10.6, an increase from 151 to 159 employees after eight years for each 100 start-ups. In other words, spin-offs *do* matter to employment – especially in the long run.

5 CONCLUSION

If spin-offs survive longer, are a more homogeneous group and show greater stability in overall job creation compared to other entrants, it would imply a relatively higher job security for spin-off employees. Moreover, if spin-offs' job creation has no trade-off between growth on one hand and size and stability on the other, then spin-offs would be relatively more significant to job creation in the economy compared to other startups. This has been the basis of the present chapter, and if proven, it could make promotion of this type of entry an interesting target for industrial policy.

By detailed investigation of younger firms' growth patterns we are able to confirm that spin-offs are a more homogeneous group showing greater stability with potential to offer higher job security to their employees compared to other entrants. In comparison to other younger firms, they not only survive longer (which in itself indicates increased stability in growth patterns), but standard deviation in growth rates is smaller and they have lower reallocation of jobs, meaning that relatively fewer spin-offs cut jobs within the same period as many others create jobs. We argue that this increased stability, homogeneity and higher likelihood of survival is the result of spin-offs being relatively less vulnerable to the liability of newness.

Despite lower gross job creation, spin-offs actually achieve higher net job creation, as gross job destruction is also below that of other entrants. The difference in net job creation is most pronounced for firms within age range one to three. Resulting from fewer exits, spin-off job destruction is significantly lower for this age group, contributing to an increased net job creation over other entrants. Furthermore, this reveals that entry of new firms is responsible for the majority of job creation accounted for by other entrants. Comparing spin-offs' share of new firms to their share of net job creation, their superiority becomes obvious. While spin-offs within age range one to three make up only a quarter of the population, their net job creation accounts for more than 40 percent. These results illustrate how spin-offs play an important role in employment in Denmark. An examination of longer-term effects to the economy emphasizes this. The tendency seems to be that the gain of spin-off entry over other start-ups is greater the further ahead we look. Overall, the results suggest that changing the composition of today's start-ups, promoting spin-offs over other entrants, could lead to substantial gains in terms of job creation.

Finally, we do not claim that our study captures the complexity of the Danish economy. Our study does not consider the overall economic effects of spin-offs. As spin-offs are founded on intellectual capital accumulated at the parent firms, they could be potentially harmful to those firms. This means that there might be an equivalent (or larger) decrease in employment at the incumbent firms once parenting and now, perhaps, competing against these spin-offs. In other words, we cannot rule out the possibility that the overall economic effect of spin-offs is in fact negative, as the negative effect on parent firm performance might outweigh the advantages of spin-offs over other entrants. On the other hand, in opposition to this, our results might fuel the discussion on non-competition clauses as a potential barrier to promote this type of entry.

NOTES

*   This research is generously supported by the Rockwool Foundation. We are grateful for discussions with Guido Buenstorf and Kristian Nielsen and comments from participants at the DRUID Summer Conference 2010. The usual disclaimer applies.
1.   IDA is merged with the Entrepreneurship Database through a third dataset, which connects the firm-level data from the Entrepreneurship Database to the establishment-level data from IDA. This implies, however, that the period of investigation must be reduced to 1995–2006.
2.   One deviation from this definition is firms which are active in 2005 but not in 2006. Since 2006 is the last year of our observation period we cannot determine whether this is a single year without activity. In these cases we consider the firms closed. As is

clarified in the following section, this deviation does not affect the overall calculation of job creation and job destruction. It can only affect the ratio of job destruction due to exit.
3. All information is generated ultimo November each year.
4. The overall employment level net change in proportion to the *average* overall employment level in year *t* and *t* − 1.
5. When investigating the actual distributions our suspicion is confirmed and we find high positive values for skewness (not reported, but available upon request). Furthermore, we see a tendency toward lower skewness for spin-offs, indicating greater homogeneity in firm size.
6. As a consequence of the enormous number of observations, outliers are not depicted in Figure 10.4. In both cases the outliers, if included, would have appeared as straight lines going to 200 and − 200, respectively.
7. Dahl et al. (2009) investigate the yearly average job creation in Denmark from 1995 to 2006, excluding job creation in the public, primary and energy sectors.
8. Note that net job creation is negative for both categories of firms within age group four to nine, but smaller for spin-offs.
9. This is the sum of employees in start-ups in 1995, 1996, 1997 and 1998.
10. This refers to the average ratio from 1995 to 1998.

REFERENCES

Agarwal, R., R. Echambadi, A.M. Franco and M.B. Sarkar (2004), 'Knowledge transfer through inheritance: spin-out generation, development, and survival', *Academy of Management Journal*, **47**(4): 501–22.

Agarwal, R., M. Sarkar and R. Echambadi (2002), 'The conditioning effect of time on firm survival: an industry life cycle approach', *Academy of Management Journal*, **45**(5): 971–94.

Audretsch, D.B. and T. Mahmood (1995), 'New firm survival: new results using a hazard function', *Review of Economics and Statistics*, **77**(1): 97–103.

Baron, J.N. and M.T. Hannan (2002), 'Organizational blueprints for success in high-tech start-ups: lessons from the Stanford project on emerging companies', *California Management Review*, **44**(3): 8–36.

Brüderl, J., P. Preisendörfer and R. Ziegler (1992), 'Survival chances of newly founded business organizations', *American Sociological Review*, **57**: 227–42.

Brüderl, J. and R. Schüssler (1990), 'Organizational mortality: the liabilities of newness and adolescence', *Administrative Science Quarterly*, **35**(3): 530–47.

Burton, D.M., J.B. Sørensen and C.M. Beckman (2001), 'Coming from good stock: career histories and new venture formation', *Research in Sociology of Organizations*, (19): 229–62.

Chatterji, A.K. (2009), 'Spawned with a silver spoon? Entrepreneurial performance and innovation in the medical device industry', *Strategic Management Journal*, **30**: 185–206.

Dahl, M.S., P.G. Jensen and K. Nielsen (2009), *Jagten på fremtidens vækstvirksomheder*, Copenhagen: Jurist-og Økonomforbundets Forlag.

Dahl, M.S. and T. Reichstein (2007a), 'Are you experienced? Prior experience and the survival of new organizations', *Industry and Innovation*, **14**(5): 497–511.

Dahl, M.S. and T. Reichstein (2007b), 'Heritage and survival of spin-offs: quality of parents and parent-tenure of founders', Aalborg Universitet working paper.

Davis, S.J. and J.C. Haltiwanger (1992), 'Gross job creation, gross job destruction, and employment reallocation', *Quarterly Journal of Economics*, **107**(3): 819–63.

Davis, S.J., J.C. Haltiwanger and S. Schuh (1997), *Job Creation and Destruction*, 2nd edn, Cambridge, MA: MIT Press.

Dunne, T., M.J. Roberts and L. Samuelson (1989), 'The growth and failure of U.S. manufacturing plants', *Quarterly Journal of Economics*, **104**(4): 671–98.

Freeman, J., G.R. Carroll and M.T. Hannan (1983), 'The liability of newness: age dependence in organizational death rates', *American Sociological Review*, **48**(5): 692–710.

Gompers, P., J. Lerner and D. Scharfstein (2005), 'Entrepreneurial spawning: public corporations and the genesis of new ventures, 1986 to 1999', *Journal of Finance*, **60**(2): 577–614.

Hager, M.A., J. Galaskiewicz and J.A. Larson (2004), 'Structural embeddedness and the liability of newness among nonprofit organizations', *Public Management Review*, **6**(2): 159–88.

Haltiwanger, J.C. (2009), 'Entrepreneurship and job growth', in Z.J. Acs, D.B. Audretsch and R.J. Strom (eds), *Entrepreneurship, Growth and Public Policy*, Cambridge: Cambridge University Press, pp. 119–45.

Hannan, M.T. and G.R. Carroll (1992), *Dynamics of Organizational Populations: Density, Competition and Legitimation*, Oxford: Oxford University Press.

Helfat, C.E. and M.B. Lieberman (2002), 'The birth of capabilities: market entry and the importance of pre-history', *Industrial and Corporate Change*, **11**(4): 725–60.

Higgins, M.C. and R. Gulati (2003), 'Getting off to a good start: the effects of upper echelon affiliations on underwriter prestige', *Organization Science*, **14**(3): 244–63.

Jovanovic, B. (2004), 'The pre-producers', NBER working paper no. W10771, Cambridge, MA.

Klepper, S. (2001a), 'Employee startups in high-tech industries', *Industrial and Corporate Change*, **10**(3): 639–74.

Klepper, S. (2001b), 'Employee startups in high tech industries', *Industrial and Corporate Change*, **10**: 639–74.

Klepper, S. (2007), 'Disagreement, spinoffs, and the evolution of Detroit as the capital of the U.S. automobile industry', *Management Science*, **53**(4): 616–31.

Klepper, S. (2009), 'Spinoffs: a review and synthesis', *European Management Review*, **6**: 159–71.

Klepper, S. and S. Sleeper (2005), 'Entry by spinoffs', *Management Science*, **51**(8): 1291–306.

Nelson, R.R. and S.G. Winter (1982), *An Evolutionary Theory of Economic Change*, Cambridge, MA: Harvard University Press.

Phillips, D.J. (2002), 'A genealogical approach to organizational life chances: the parent–progeny transfer among Silicon Valley law firms, 1946–1996', *Administrative Science Quarterly*, **47**(3): 474–506.

Roberts, P.W., S. Klepper and S. Hayward (2011), 'Founder backgrounds and the evolution of firm size', *Industrial Corporate Change*, **20**(6): 1515–38.

Schein, E.H. (1983), 'The role of the founder in creating organizational culture', *Organizational Dynamics*, **12**(1): 13–28.

Shane, S. (2003), *A General Theory of Entrepreneurship: The Individual-Opportunity Nexus*, Cheltenham, UK and Northampton, MA, USA: Edward Elgar.

Stinchcombe, A.L. (1965), 'Social structure and organizations', in J.G. March (ed.), *Handbook of Organizations*, Chicago, IL: Rand-McNally, pp. 142–93.

Stuart, T.E., H. Hoang and R.C. Hybels (1999), 'Interorganizational endorsements and the performance of entrepreneurial ventures', *Administrative Science Quarterly*, **44**(2): 315–49.

Westergård-Nielsen, N. and R. Ibsen (2005), 'Jobskabelse', Center for Corporate Performance Århus Business School working paper.

11. *Innovationes Jenenses*: some insights into the making of a hidden star

Uwe Cantner*

1 JENA: GENERAL SETTING AND AMBITIONS

The years after the German reunification in 1989 have been characterized by a sharp difference in the economic performance of the two formerly separated parts of Germany, with the West flourishing and the East having to cope with outdated industrial structures which resulted in its lagging far behind in almost all sectors of the economy. An improving and prospering development in the East in the years following appeared to be slow and unevenly distributed. Exceptions were mainly related to some of the major cities or capitals of the East German Bundesländer, such as Dresden, Leipzig and Berlin on a first view, and Erfurt and Potsdam on a second. One notable and maybe surprising exception has been the city and region of Jena, neither one of the big cities nor a capital, but a city with a long tradition of optics and glass production, with one of the oldest universities in Germany, the Friedrich Schiller University (FSU). The way the Jena development after 1989 was received by the public has been reverential, astonishing and sometimes exaggerated. 'Boom town Jena' and the 'hidden star' on the one hand, and 'science city' and 'learning city', on the other, are examples from newspapers and TV programs. This all indicates an exceptional development within the East German states as well as within Germany as a whole – perhaps a kind of 'miracle'.

Jena's recent extraordinary development calls for closer scrutiny and analysis of the facts. This is the task in the next sections. We start with a brief characterization of Jena's development in Section 2, and then go into a deeper analysis of the core mechanisms of development.

2   JENA'S ECONOMIC AND INNOVATIVE PERFORMANCE AFTER 1989

Trying to make sense of the characterization of Jena as being a 'Boom town',[1] we can first look at economic prosperity, as measured by per capita GDP. Jena's economic development during the mid-1990s reflected the backwardness of other East German regions, as compared to the West. By the New Millennium, Jena managed to cut across the German average. Among the group of East German cities, such as Halle, Rostock and Dresden, Jena has been making good progress, coming quite close to Dresden. Within the state of Thuringia, Jena has always been among the top regions in per capita income, although always behind the capital, Erfurt; it was superseded by the Eisenach region (a location strong in automobile production) by 2002. Whether Jena's obviously remarkable progress deserves the characterization as a town among the stars in Germany is open to question. Characterizing it as a 'hidden star'[2] might be more appropriate, thus raising the question of hidden factors. Here other characterizations may be indicative, such as 'the spirit is in the air',[3] 'learning city',[4] or 'science city'.[5] They seem to suggest that the key lies in innovative potentials, the creation and usage of new knowledge, and an exceptional-spirit with regard to performance.

Looking at these dimensions of innovative performance, we distinguish the historical heritage and the concurrent innovative context in Jena. With respect to the former, Jena has quite a tradition in innovative activities above the normal. Carl Zeiss, Ernst Abbe and Otto Schott were the initiators of an innovation-oriented cooperation between two large manufacturing firms (Zeiss optics and Schott glass) and the university (Ernst Abbe, and Matthias-Jacob von Schleiden) (from 1846 to 1900). This cooperation had led to one of the most successful optical firms (Zeiss) and one of the most successful glass producers (Schott) in the world. After the Second World War, these firms were split up into parts operating in the Federal Republic of Germany – Zeiss Oberkochen and Schott Mainz – and, in the German Democratic Republic, those that had been integrated into a large business trust, the Zeiss Kombinat, located in Jena. The economic success of Zeiss Oberkochen and Schott Mainz was prodigious and pushed the two towards the frontier in the optics and glass industries. The Zeiss Kombinat was technologically successful even if for the political reason that not all potentials could be exploited – in today's terms, 'intrapreneurship' combined with a politically guided internal selection. After the reunification, the Zeiss Kombinat was split up into a number of large and even more small and medium-sized firms. Afterwards, the two Zeiss firms as well as the two Schott firms merged again, with Zeiss Oberkochen/

Schott Mainz taking the lead and Carl Zeiss GmbH and Schott Jenaer Glas GmbH enjoying some, although not total, independence. Today these two firms continue to influence the economic scene in Jena and have a considerable impact.

The second dimension on innovation is to be seen as a continuation of the historical process described above, and looks at the innovative activities going on in Jena since the reunification. First, we look at the patents per 100,000 inhabitants and compare Jena with other German regions. Figure 11.1 plots these numbers, where the darker the region, the higher the patent output (per 100,000 inhabitants). Quite obviously, Jena stands out with respect to both East and West German regions. With regard to the former, only Dresden comes somewhat close, and in the latter, Jena performs very similarly to regions such as Stuttgart, Mannheim, Erlangen and Munich. Hence, the innovative potential of Jena is quite outstanding. Refining the analysis somewhat, we find that, with regard to cooperative patents (that is, patents with more than one applicant), Jena is above average; in cooperative patents with research institutes, far above average; and in cooperative patents with partners from the same region, far above average. In Cantner and Meder (2008), we analyzed the determinants of cooperative patenting by distinguishing between an effect based on a region's industry composition and an effect indicating some purely regional factors. For Jena, we find this regional factor to be exceptionally high and persistent over time. Explaining this regional factor, the coherence of the regional knowledge base shows a significant inverted-U shaped influence. From these results, we conclude that in searching for factors that make Jena unique, one has to address issues such as cooperative invention/innovation and the coherence of the knowledge base. Other factors, such as a region-specific spirit or attitude, may also deserve attention, as will briefly be addressed in the conclusion.

An analysis of these factors will be undertaken in the next sections at the firm or sector level. In order to embed the results into Jena's economic development, a few remarks on the sectoral- and firm-level-related changes in Jena since 1989 are appropriate. The German reunification in 1989 provided a major structural change in Jena's industry. Following the domination of the multi-technology Zeiss Kombinat during the GDR period, in the early 1990s its breakup created a few larger and a number of smaller units, with technological restructuring around some highly valued core technologies such as optics. These changes were not always easy to make, but they had all the features of creative destruction – unemployment, income decline, frustration, social problems, and so forth. Nevertheless, on a broad scale, this restructuring was accomplished by former Zeiss Kombinat employees who had to be laid off but were provided with some

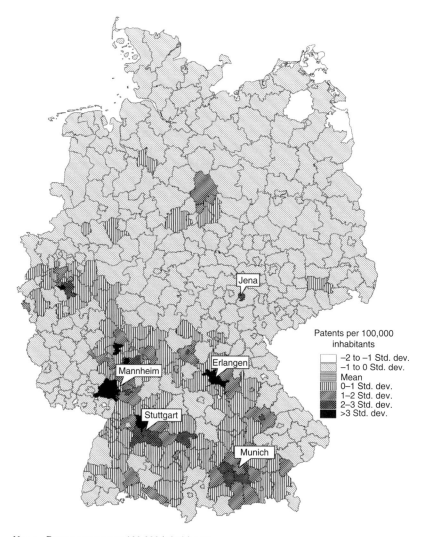

Note: Patent output per 100,000 inhabitants.

Source: Cantner and Graf (2003).

Figure 11.1   Regional patent output

seed capital for founding their own businesses, partly monetary compensation and partly remuneration in terms of machines and factory space.
This led to a larger number of newly established firms, which we might
call 'enforced spin-offs', as the founders were former employees. Since

then, this basic spin-off structure of the Jena economy has been in the process of development, with some exits and mergers, on the one hand, and new-firm formation, on the other. With respect to firm formation, it is interesting that new firms entering from outside of Jena are quite rare. The majority of new firms have been spin-offs (from established firms and from academia) (Cantner et al., 2003), as well as start-ups by local founders.

This brief characterization of the Jena microlevel development in the aftermath of 1989 indicates that Jena's success story is based on a breeding mechanism, relying more (if not nearly entirely) on Jena-related or -specific factors than on external forces or investments – founding of firms mainly from within, innovative activities very much cooperative and oriented within the Jena system. In the sections to follow, we shall explore these issues more deeply by focusing on innovation activities in Jena and the related network of cooperating inventors/innovators. We look at the development of this network over time (Section 3), the driving mechanisms behind it (Section 4), and some corroborating evidence with respect to sustaining institutions and performance (Section 5). Section 6 concludes briefly and puts together the Jena dimension, the innovative heritage of the Zeiss/Schott initiatives, and the established innovative power after the reunification.

3   GENERAL NETWORK DYNAMICS: POTENTIALS, REALIZATIONS AND COMPLEMENTARITIES[6]

The strength of an innovator network is basically determined by (i) the potentials for (potential) network actors to interact and to exchange knowledge, and (ii) the degree to which these potentials are exploited. First, the potentials for knowledge exchange are related to the technological overlap between partners. We define this overlap as the number of technological classes in which two actors both hold patents. These classes are defined by the International Patent Classification (IPC) codes stated on the actors' patents, which we used for a classification distinguishing between 30 technological classes.[7]

Figure 11.2 visualizes the Jena network of potential cooperations for two periods, p1 (1995–97) and p2 (1998–2001). Here, the network nodes are innovators, and edges result from an overlap in at least two technologies. At the center of these networks are the larger innovators – with Jenapharm, a large specialized pharmaceutical firm, being the only exception. Carl Zeiss Jena and Jenoptik are the successors of the former Zeiss Kombinat at the core of both networks, both with a tendency to move toward the periphery of the network from p1 to p2 as they follow a

(a) Period p1   (b) Period p2

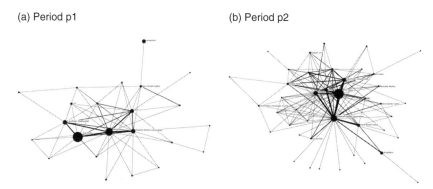

Note: Nodes are innovators (some with a name label) and lines connecting indicate overlapping technology classes according to the IPC.

Figure 11.2   Cooperation potentials

Table 11.1   Descriptive statistics of the networks of technological overlap

	p1	p2
Number of actors	139	189
Number of components	4	4
Size of largest component	135	179
Number of isolates	2	1
Density	0.15	0.17
Mean degree[a]	19.20	28.70
Network centralization[a]	0.60	0.72
Overall graph clustering coefficient	1.23	1.20

Note: [a] Networks have been dichotomized.

strategy of higher specialization. Another core actor is the FSU, moving from p1 to p2 towards the center of the network. On more general terms, we find an increasing cohesion, which is interpreted as a stronger focus on core competencies, where the activities of the central actors become increasingly important for the whole network. This is evidenced by several network statistics summarized in Table 11.1, which are based on a network which is dichotomized and where an overlap in one technology class establishes a link.

The number of potential partners increases over time from 139 to 189. We observe four components, that is, disconnected parts of the network, in each period, and one or two isolated actors, respectively. In both periods, about 95 percent of the actors are part of the largest component. Over time, the network has become increasingly connected, as the increase in the density (from 0.15 to 0.17) and the mean degree (from 19.2 to 28.7) indicate.[8] Looking at the degree of centralization of the network, we find an increase (from 0.60 to 0.72), which means that peripheral actors are more strongly connected to actors in the center and/or less connected to other peripheral actors.[9] Another structural network measure, the overall clustering coefficient,[10] decreases slightly (from 1.23 in p1 to 1.20 in p2), indicating a higher connectedness among all actors.

Analyzing the exploitation of the potentials to cooperate, we look again at the patents of the actors in the Jena innovation system and again we distinguish the two subperiods, 1995–97 and 1999–2001. Actors (innovators) are connected to each other via the scientists and engineers involved in the creation of the knowledge that led to this patent (inventors). We distinguish two different possibilities as to how this relationship is established. The first is by direct cooperation, whereby the connected actors rely on the same inventors in a common project – all the inventors (stated in the patent) are then a 'common event' of all the innovators. These cases are easily identified by patents with more than one applicant (co-application). We assume that these actors have been cooperating and, consequently, we call the resulting network 'cooperation' (*co*). The other possibility is less direct. If an inventor is mentioned on patents applied for by different, not co-applying, innovators we end up with a link between those innovators that is referred to as 'scientist mobility' (*sm*). Aggregating the two types of relationships leads to the network 'personal relationships' (*pr*).

Figure 11.3 visualizes the two different networks together (black the network based on cooperation, and grey the network based on scientist mobility) and separately for the two subperiods: (a) for p1 and (b) for p2. Besides the obvious increase in size of the total network, both types of network are characterized by a different development of the network structure. In Table 11.2, we report the statistics for the networks of cooperation (*co^t*), scientist mobility (*sm^t*), and personal relationships (*pr^t*).

The analysis of components shows a trend toward less fragmentation. The share of innovators that are part of the largest component of the cooperation network increases from 9 to 32 percent, and the share of innovators connected by scientist mobility in the largest component increases from 25 to 32 percent. If we abstract from the type of interaction, the share of innovators that is part of the largest component of the network increases from 42 to 50 percent. The share of isolates, however, remains roughly constant in all three types of network. The density of the cooperation network decreases (from 0.029 to 0.027), while it remains constant for the scientist mobility network (0.010). The overall effect is dominated by

(a) Period p1   (b) Period p2

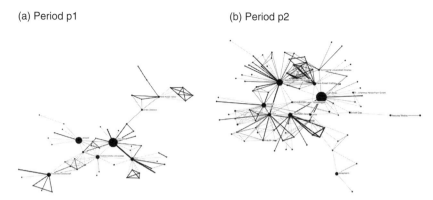

Note: Nodes are innovators (some with a name label) and lines connecting them indicate co-patenting (black line) or having an inventor in common (grey line).

Figure 11.3   Realized cooperations

Table 11.2   Descriptive statistics of the interpersonal networks

	pr		*co*		*sm*	
	p1	p2	p1	p2	p1	p2
Number of actors	139	189	139	189	139	189
Share of actors in the largest component	0.420	0.500	0.090	0.320	0.250	0.320
Share of isolates	0.300	0.300	0.510	0.580	0.550	0.550
Density	0.040	0.037	0.029	0.027	0.010	0.010
Mean degree[a]	2.200	2.800	1.100	1.500	1.100	1.300
Network centralization[a]	0.109	0.184	0.051	0.137	0.102	0.057
Overall graph clustering coefficient	2.452	2.191	3.634	2.833	0.856	0.648

Note: [a] Networks have been dichotomized.

the effects of cooperation, which leads to a network of personal relationships less dense in the second period (from 0.040 to 0.037). Taking control of the size of the actors, we calculate the mean degree. While, in the first period, each actor had an average of 2.2 connections to other actors, in the second period we observe an average of 2.8 connections via personal relationships. The overall network becomes more centralized (from 0.109 to 0.184), which is due to the development in formal cooperation (from 0.051 to 0.137), whereas centralization decreases in the scientist mobility network (from 0.102 to 0.057). Finally, all networks show a tendency towards less clustering – the overall graph clustering coefficient decreases for the overall network (from 2.452 to 2.191), for the formal cooperation network (from 3.634 to 2.833), and for the mobility network (from 0.856 to 0.648). Interpreting these observations, it would seem that the large, core actors within the network increasingly focus on formal cooperation, while the smaller, surrounding or peripheral actors rather have contacts through informal, personal relations.

This general tendency of the Jena innovation system to become less fragmented, and more centralized, connected and clustered can be related to the analysis focusing on the relationship between the degree of specialization of a system's knowledge base and its degree of fragmentation.[11] Comparing the Jena system with those of another German region, Northern Hesse, and the region around Sophia Antipolis, Alpes Maritim, suggests that Jena, as a region that is relatively specialized in a number of broad technology fields, exhibits the least-fragmented network structure. By contrast, the example of Northern Hesse suggests that a very heterogeneous knowledge base is associated with a very fragmented regional network. The positive impact of a common technological knowledge base on the cooperation propensity is in line with earlier studies on the interorganizational (for example, Mowery et al., 1998; Cantner and Meder, 2007) as well as on the aggregate (Fritsch and Franke, 2004) regional levels.

4   PROCESSES OF NETWORK DEVELOPMENT

The development of the Jena innovator network is characterized by an increase in the number of actors, a higher degree of relatedness and centralization, as well as a lower level of clustering. In the following, we look at some basic mechanisms on the actor level which may be causal for these patterns. For this, we distinguish actors that are permanently in the network from those that enter in the second period and those that exited after the first period; furthermore, we distinguish actors located in Jena from those located elsewhere. Accordingly, we look at the persistence of cooperative activities, the entry–exit dynamics and the relationships with Jena's external actors.

Persistence of Cooperation[12]

We first turn to the question whether certain linkages between the actors in one period will lead to stronger interactions in the following period. More specifically: how can we explain the linkages between innovators in Jena that arise through co-applications during one period by various linkages between these actors in a preceding period?

Our analysis of partner selection is pursued within a knowledge-based approach. The basic criterion for selecting a cooperation partner is its capability to increase the probability for the success of a common research project. In a knowledge-based approach for a searching firm this implies that the technological knowledge of a partner has to be complementary to its own knowledge. In addition to complementarity and in order to facilitate knowledge exchange and joint development, the potential cooperation partners require some level of technological 'overlap' (Cantwell and Barrera, 1998; Mowery et al., 1998; Cantner and Graf, 2004). The identification of appropriate partners and the matching of competences and capabilities is by no means only a marginal problem. Powell et al. (1996, p. 117) mention 'each partner's size and position in the "value chain," the level of sophistication, resource constraints, and prior experiences with alliances' as factors influencing the partnering decision. Gulati (1998) stresses the relevance of firms' embeddedness in social networks in shaping their collaborative actions and choice of partners. Hence different types of actor as well as cooperation experience serve as important determinants. In the following, we shall examine the role of existing relations between actors as an explanation of future cooperative activities.

The econometric approach we pursue is multiple regression analysis with dyadic data (for example, Krackhardt, 1988).[13] The dependent variable is the number of interpersonal linkages between innovators i and j which result from a formal cooperation of both in the second period. As independent variables, we use cooperation, scientist mobility, and technological overlap from the first period, scientist mobility from the second period, as well as dummy variables for linkages between public funded research institutes (public linkages) and private organizations (private linkages).

We estimated three models (I–III); the results are reported in Table 11.3. In the first model, we include only the explanatory variables from the first period (Cooperation 95–97, Scientist mobility 95–97, Tech. overlap 95–97), thereby assuming that long-term relations are relevant for cooperative linkages. In the second regression, we additionally control for scientists changing their job (Scientist mobility 99–01) in the same period as the dependent variable, cooperations (Cooperations 99–01). In the third model, we additionally account for an inverted-U relationship in the technological overlap (Tech. overlap 95–97) by including a respective squared term (Tech. overlap 95–97-squared). In all three models, we control for only public and for only private linkages.

Table 11.3   Network regression

Dep.var. co99–01	I	II	III
(Intercept)	0.010**	0.010**	0.051
Cooperation 95–97	−0.103***	−0.099***	−0.082***
Scientist mobility 95–97	−0.131***	−0.076	−0.136**
Scientist mobility 99–01		0.404***	0.410***
Tech. overlap 95–97	0.291***	0.242***	0.075*
Tech. overlap 95–97-squared			0.038**
Public linkages	0.337**	0.250*	0.277*
Private linkages	−0.093	−0.100	−0.109
Res. std err.	0.866	0.851	0.847
Mult. R^2 (adj.)	0.111	0.142	0.153
F-statistic (p-value)	12.260	13.530	12.590
Obs. (nodes)	496 (32)	496 (32)	496 (32)

Note: * Significance levels ≤ 0.01 (according to QAP); ** Significance levels ≤ 0.05 (according to QAP); *** Significance levels ≤ 0.1(according to QAP). Significance is the minimum of $Pr(\geq\beta)$ (which is documented) and $Pr(<\beta)$; number of permutations: 1,000. The null hypothesis is QAP; that is, the probability of observing a coefficient of this magnitude or larger under the assumption of random assignment of actors to nodes.

With respect to the explanatory power of our models, we observe a slight increase in the R^2 when controlling for short-term mobility. The variance in the data, explained by our model, increases from about 0.11 to 0.15, which is rather small but seems acceptable given the restrictions of the data (see Krackhardt, 1987). The estimated coefficient for cooperations in the first period (co95–97) is negative in all three models and significantly different from what we should expect under the random assignment hypothesis. This implies no persistency in innovation cooperation, but a switch in partners.

The influence of personal linkages through scientist mobility on the network of cooperations seems to depend on the time between the change of jobs and the cooperation. The respective coefficients in the first period (Scientist mobility 95–97) are negative in all three regressions.[14] This negative influence on the network of cooperations remains when we control for the mobility of scientists in the same period as the observed cooperations (Scientist mobility 99–01 in models II and III). In contrast to long-term personal relations through mobility, Scientist mobility 99–01 has a strong and significant positive influence in our models. This result speaks strongly in favor of the prominent role of short-term interpersonal linkages in shaping networks of cooperation or local innovation systems as a whole.

The results (in all three models) concerning technological overlap in the first period (Tech. overlap 95–97) come as no surprise and affirm our predictions that actors have to share a common knowledge base. The inclusion of a squared term (Tech. overlap 95–97-squared in model III) does not lead to a large increase in explanatory power. The quadratic term is positive but rather small, which is different from that found in previous studies: Mowery et al. (1998), for example, find an inverted-U relationship between technological overlap and the propensity to cooperate. The reason for these differing findings should lie in the specificities of our data. Our sample includes not only private firms but also universities and public research institutes. For cooperation between private and public actors, a strong technological closeness should not be problematic, as the partners do not compete on the market for goods. Finally, in all three models, collaborative agreements between two public organizations (public linkages) or between a public and a private partner (intercept) are more likely than between two private ones (private linkages).

Summarizing our results, we find that a shared knowledge base is an important prerequisite for cooperation in R&D. A network of technological overlap can therefore be viewed as the potential for cooperation and knowledge exchange. In contrast to previous studies (Gulati, 1995a,b), we do not observe persistent linkages through cooperation, meaning that actors do not tend to cooperate with previous partners. The importance of trust in the formation of cooperation is not neglected but shows up in our estimates for scientist mobility. As workers or scientists change their job, they carry knowledge about competencies and the trustworthiness of previous colleagues or the previous employer.

The results of easy mobility of inventors as well as of the non-persistence of bilateral cooperative arrangements fit quite well to the Jena-specific structural transition of the firm population after 1989, with enforced spin-off firms at the core. The founders, managers and employees of these firms often knew each other from former times at the Zeiss Kombinat. This enabled trustful relationships to develop which still allow for an uncomplicated access to one another and to vital networking activities.

Entry–Exit Dynamics

A further issue related to the increasing connectedness of the Jena innovator network is with actors entering and leaving the system. We can characterize the innovators according to their innovator status, that is, entry, exit, and permanent. If network positions really matter for the performance of single actors, one would suspect that innovators who exit the system have to do this because of a weak position – in the sense of being less connected or in the periphery (Powell et al., 1999). For the entering firms, we should observe a higher number of connections to the core of the existing network. The analysis is performed for the networks of personal relations.[15]

To analyze the effects of entry and exit, we look at the relative positions of different groups – entrants, exiters, and incumbents – in the networks of cooperation and scientist mobility. We expect entrants to be closer to the core (incumbents) than exiters. For the theoretical argument, we distinguish between local entrants and entrants who relocate. With regard to the former, we know from a related study (Cantner et al., 2003) that a large number of local high-tech firms in Jena are spin-offs or academic start-ups. Those new ventures are characterized by the previous employment of their founders in incumbent firms or research institutes. If a scientist has worked and patented for members of the network and then starts his/her own firm with a patented innovation, it will show up as scientist mobility in our data. Such an actor gained insight into the network of innovators during previous employment and might therefore make use of this type of know-who to form cooperations. Firms relocating to Jena might have learned about the location via previous contacts with network members, for example, through cooperation. Involvement in these networks of personal relationships provides access to knowledge external to the firm. With respect to the exiters, those firms may lack such contacts and are therefore cut off from important knowledge channels. We expect them to be less innovative and to consequently exit from the network. However, an opposing argument could be that, since exiting innovators are presumably older than the entering innovators, they had more time to establish linkages through cooperation and scientist mobility.

Calculating mean degrees for the different groups mentioned above – entry, exit, and permanent – we distinguish between relations within the group and between the groups. The resulting values and tests for the significance of differences between the mean degrees are given in Tables 11.4 and 11.5.[16]

Our first observation regards the comparison of the connectedness between exiting and entering innovators within their respective group (column 1 in each table). The exiting innovators have significantly ($p = 0.066$) more linkages through cooperation than the entering group (3.084 versus 2.242) and slightly, but not significantly, more linkages through scientist mobility (0.561 versus 0.497). While this can be explained by the age of the exiting innovators, the more interesting result regards the connections of these two groups with the permanent innovators. Compared to the exiting innovators, the entering innovators cooperate significantly

Table 11.4   Cooperation: mean degree (within and between blocks)

	Within	Between	Between	Within
1995–1997	Exit	Exit and permanent	Permanent and exit	Permanent
N	107	107	32	32
Mean degree	3.084	0.710	2.375	2.563
S.D.	(5.207)	(1.873)	(5.375)	(5.346)
1999–2001	Entry	Entry and permanent	Permanent and entry	Permanent
N	157	157	32	32
Mean degree	2.242	1.516	7.438	3.938
S.D.	(4.424)	(2.623)	(17.005)	(6.710)
Significance of difference between mean degrees				
	Mann–Whitney		Wilcoxon rank sum test	
W	9191.5	7111	34.5	49
p-value	0.066	0.003	0.136	0.1

Note: One-sided tests are performed with H_0 as no difference between samples and H_1 in the direction of the observed differences.

($p = 0.003$) more with the permanent ones (1.516 versus 0.710) and also have more linkages through scientist mobility (0.637 versus 0.514), although not to a significant degree. A glance at Figure 11.3 shows that these linkages with permanent innovators are mostly with few large actors in the center of the network, which explains the large standard deviation of the mean degree between permanent and entering innovators (third column in Table 11.4). The permanent innovators themselves (fourth column in Tables 11.4 and 11.5) show a significant increase in linkages through cooperation (from 2.563 to 3.938) and especially in scientist mobility (from 0.938 to 2.500).

Overall, innovative entrants in Jena seem to be better integrated into the network of personal relations than actors who, for whatever reasons, stopped innovating. The finding on exiters is consistent with our above reasoning and the results of Powell et al. (1999) that the network position has an important influence on firm performance. Taking into account the spin-off dynamics in Jena (enforced in the early 1990s and then marked by a high share of academic spin-offs) the closeness of entrants to incumbents does not come as a surprise. The observations regarding the connectedness of entrants and exiters within their group do not contradict our argument. Actors that enter such a network are certainly more aware of incumbents than actors entering during the same period.

Table 11.5   Scientist mobility: mean degree (within and between blocks)

	Within	Between	Between	Within
1995–1997	Exit	Exit and permanent	Permanent and exit	Permanent
N	107	107	32	32
Mean degree	0.561	0.514	1.719	0.938
S.D.	(1.361)	(0.883)	(2.976)	(1.900)
1999–2001	Entry	Entry and permanent	Permanent and entry	Permanent
N	157	157	32	32
Mean degree	0.497	0.637	3.125	2.500
S.D.	(0.965)	(1.415)	(4.030)	(2.700)

Significance of difference between mean degrees			
	Mann–Whitney		Wilcoxon rank sum test	
W	8166.5	8613	66.5	20
p-value	0.695	0.668	0.008	0.000

Note: One-sided tests are performed with H_0 as no difference between samples and H_1 in the direction of the observed differences.

Development of External Relations[17]

Regarding the increasing connectedness of the Jena innovator network, one may ask whether this is due to an increase of internal relationships or whether more external partners are responsible for this development. In the former case, this could be an indication of the danger of getting into a technological lock-in situation, while in the latter case, external pipelines may protect against such an unfortunate situation (see Bathelt et al., 2004). The general tendency of external relations of the Jena network of innovators shows a slight increase in external collaborators, from about 54 percent in p1 to 58 percent in p2, suggesting that knowledge exchange with external partners tends to intensify over time. For a more fine-grained analysis of these external relations, we distinguish relations between only internal actors (*internal*), on the one hand, and between an internal and an external partner (*external*), on the other. Furthermore, we look specifically at the two different types of relations, *co* and *sm*, and at different types of actors, private versus public and persistent versus non-persistent. In general, the number of internal and external relations rose from p1 to p2, independently of whether we look at the different networks or the different

Table 11.6   Internal and external relations in the network

	co network		sm network	
	p1	p2	p1	p2
All	1.682	1.563	2.000	1.605
Private	1.649	1.593	2.091	1.741
Public	1.857	1.524	1.769	1.273
Non-persistent	1.929	2.140	1.958	2.367
Persistent	1.250	0.935	2.045	1.109

actor groups. Table 11.6 shows some descriptive statistics of respective developments from p1 to p2, looking at the *external/internal* ratio.

For the *co* network, we find a decrease in the *external/internal*, ratio indicating an increasing inward orientation in relative terms (from 1,682 to 1,563). The same holds true for the *sm* network (from 2,000 to 1,605). In view of these results, a distinction between private and public actors delivers an increasing inward orientation (the *external/internal* share always decreases) for both. However, comparing the decline for public actors in the *co* network (*sm* network) – from 1.857 to 1.524 (from 1.769 to 1.273) for the public actors to the decline from 1.649 to 1.593 (from 2.091 to 1.741) for the private actors – shows that the inward orientation is more pronounced for the public actors.

If we alternatively distinguish between persistent innovators and those that exit or enter (non-persistent), we find that, for these groups, the development goes in different directions. For non-persistent actors, we find an increasing outward orientation regardless of the type of relation (from 1.929 to 2.140 in the *co* network and from 1.958 to 2.367 in the *sm* network), which is mainly driven by the entrants' higher outward orientation compared to actors exiting the network. The persistent innovators, on the other hand, increasingly focus on internal relations, which is especially true for linkages through mobility. One of the reasons for this development might be initiatives to foster academic start-ups and a culture of entrepreneurship in general during that period.

Summarizing these results, we find that even though the share of external actors in the Jena network of innovators increased slightly over time, linkages within the region enlarged their share, especially when public actors are concerned. The more internal orientation is also emphasized by persistent actors, while for non-persistent actors we find that entrants are more outward oriented than the exiting innovators. The antenna function that persistent and central actors – especially universities – are assumed to fulfill seemingly shows diminishing importance, at least in relative terms.

Also, this development of external relations seems to be consistent with the structural dynamics of the firm population in Jena being quite reliant on internally oriented factors and mechanisms.

5   SOME CORROBORATING EVIDENCE: SUSTAINING INSTITUTIONS AND PERFORMANCE

The results obtained so far from the analysis of the Jena innovator network find some corroboration by further comparative analyses of Jena firms with respect to the role of intermediaries/political actors and the role of the cooperative embeddedness in the value chain (see Cantner et al., 2010a, 2011). Moreover, an analysis of the innovative performance of Jena firms has been carried out (see Cantner et al., 2010a). These studies have been performed on data gathered within a research project comparing the innovation systems of Jena with those of Sophia Antipolis/Alpes Côte Azur (France) and of Kassel/Northern Hesse (Germany).

Looking first at the relationship between the external relationships of Jena firms and their ability to perform innovative activities successfully in Cantner et al. (ibid.), we focus on a firm's innovation cooperation network (number of research relations), on relation to research centers (binary, with 1 for having that kind of relationship), and social

Table 11.7   Cooperation network and a firm's innovative capacity

Dep. variable	Firm's innovative capacity
Intercept	-0.357
Firm's innovative cooperation network	$0.200***$
(Firm's innovative cooperation network)^2	$-0.007***$
Firm's innovative cooperation network $\times$ optic	$-0.109***$
Relationships with research centers	$0.100**$
Social relationships	0.029
Share of R&D staff	$0.020***$
Future development	$0.243***$
Number of employees	0.096
Optic instruments sector	-0.266
Service sector	-0.023
Pseudo R^2	0.346
Observations	153

Note: ** ≤ 0.05 significance; *** ≤ 0.1 significance.

relationships (intensity of social relationships with regional stakeholders), as well as two transformations of the extent of the network of co-innovators, the squared number of relations and the interaction with the optics sector.

As shown in Table 11.7, we first find strong statistical evidence supporting both the association between the innovative capacity of firms and the number of co-innovators and the inverted U-shaped relation. First, the regression coefficient related to a firm's innovative cooperation network is statistically significant at the 1 percent level, showing that pursuing innovation with partners increases innovative performance, *ceteris paribus.* Second, the regression coefficient of the squared term is also significant at the 1 percent level and is negative, meaning that the rate of positive returns deriving from extending the number of co-innovators decreases with a firm network's growth. Indeed, first, due to the increase in information and knowledge sources, firms face greater costs of selection; and second, the degree of novelty of the exchanged information tends to decrease with an increase in a firm's innovative cooperation network, and, consequently, the effect on innovative capacity follows the same trend.

Taking into account that Jena is specialized in optics, the interaction term between a firm's innovative cooperation network and the dummy related to the optics sector is unexpectedly significantly negative. This indicates that the positive effects of innovating by interacting with regional partners, albeit not strongly significant, are diminished in the case of the optics sector. A reinforcement of the positive relation between cooperating and innovative capacity is found with respect to the contact intensity with research centers. However, a more general integration into the regional community is not significantly related to innovative capacity. With respect to the control variables, the share of R&D employees as well as a firm's expected gains are positively related to the innovative capacity. The firm-size variable and the sector dummies do not show significant coefficients. This can be justified by the fact that the sample under analysis is already limited to highly innovative sectors.

Looking more specifically at the role of political actors and intermediaries, the firms in Jena compared to those in the two other innovative regions perceive regional intermediaries ('chamber of commerce and industry' and 'business promotion agencies') as positively contributing to firm development in general (Cantner et al., 2011). However, a direct effect of intermediaries on the cooperative success of firms is not observed. Hence, we conclude that the general economic atmosphere intermediaries are influential, but not the direct cooperative activities in cooperative arrangements and networks. With respect to the latter, the issue that, in innovation networks, efficacy often requires intermediaries in order to enable cooperation, seems to be absent in Jena – cooperation partners seem to know each other already.

Shifting the focus on the type of cooperation partners that sustain the cooperation success of firms, we find that the cooperation with partners along the value chain (customers and suppliers) is significantly positively related to the cooperation success of firms (ibid.). In addition, the innovative performance or capacity of firms shows a significantly positive relation to contact with university and research institutes (Cantner et al., 2010a). These two findings nicely substantiate our above findings that, first, the complementarities of the Jena actors seem to be high (which might be due to value chain relationships) and, second, that research institutes are important actors in the Jena innovator network. Hence, the firm and actor structure in Jena evidently is conducive to a quite high inclination to successfully cooperate in innovation.

6   CONCLUSION

The development of Jena after the German reunification 1989 has always been considered outstanding. A closer look showed that it has not been the economic development directly but the development of innovative capacities and potential which gives Jena its exceptional status. Some more insights into the mechanisms behind this are given by combining the principal structural development of the firm population just after 1989 through the early 1990s with the quite powerful network of collaborative innovative activities.

High technological opportunities – also created during the Kombinat years in the former GDR (see Kogut and Zander, 2000) – have mainly been exploited after 1990 by an agglomeration of spin-offs (largely from the Zeiss Kombinat), which quite easily and quickly, but also without many alternative options, built up a network of innovators. Over time, this network has become attractive for other actors trying to integrate close to the core. It has influenced the performance especially of spin-offs and new-firm founding nearby, but it has also shown an inward orientation, especially by the core actors risking a lock-in.

Further developments in Jena depend mainly on how it is able to manage being a spin-off agglomeration with a Zeiss and Schott heritage, on the one hand, and, at the same time, an open entrepreneurial site on the other. The key to staying successful has to do with the ability to reconcile different attitudes or role models. A first one, 'cooperate', historically draws on the firm leaders Carl Zeiss and Otto Schott and researchers Ernst Abbe and Matthias-Jacob von Schleiden, who formed the first cooperation between a university and firms. This cooperative attitude has been a major success factor for Jena, but bears the risk of lock-in. A second role model is the so-called 'Zeissianertum', a certain, already traditional attitude toward the usage of technique and the pursuit of technological change, claiming that the Zeiss employees are 'highly precise and better than others'. This attitude serves as a major focusing device which, on the one hand, may provide for excellence but, on the other, may also run the risk of forgetting the outside world – by hinting at exclusiveness. The third role model is more recent and entrepreneurial. It is related to the successful start-up Intershop and serves as a role model for firm-founding activities in Jena. It is an attitude of attempting to be different and to break with the old or the traditions, pursuing an opening-up and search for new, alternative ways. Combining these attitudes and balancing them may provide for a fruitful further development of the Jena region.

NOTES

*   When Guido Buenstorf in 2007 started organizing the EMAEE Conference Jena 2009, he asked me to provide a keynote shedding some light on the performance of Jena since the reunification in 1989. Having done some research on Jena, together with Holger Graf, Andreas Meder, Kristin Joel, Anne ter Wal, Dirk Fornahl, Elisa Conti, and Tina Wolf, I am happy to put that work together and provide some insights into the determinants of the spectacular development in Jena in the last two decades.
    I would like to thank Guido Buenstorf for commenting on the first draft of this chapter and Charles McCann for editing it and improving the English. The usual caveats apply.
1.   *Frankfurter Allgemeine Sonntagszeitung*, no. 5, 5 February 2006, p. 39.
2.   'Stille Stars', *Handelsblatt*, 29 July 2004.
3.   'Der Geist der durch die Luft fliegt', *Der Spiegel*, 18/2000, 1 May, 86–101.
4.   OECD (1999).
5.   'Stadt der Wissenschaft 2008', as awarded by the Stifterverband für Deutsche Wissenschaft.
6.   This section draws on Cantner and Graf (2006).
7.   This very simple measure of technological closeness might be interpreted as a necessary condition for cooperation, as actors share a minimum of common knowledge needed for understanding each other. We know that this is not an ideal measure, but we consider it as a minimum requirement for communication. Since our data do not include patent citations, we cannot follow the more elaborate methodology of Mowery et al. (1998).
8.   The mean degree is the average number of ties an actor holds.
9.   The degree of centrality of actor i is the number of its ties divided by the number of possible ties.
10. It is calculated by averaging the clustering coefficients of all actors within the network. The node level clustering coefficients are calculated as the density of the neighborhood, that is, the network of actors directly linked to the respective actor.
11. This interpretation draws on Cantner et al. (2010b).
12. This section draws on Cantner and Graf (2006).
13. For details on the method and its application, see Cantner and Graf (2006). This model

is estimated using a standard OLS procedure with the usual interpretation of the coefficients. As opposed to regular regression data, a problem of structural autocorrelation might appear either in rows or in columns of the network matrix (Krackhardt, 1987) – since observations are no longer independent. Therefore, the significance levels of the regression coefficients as provided by the t-statistic or the p-value have to be treated with caution. In this context, Krackhardt suggests a different method to evaluate the significance of the coefficients. QAP tests (quadratic assignment procedure) (Hubert, 1987) are applied to make more correct inferences about the significance of the coefficients. In these tests, the null hypothesis is that the t-statistic of association equals the expected value of the t-statistic under a permutation distribution. For details on the method and its application, see Cantner and Graf (2006).

14. Here, we can also observe the difference between the standard p-value based on the t-statistic, which would suggest no significant influence of scientist mobility on cooperations, and the significance provided by testing the QAP hypothesis

15. The following is based on Cantner and Graf (2006).

16. Since we cannot assume a normal distribution of the degrees of the network members, we perform the nonparametric Mann–Whitney or Wilcoxon rank sum test to examine our above reasoning. The tests are performed by column, that is, we compare exiting innovators of the first period with the entering innovators of the second period, and so on.

17. This section draws on Cantner and Graf (2010).

REFERENCES

Bathelt, H., A. Malmberg and P. Maskell (2004), 'Clusters and knowledge: local buzz, global pipelines and the process of knowledge creation', *Progress in Human Geography*, **28**, 31–56.

Cantner, U., E. Conti and A. Meder (2010a), 'Networks and innovation: the role of social assets in explaining firms' innovative capacity', *European Planning Studies*, **18**: 1937–56.

Cantner, U., D. Fornahl and H. Graf (2003), 'Innovationssystem und Gründungsgeschehen in Jena: Erste Erkenntnisse einer Unternehmensbefragung, Jenaer Schriften zur Wirtschaftswissenschaft', FSU Jena, 6/2003.

Cantner, U. and H. Graf (2003), 'Innovationssysteme und kollektive Innovationsprozesse', in U. Cantner, R. Helm and R. Meckl (eds), *Strukturen und Strategien in einem Innovationssystem – Das Beispiel Jena*, Sternenfels, Germany: Verlag Wissenschaft & Praxis, pp. 21–44.

Cantner, U. and H. Graf (2004), 'Cooperation and specialization in German technology regions', *Journal of Evolutionary Economics*, **14** (5): 543–62.

Cantner, U. and H. Graf (2006), 'The network of innovators in Jena: an application of social network analysis', *Research Policy*, **35**: 463–80.

Cantner, U. and H. Graf (2010), 'Growth, development and structural change of innovator networks: the case of Jena', in R. Boschma and R. Martin (eds), *The Handbook of Evolutionary Economic Geography*, Cheltenham, UK and Northampton, MA, USA: Edward Elgar, pp. 370–87.

Cantner, U. and A. Meder (2007), 'Technological proximity and the choice of a cooperation partner', *Journal of Economic Interaction and Coordination*, **2** (1): 45–65.

Cantner, U. and A. Meder (2008), 'Regional and technological effects on cooperative innovation', Jena Economic Research Papers 014-2008.

Cantner, U., A. Meder and A. ter Wal (2010b), 'Innovator networks and regional knowledge base', *Technovation*, **30**: 496–507.

Cantner, U., A. Meder and T. Wolf (2011), 'Intermediation, reciprocity and innovation cooperations of firms', *Papers in Regional Science*, **90** (2): 313–30.

Cantwell, J.A. and P. Barrera (1998), 'The localisation of corporate technological trajectories in the interwar cartels: cooperative learning versus an exchange of knowledge', *Economics of Innovation and New Technology*, **6** (2–3): 257–90.

Fritsch, M. and G. Franke (2004), 'Innovation, regional knowledge spillovers and R&D cooperation', *Research Policy*, **33** (2): 245–55.

Gulati, R. (1995a), 'Social structure and alliance formation patterns: a longitudinal analysis', *Administrative Science Quarterly*, **40**: 619–52.

Gulati, R. (1995b), 'Does familiarity breed trust? The implications of repeated ties for contractual choice in alliances', *Academy of Management Journal*, **38**: 85–112.

Gulati, R. (1998), 'Alliances and networks', *Strategic Management Journal*, **19**: 293–317.

Hubert, L.J. (1987), *Assignment Methods in Combinatorial Data Analysis*, New York and Basel, Switzerland: Marcel Dekker.

Kogut, B. and U. Zander (2000), 'Did socialism fail to innovate? A natural experiment of the two Zeiss companies', *American Sociological Review*, **65**: 169–90.

Krackhardt, D. (1987), 'QAP partialling as a test of spuriousness', *Social Networks*, **9**: 171–86.

Krackhardt, D. (1988), 'Predicting with networks: nonparametric multiple regression analysis of dyadic data', *Social Networks*, **10**: 359–81.

Mowery, D.C., J.E. Oxley and B.S. Silverman (1998), 'Technological overlap and interfirm cooperation: implications for the resource-based view of the firm', *Research Policy*, **27** (5): 507–23.

Organisation for Economic Co-operation and Development (OECD) (1999), *Economic and Cultural Transition Towards a Learning City: The Case of Jena*, Paris: OECD.

Powell, W.W., K.W. Koput and L. Smith-Doerr (1996), 'Interorganizational collaboration and the locus of innovation: networks of learning in biotechnology', *Administrative Science Quarterly*, **41**: 116–45.

Powell, W.W., K.W. Koput, L. Smith-Doerr and J. Owen-Smith (1999), 'Network position and firm performance: organizational returns to collaboration in the biotechnology industry', in S.B. Andrews and D. Knoke (eds), *Research in the Sociology of Organizations*, Greenwich, CT: JAI Press, pp. 129–59.

Index